Craig Lesley received the Pacific Northwest Booksellers Association Book Award for *The Sky Fisherman, Winterkill,* and *Talking Leaves.* He lives with his wife and two daughters in Portland, Oregon, where he teaches at Portland State University.

ALSO BY CRAIG LESLEY

Storm Riders

River Song

Winterkill

The Sky Fisherman

BURNING FENCE

A Western Memoir of Fatherhood

CRAIG LESLEY

PICADOR

———

ST. MARTIN'S PRESS

NEW YORK

www.picadorusa.com

Picador® is a U.S. registered trademark and is used by St. Martin's Press under license from Pan Books Limited.

For information on Picador Reading Group Guides, as well as ordering, please contact Picador.
Phone: 646-307-5629
Fax: 212-253-9627
E-mail: readinggroupguides@picadorusa.com

Design by Phil Mazzone

LIBRARY OF CONGRESS CATALOGING-IN-PUBLICATION DATA

Lesley, Craig.
    Burning fence : a Western memoir of fatherhood / Craig Lesley.
        p. cm.
    ISBN-13: 978-0-312-42625-5
    ISBN-10: 0-312-42625-9
    1. Lesley, Craig. 2. Novelists, American—20th century—Biography.
3. College Teachers—Oregon—Biography. 4. Oregon—Social life and customs.
5. Violence in children—Oregon. 6. Fathers and sons—Oregon. 7. Foster
children—Oregon. 8. Indian children—Oregon. 9. Lesley, Craig—Family.
10. Trappers—Oregon. I. Title.

PS3562.E815Z47 2005
813'.54—dc22   2005047054
[B]

First published in the United States by St. Martin's Press

First Picador Edition: September 2006

10 9 8 7 6 5 4 3 2 1

For Katheryn Ann Stavrakis and
our daughters, Elena and Kira

CONTENTS

II   BACK TO MONUMENT

The author would like to thank the Regional
Arts & Culture Council for its generous support.

I

TRAIN TIME

1

BURNING MONUMENT

When we held my father Rudell's funeral service in the Monument cemetery, raging forest fires surrounded the town, and we could hear the burning wood crackle. Smoke filled the air, and through stinging eyes, I could see only about a hundred feet. Ormand, my half brother, set the box containing my father's ashes next to the headstone. He kept looking around, but neither of Rudell's former wives had made the effort to attend. My half sisters didn't show, either. Just us boys.

As Ormand read the Bible parable of the workers in the vineyard, I stood off a ways, since it was Ormand who grew up with my dad, not me. As far as I was concerned, this was Ormand's show. Anyway, he was an apprentice preacher, and this was his first funeral. Besides, I didn't want to stand too close because one of the Lesley bad-luck demons might crawl into my bones.

Ponderosa, lodgepole, red pine, juniper, sagebrush—all burning. The wind carried the smell like a campfire, but bigger and more ominous. The Forest Service had sent 450 firefighters into Monument and they had taken over the whole town, except the cemetery. Mexicans, Indians, Alaskans, prisoners with crew cuts and jug ears—guys who hadn't seen anything outside but brick walls and razor wire in years. None of them could do a thing with the fire because of the wind. They sat around, dirty and defeated, complaining about the wind shifts and lightning strikes.

Nobody could handle that fire. The wind gusts topped thirty miles an hour and the blazing embers touched off spot fires everywhere—in the canyons, on the scablands, the far hillsides. Johnnycake Mountain was burning, and the Boneyard, Sunflower Flat, even Cupper Creek, where my dad claimed he saw Bigfoot back in 1980, when Mount St. Helens blew. He said old Bigfoot knew the blast was coming so the creature hightailed it four hundred miles away, into the Umatilla Forest near my father's fence-building camp. How it crossed the Columbia, he couldn't figure. Maybe it swam, or paid a bridge toll like everyone else. Ormand swears my father didn't meddle with the truth, but I've always been skeptical. The old man ran off and left my mom before I grew teeth, so I didn't owe him anything, not even the benefit of believing his wild stories.

Right then, Ormand kept droning on about the vineyard workers who never started until an hour before quitting time. Even so, they got paid for a full day's wage, and the other workers complained that the latecomers got the same pay for less work.

Nothing's fair, I thought.

My feet were wet because some yahoo had turned the sprinklers on in the wrong part of the cemetery and flooded the section where we held the service. They could have used that water on the fire lines, I figured, but I was wet-footed instead. Maybe it would soak into the wooden box that held my father's ashes and make a soggy mess for us to scatter.

And I thought Ormand made an okay preacher, the way his voice kept getting low and serious when he was making a point about how my father had come to believe late in his life—at the eleventh hour—but he was still saved, paid the same wages as those who had started laboring in the vineyards early in the morning. My half brother was thinking about studying preaching at a little Bible-thumping school over near Boise. And I smiled just a hint, wondering if Ormand would give up poaching deer and elk when he starting preaching for serious full-time, and small-town people criticized his every move.

But I was thinking hardest about something else: all the range fences my father had built in his lifetime. Each post split and fashioned from ornery juniper was burning now, and as the posts burned and the barbed wire sagged, frantic horses and cows ran helter-skelter all over the mountainside and up the canyons, ran until they tangled in wire and dropped, rolling their panicked eyes and frothing at the mouths as the fire blazed toward them.

And then I thought about Ormand helping my father build most of those fences, flunking out of school while my father used him like a horse, packing posts and wire spools, sledges and post-hole diggers. My brother was all crippled up from that wretched work and being smacked by a car when he was eleven while walking out of the Irrigon hardware store. He should have been in school, but he was a huge, rawboned boy capable of a man's work, and my father took advantage.

"Long-suffering," my uncle Oscar called my father and his brood. And it was true. Opal didn't make the funeral because we couldn't find her. Yuba-Jean was slaving as a motel maid down in Weed. None of us was young anymore. All of us had snuck past fifty when the devil wasn't looking.

So I was thinking about all this, mostly those miles of burning fence line, when Ormand banged his Bible shut.

Everyone stared at me. Ormand nodded, and I knew that come hell or high water, I had to say something about my father. But I couldn't speak, so I read John 14:2:

In my Father's house are many mansions; if it were not so, I would have told you. I go to prepare a place for you.

Everyone seemed satisfied, except for me. I know that Ormand said God had forgiven Rudell, but I hadn't.

■ ■ ■

My mother seldom mentioned my father—coyote trapper, fence builder, backslider. She believed in keeping quiet if she couldn't find anything good to say. "Weak as water," or "That loser," she let slip a couple of times when I was growing up. Then she hastened to add, "But there wasn't a mean bone in his body." Of course, that was wrong.

"Shell-shocked," "not good in his mind," "no-count," other relatives suggested over the years, and they were on *his* side of the family. When I first workshopped with Raymond Carver and showed him stories with a character similar to Rudell, Ray called him "shiftless." Then he crinkled a smile. "Or still working up to it."

If anybody asked, I told them my father was in the fur business. My mother claimed he worked as a security guard at the Umatilla Army Depot, where the army stored thousands of tons of chemical weapons. This suggested that he served an important role keeping the U.S. safe from the evildoers of the world. True, he did work a spell as a security guard, but long after she was married to him, when he tried to maintain a second family. Eventually, his other wife took my four half siblings and ran off to California with a long-haul trucker.

After that blow, my father claimed his nerves were shot, and he collected a small government disability check. Moving back to Monument, he tacked a lean-to shed onto a banged-up trailer and started trapping coyotes and poaching deer. "Oregon Appalachia," my mother called it.

■ ■ ■

My birth certificate is the only official document I have that holds Rudell's scrawled signature and birth date: March 18, 1914. Ormand has my father's discharge papers from the service. Rudell served with distinction in France and faced severe fighting in the Battle of the Bulge and the Ruhr Pocket. He received several medals and an honorable discharge after fighting the Germans all the way to Berlin. I was born on July 5, 1945, and my father left eight months after that with what my mother called "shell shock."

My mother raised me, providing groceries, shelter, discount shoes, and most important, unconditional love. She believed in my success and encouraged me to attend college. So why write about my father at all when she's the hero? Even though I had only eight meetings with my father until I was well past forty, his influence on me was enormous. Since my mother had criticized him for being "weak," I vowed to be strong. Fear of backsliding motivated me to become high school and college student body presidents, to keep moving ahead at all costs. This also fueled my obsession with becoming a writer and chronicling the lives of Westerners similar to my father.

Rudell's neglect motivated me to raise an alcohol-damaged Indian boy just to show the old man I could succeed as a father where he had fallen down. To be truthful, it was harder than I thought. I stood trapped middle ground between a man who wouldn't communicate and a boy who couldn't.

Tricky business, fathers and sons. In my case, a lot needed settling.

2

CHERRY TREE

Lifting me high above his head, my father placed me in the crotch of the Bing cherry tree growing beside my mother's parents' house in The Dalles. A little frightened at that dizzying height, I pressed my palms into the tree's rough, peeling bark. My father stood close, reassuring. I could see his olive skin, dazzling smile, and sharp-creased army uniform.

"Rudell, don't let him fall." My mother watched, her arms held out halfway, as if to catch me.

"Look at that big boy. He's taller than me." My grandfather Lange spoke around his crook-stemmed pipe filled with Prince Albert tobacco. Wearing her kitchen apron, my grandmother stood close by, ready to serve a pitcher of lemonade.

The cherries were ripe and robins flittered through the dark green leaves, pecking at the Bings. Tipping my head back, I could see blue sky beyond the extended branches.

"That's enough. Bring him down now." My mother's arms reached out farther.

Laughing, my father grabbed me under the arms, twirled me

around, and plunked me onto the grass. I wobbled a little. Imprinted on my palms was the pattern of the tree bark, and I brushed off the little bark pieces on my dungarees.

In a moment, my grandmother gave me a small glass of lemonade. When I drank, it tasted tart and sweet at the same time.

This first childhood memory of my father remains etched in my mind.

Other memories followed. Every morning, Grandmother Lange lifted me onto a kitchen chair so I could see the Columbia River and the Klickitat Hills. In summer, the two of us planted crocuses in the back yard; in winter, we watched their yellow and purple flowers spring from the snow. Two days a week, I helped her clean the roomers' quarters, and as I emptied the waste baskets and ashtrays, I smelled aftershave and old cigarettes.

Every lunch hour, my grandfather walked home from the newspaper to give me cod liver oil, because I had rickets. I refused to take the fishy liquid from anyone but him. Brandishing a bottle and spoon, he chased me from room to room while I laughed. After I swallowed, I became the pursuer, and he lumbered away shouting, "Don't give me any of those lutefisk kisses!" When I caught and kissed him, my grandfather wiped his mouth and made terrible faces. My cheeks burned from his heavy whiskers and the delight of the chase.

Each afternoon, I waited for him to come home and read me my favorite book *Peppy the Puppy*. Relaxing in his easy chair, he filled his crook-stemmed pipe and smoked while he read. To this day, the smell of pipe smoke conjures those wonderful times.

When I grew older, I realized that my father had never lifted me into the cherry tree. After Rudell left, I never saw him until I was fifteen. My grandfather had put me in the tree. Still, the memory of my father lifting me into the tree persists. Even today, I remain half-convinced by the details: the press of bark against my palms, the taste of lemonade, the texture of my father's serge uniform. Apparently, my mind has cross-wired the photographs of my handsome father in his army uniform with the logical reality that my grandfather set me in the crotch of the tree.

Why can I remember the event so vividly? I guess because I wanted so much for my father to be there. I have no easy answers.

■ ■ ■

At eight-seven, my mother, Hazel, has a perfectly clear mind, but she refuses to talk about Rudell.

"How did you two meet?"

"I can't remember."

I decide to prompt her out of her stubbornness. "You were in Vancouver, right? Working at the county courthouse? Rudell was in the army, stationed at the Barnes Veteran's Hospital. Did you meet at a dance for servicemen? A bar? Church?"

"I just can't remember."

"But it was in Vancouver?"

A long pause. "It must have been."

"Before he came to Vancouver, he worked on the Alcan Highway. He said the mosquitoes were as big as horses. So you met him after he worked on the highway and before he went overseas."

"When was the highway built?"

"Nineteen forty-three was when he worked on it. Aunt Sally and Ormand told me. She said you and Rudell came to visit her in Portland when you were going together."

"Well then, I guess maybe we did."

"It would help if you said a little more about him."

"I don't have anything more to say about him. He just didn't give a damn."

"You always told me he had shell shock after the war."

"Listen. All I want you to put in that book is that I'm your mother, and I was a single working parent. When your father ran off, I tried to raise you, and after I was married to Vern . . . well, you know what he was like. Then I had Ronna and tried to raise you both."

"Well, do you want to talk about Vern a little?"

"He was a stinker. But you're a good person, and Ronna is a good person, and I'm a good person."

Of course, I remember my stepfather all too well, but I want her to say a little more. "What are some of the things you remember about him?"

"I did the best I could, under the circumstances. That's all anybody can do."

"I know. I've always admired you for that. Ronna has, too."

"I want to read what you write. Before it goes to publication, or whatever that's called. I want to read it."

Maybe it was a request, but the edge in her voice made it sound more like a threat.

■ ■ ■

I remain amazed at how little I know about my father from my mother's side of the family. My grandmother said nothing. Twice, my grandfather told me that he was a good hunter with keen eyes. My aunt Mac said she thought he was an Indian. My mother told me he suffered shell shock following the Battle of the Bulge and left us because of his illness. Then she added, "But there wasn't a mean bone in your father's body."

Much later, she told me, "After the war was over, he just hung around the house [my grandparents' home in The Dalles]. Your grandfather finally got him a job with my uncle out at the cement works, and he wouldn't do what he was told."

When I was in my fifties, she added that he left the cement works job to go deer hunting. "And when he came back, he remembered that he'd left a flashlight with his cousin down in Molalla. He left to get it and never returned."

Most details about my father have come from my grandmother Anna Lesley, his eleven brothers and sisters, my half brother Ormand, and the few meetings I had with the old man himself. In 1946, shortly before he sent divorce papers to my mother, Rudell sat on a park bench outside the Pendleton courthouse, waiting for my aunt Sally to get off work. They were close to each other because my grandfather Newton Lesley had been cruel to both of them, forcing them to become allies. Later, Sally offered Rudell help in going to college, but he felt college was a waste of time.

"I saw your father out the window, just sitting on that bench," Sally told me. "It was about three o'clock in the afternoon. I could tell he had something heavy on his mind and I'm sure it was about your mother."

"So what did he say?"

"I wanted to go outside and talk with him, but I couldn't right then. I had all this work to do for the judge and I didn't want to get in trouble."

Sally looked down at her folded hands. I could tell she felt that she had made the wrong decision.

"About four, Rudell left the bench for a while and came back with a cup of coffee. I figured that would hold him."

When 5:30 came, Sally hurried out of her office and across the street to the bench. My father was gone, the half-drunk cup of coffee left behind.

"I hoped he'd be up at the house. DeAnna was just a baby then, and I thought he might stop by to see her. I called Jim at work, but he hadn't seen him. Later, we found out he'd gone back to Monument."

Maybe my aunt Sally could have persuaded Rudell not to leave. How much convincing would it have taken? I'd like to believe that somehow he would have stayed, that he cared for me more than he wanted that flashlight.

3

THE CARNIVAL

Grandma Lesley made the world's best cinnamon rolls. Everyone raved about them. Old-timers in Monument today, people who knew her as children, still speak wistfully of those rolls. On the farm, she baked rolls, bread, pies, and cookies every day, so her children had treats when they walked home from school.

She sold the farm in 1947 because the children had grown and moved away. Tired of farm work, none of them wanted to run the place. She traveled from one relative's home to another by bus, always baking her famous rolls, helping with new babies, applying her homemade tonics and remedies to upsets and aches.

I loved her visits to my mother's parents' home, where we had moved after the divorce. I listened eagerly for Grandma Lesley bustling around the kitchen, the clanking of bowls and pans. Cinnamon rolls! Soon the house filled with their wonderful aroma. All the ingredients seemed ordinary enough, except for her insisting on sweet creamery butter and brown farm eggs. But she had magic in her recipe. Her rolls melted like soft sunlight in my mouth.

A tiny woman with quick birdlike movement, she always sang while she worked. She taught me "Billy Boy," which she said was my father's favorite, "Onward Christian Soldiers," and "The Strawberry Roan."

Not everyone was enchanted by her cooking. "She dirtied every pan in the house," my mother told me when I got older. "She made deep gouges in the porcelain sink."

Any art requires some sacrifice, I thought. And my grandmother had perfected the art of the cinnamon roll.

My grandmother's doctoring art was more ferocious. Her soft suitcase bulged with tonics, elixirs, purgatives. She believed most diseases came from "bad blood" or constipation, and she had methods to cure each unhappy condition with potions concocted of watercress, dandelion greens, rhubarb, and plenty of alcohol. Buckshot boiled in milk fixed most aches, including back and tooth (you drank the milk after the buckshot was caught in a sieve). Straight alcohol rubbed in the eyes and nose was good for a cold. Warm molasses stopped an earache.

"Don't ever say you're sick when Grandma Lesley is coming to visit," my mother cautioned sternly. Although I suffered from tonsillitis, fevers, and sore throats, I tried to hide any symptoms from our annual visitor.

She never missed my birthday, and I could always rely on her sending a dollar, sometimes two. When my mother and I lived with my grandparents in The Dalles, Grandma Lesley once showed up with a five-dollar bill she had saved to take me to the carnival. Every penny must be spent, she insisted. I was to do anything I wanted, but my mother forbid me to ride the Ferris Wheel and small roller coaster.

My grandfather pointed out that I wasn't to attend the sideshow, either. He had seen the Tattooed Lady and she was not a proper sight for young boys. I promised to avoid the banned attractions.

Grandma Lesley wore a large sunhat with a ribbon and matching bow for her dress. She planned on sitting in the shade and reading while I squandered my riches. Nearly everything cost a dime except the penny pitch for milk-glass dishes, and I jingled fifty dimes in my pocket after seeing the change maker. At six years of age, I had never luxuriated in such freedom.

She chose a bench in the shade and sat, then patted the place beside her so I would sit, too. Even though I was eager to explore, first I wanted to hear about my father.

"Your father caught the biggest fish you ever saw." She stood, stretching her hand high above her head. "A sturgeon seven feet long. He smoked most of it, and that fish tasted delicious."

I liked fishing. My grandfather Lange had taken me a couple of times, but we didn't catch anything, and he grew impatient with all the snarls in my line. A fish twice my height was enormous, a real prize.

My grandmother Lange fried the small fish my grandfather occasionally caught when I wasn't with him. She made the tails crisp and salty. They were my favorite part because they didn't have bones.

"What else did my father do?"

"Well, he got a job fighting forest fires this summer. I worry when he does that but it's good money. A lot of that forest out there by Monument went up in a big blaze."

I tried to picture the fire in the trees. Sometimes I helped my grandfather rake leaves and small limbs for a bonfire back in the alley, but after he lit the pile, I couldn't go near.

She shifted on the bench and fixed me with her dark brown eyes. "Honey, I thought I should tell you your father is fixin' on getting married again."

"To my mother?" I knew that my father, mother, and I had lived with my grandparents for a while when I was a baby. Now only my mother and I lived there.

Grandma Lesley put both arms around me and hugged. "Not to your mother, honey. He's fixin' on marrying somebody else. But don't worry. He loves you and he thinks about you all the time. I always tell him how you're growing up to be such a stout, sweet boy."

"Maybe I can go see him and his new wife."

"I'm sure you can. But you like it here with your grandparents, don't you? They're real good to you."

I scuffed my shoes in the dirt. "Sure. I just want to see my father sometime. Does he still wear that army uniform like in the pictures?"

"Sometimes he does."

"Maybe he'll come and take me fishing."

"I wouldn't be surprised. Not one bit." She patted my back. "Now, you go and have fun."

"How about coming on some rides, Grandma?"

She shook her head. "I'm all give-out from the walk here. Don't worry about me. You go."

I rode Cups and Saucers, Bumper Cars, the Ferris Wheel (although they insisted on having an adult ride with me in the cage). I couldn't go on the Roller Coaster because I was too short. I squandered seventy-five cents at the penny pitch before I won an ashtray for my grandfather, who always smoked a crook-stem pipe, a cake dish for my grandmother, a soap dish for my mother, and a candy dish with an elephant's head for Grandma Lesley.

I couldn't decide what to win for my father. Grandma Lesley could take it to him and then he'd come see me. I spotted a dish shaped like a fish and spent forty-five cents throwing pennies at it, but I was too nervous. Finally, the man in the booth just gave it to me.

"Go on the rides, kid. See the sights."

Forgetting my grandfather's warning, I carried my booty to the sideshow tent and marveled at the posters plastered outside. Too young to be attracted to the Tattooed Lady, I concentrated on the Fat Man, Bearded Lady, Siamese Twins, Magician, and Strong Man. Each spectacle cost a dime.

The illustrated poster that fascinated me most featured a Two-Faced Man with fair features and blond hair at what should have been the back of his head, swarthy features and coal black hair at the front. He was the one I wanted to see.

But first came the Siamese Twins, Lonny and Donny. Inside the dark tent, the spotlight illuminated the two, who were joined near the hip and pelvis. The crowd roared as they made fun of each other, told jokes. Lonny or Donny ate an onion and blew in his twin's face, producing a laugh-getting grimace. For revenge, the second twin ate some sardines and paid his brother back. They concluded the show by saying how happy they were to be in The Dalles, where people were polite. In Longview, Washington, they complained, members of the audience had thrown trash at them. I was proud to live in The Dalles.

When they offered to shake hands with members of the audience for a dime, a lot of people pressed forward to pump their hands. I gave my dime to the manager and shook each twin's hand. "I'm sorry they treated you like that in Longview," I told them.

I wanted to tell my grandparents, but I knew my grandfather would be angry, so I'd have to settle for telling Grandma Lesley and hope she kept quiet.

Before the next show started, I squeezed to the front railing so I would have a close-up view. When the Two-Faced Man appeared under the spotlight, he didn't look much like the poster. His black hair resembled a wig and his mouth never moved when he talked. He told the audience that he had not always been a Two-Faced Man. Once he'd had a single face exactly like we had.

His words sent a shiver through me. I was growing so fast my grandparents had to buy me new shoes all the time. Would I grow a second face?

An orange cloth covering the back of his head concealed the second face, so I couldn't see his fair features and blond, curly hair yet. When it was time to reveal the second face, he turned his back to the audience and removed the cloth with a flourish.

I saw no second face at the back of his head, just odd-colored purplish flesh. Suddenly, he whirled around, whipping off a mask and wig. As he confronted the audience, my curiosity changed to horror, and I pushed back from the railing—terrified.

He had no face, just a second mask of scarred flesh. Deep pits for eyes, a deformed, cavernous mouth without lips, no ears or nose. He was ghastly.

He had been smoking in bed, the Two-Faced Man explained in a calm voice, and there had been a horrible fire.

"My face melted," he said. "What you are witnessing is the result of carelessness. After the fire, no one would hire me, but the carnival offered me a job. . . ."

I don't know what he said after that, because the shock sickened me. I pitched forward to the rail and threw up. Hot dogs, strawberry pop, funnel cake, and ice cream gushed forth over the railing and onto the tent's sawdust floor.

"For God's sakes, who let that kid in here?" the Two-Faced Man said. "Get him the hell out!"

Someone took my arm and began pulling me toward the tent flap. I kept staring back, hypnotized by the horror.

The Two-Faced Man pointed in my direction. "Don't ever play with matches, young man. And never smoke in bed."

Out in the bright sunlight, I gasped for air. The man who had led me out steered me toward a rest room. At the small sink, I dabbed the vomit on my shirt with a wet paper towel.

"Are you here with somebody?" the man asked. "Do you have anyone to take you home?"

"My grandmother," I said.

"A boy your age doesn't belong at the sideshow," he said.

Suddenly, I realized that I had dropped the milk-glass prizes I had won, but I was terrified of going back inside the tent. The man agreed to retrieve them for me, and he did.

I found Grandma Lesley reading her book. "What on earth happened to you? You look white as a sheet."

"I threw up," I said.

"Too much carnival food," she said. "I have some tonic that will fix you straight away."

"Look what I got." I handed her the fish dish. "I want you to take it to my father. Do you think he'll like it?"

"Honey, he's going to love it."

Once safely back at my grandparents' house, I was reluctant to swallow the tonic, but she insisted. Both my mother and grandfather were at work, and my grandmother Lange was taking a nap, so there was no one to stop Grandma Lesley.

She washed the shirt in the sink and put it on the line to dry. I could hear her singing "The Sinking of the Maine." Fearing a fire, I checked my grandfather's ashtray for smoldering tobacco. Then I went to each room and checked the other ashtrays.

That night I couldn't sleep. Grandma Lesley warmed some milk and laced it with valerian. "A troubled stomach will cause nightmares," she said.

My nightmares about the Two-Faced Man lasted for months. In those horrifying dreams, my father suffered terrible burns in a forest fire. He wouldn't come to see me because he looked so frightening. No one would hire him except for a traveling carnival. But anytime I tried to see him, a gang of adults kept pushing me away from the tent.

4

COWBOY COFFEE

When I turned five, my grandfather set up the cowboy room as a playroom. This was in the basement, where I heard the deep hum of the freezer chest, the hiss of the coal furnace, my grandfather's soft cursing as he sawed and nailed projects back in the shop.

The room's wallpaper featured colorful cowboys gathered around a chuck wagon fixing breakfast, or mounted on horseback keeping an eye on the grazing herd. All the cowboys wore bright shirts; the riders carried weapons. I named them Rex, Charley, and Joe.

Lincoln Logs, a Texaco service station and garage, twin six-shooters that fired strings of caps, and a cowboy hat were my favorite toys. Although I played some with the garage, most of my hours went to building forts, helping the cowboys keep the herd gathered, and watching out for danger. When renegade Indians attacked the fort, I blazed away with the six-shooters until the room grew hazy from fired caps. I loved the smell of gunpowder.

One day, my grandfather came in wearing his battered hat and smoking his crook-stemmed pipe. He put me on his knee and told me I was going to have to move my toys back upstairs into my mother's room. Money was tight and my grandparents were taking in another roomer to help with expenses.

At first, I resented the new roomer, a railroader from Pocatello named Vern Hecker, but one day he brought me a railroader's blue bandanna and an old telegraph. After that, we got along. When he understood that the cowboy room had been my play area, Vern told me I could come visit the cowpokes whenever I wanted.

I didn't think he meant it, but the first time I visited he told me to take my time, and then he left to go buy some cigarettes. Lined up on his bureau were bottles of Old Spice aftershave, Vitalis hair tonic, and a tube of Pepsodent toothpaste. A calendar featuring Union Pacific locomotives hung on the wall, and two decks of UP playing cards rested in the drawer.

When I talked to the cowboys, they told me Vern was okay. The room smelled like Chesterfields instead of caps, but they said Chesterfields were good smokes.

My mother and Vern started seeing each other. He didn't go to church, but on Sunday afternoons he took both of us out for picnics up Mill Creek. Another time, we hiked from Hermit's Cave to Eagle Cave, and my mother spread a blue-and-white-checked tablecloth on the flat bench above the cave. She had fixed deviled-ham sandwiches and fried chicken. Vern ate both, but I just ate the chicken because the ham had a funny texture.

While my mother lay in the sun, we hiked a little and picked a bouquet of bachelor's buttons for her, a second one for my grandmother. "Women always like you to bring them flowers," Vern said.

Early one Sunday morning, I slipped down to the cowboy room. Vern lay in bed smoking and reading *Argosy* magazine.

"You're up before the cows," he told me.

"What were the cowboys doing last night?"

"There was a big thunderstorm and a wild cattle stampede. But things have quieted now."

I shivered while he told me of the frenzied stampede, how Rex had nearly been trampled by the crazed herd, how Joe had saved him by riding alongside the wild-eyed cattle, firing his pistol to head them off.

"I saw cattle stampede like that in Idaho," Vern said. "It was dangerous, nothing to fool around with."

By the serious look in his green eyes, I knew he meant it.

"It got mighty cold last night, but this morning the boys are cooking bacon and pancakes. Soon everyone will warm up." He lit another cigarette. "Hot coffee. Cowboys drink their coffee black on the trail."

I got under the comforter. "I'm glad they're getting a hot breakfast."

"What's your grandmother feeding you?" he asked.

"Oatmeal," I said. "Maybe cracked wheat." I was disappointed we weren't having pancakes with bacon or ham. Those were special treats for days like my birthday.

"You can't feed a real cowboy oatmeal," he said.

"I know," I said, but I hadn't known it until then.

"If you're good, I'll buy you a new cowboy hat for your birthday."

"And a shirt, too," I added. "Blue-and-white plaid, or maybe red, just like the cowboys on the wall."

"Okay," he said. "Buckaroo britches, too. We'll go to the rodeo and parade. You'll look just like all the other cowboys, only better."

"Great," I said, imagining wearing my new outfit and showing off to Johnny Maris and Sam Bishop. I'd have a new dad to show off, too. My mother had discussed it with me.

Johnny's father treated strep throat and Sam's father ran Pinky's store. But Vern telegraphed the trains, telling them when to come through The Dalles and when to switch onto a siding. Over thirty trains a day, my mother said. That was more important than being a doctor or running a store. I listened for the locomotives' whistles.

Now Vern grabbed my arm. His face turned solemn. "Early this morning Charley saw smoke signals. Like this." He tipped his head back and blew three smoke rings. I had never seen him do that before.

"It's a bad sign. Rex thinks the Indians will try to steal the cattle today."

"Tell me what happens," I said.

"Sure," he said, blowing another smoke ring. "That's how the Indians talk. Smoke signals mean danger."

"I'll bet you've seen smoke signals in Idaho," I said.

"More than you can imagine."

As Vern began to talk about the Indians, I felt afraid. Their names were scary—Apache Jack, Blind Owl, Bloody Knife.

His voice stayed calm as he described the Indian trouble. Under the covers, he touched me, reaching inside my pajamas. I began to shiver.

"Now that I'm going to be your father, we can do this," he said. "But you can't tell anyone. It's just between us. Like cowboys, you and me."

His green eyes had grown more serious and he snubbed out his cigarette with his other hand. "If you tell anyone, even a whisper, we'll have to stop. Then maybe I can't be your father anymore. You wouldn't like that, would you?"

I stopped shivering and shook my head. His hand felt okay, and I wanted a father, just like my friends had.

He took my chin, turning my head toward him.

"Do you promise, Craig?"

I smelled Old Spice, Vitalis, and Chesterfields. I tried looking at the cowboys, but all I saw was his face. "I promise," I said.

"I believe you, so we trust each other," he said. "But nobody loves a liar. Don't ever be a liar, or you won't have a father or any friends."

"I won't ever be a liar."

"Good deal, then." He lit another cigarette. "Now I'll tell you about the Indians."

The three cowboys managed to chase off the Indians, but Joe got struck in the shoulder by an arrow. They had trouble cutting it out. When they reached town, the doctor put in a dozen stitches. After that, Joe was all right—just stiff and plenty sore.

Upstairs, my grandmother called me for breakfast.

Vern grew quiet.

She called a second time.

Maybe I wanted to stay in the basement with Vern and the cowboys.

"You go on, son," Vern said. "Later today, we'll take a drive with your mother. Stop at some creek so you can throw rocks in the water, try fishing a little."

As I got out of bed, he held up his finger. "Remember our cowboy secret."

I nodded.

Back upstairs, I slipped into my scratchy wool trousers, my Sunday white shirt, and the stiff black shoes my grandfather had polished along with his own. My mother sang quietly in the bathroom. At the kitchen table, my grandfather had a napkin stuck in his shirtfront to protect his tie. My grandmother wore silver earrings shaped like crosses.

I stared at the oatmeal and milk, unwilling to eat.

"Better hurry," my grandmother said. "We don't want to be late." She sprinkled a spoonful of brown sugar on the oatmeal. "How's that?"

I didn't say anything.

My grandfather scowled. "Speak up. Cat got your tongue?"

"No oatmeal. I want bacon. Bacon and black coffee."

My grandmother put her hand to her cheek as if I'd slapped her.

My grandfather reached across the table and shook my shoulder. "What's gotten into you this morning, boy?" His napkin fell away. His wide red tie hung like a silent tongue.

Many years later, my cousin Annette bought my grandparent's house and had it remodeled. She saved me a section of the cowboy wall roughly three feet square. She thought I would want it as a remembrance.

I never could figure out what to do with that section, how to face the mix of emotions. For a while, I kept it propped up in my writing study. Then I carried it out to the garage, where it stayed for many years. Eventually, I brought it inside again and studied the cowboys' expressions carefully.

Rex seems content drinking his coffee. Charley is about ready to take the bacon out of the long-handled skillet. Joe's arrow wound still gives him trouble sometimes, sleepless nights. He always keeps a wary eye on the cattle, watching for danger.

5

IODINE

Shortly after my mother and stepfather were married, the three of us moved to Pendleton. My mother called this "a fresh start." She was eager to begin a new life with Vern and to have another baby. And she was ready to live in her own house, away from her parents. Vern was ready to move, too. He had work conflicts with the stationmaster at The Dalles and he wanted to get my mother away from her parents' influence.

He didn't work at the main Union Pacific station in Pendleton, but out at Rieth, a siding and small settlement just west of town. Usually he worked graveyard, midnight until eight, but for a few months, he worked swing shift, getting off at midnight and staying in a pretty good mood because his sleep was regular. A few times, he took me out to Rieth and introduced me to the railroaders who drank at the tavern. Vern seldom drank to excess, but he'd have a beer, sometimes two. He ordered Green Rivers for me because he said Green River, Wyoming, was an important railroad town.

I loved Pendleton and the freedom I found there. Mom wasn't

as strict as my grandparents had been. In addition, she had terrible allergies, or hay fever, and spent a good deal of her time sick in bed.

Tom, an older boy who lived in the same duplex, took me fishing and wading in the Umatilla River. He had a dog, Thumper, which I adored, and the dog followed us as we rode our bikes all over town.

In September, the excitement over the Pendleton Round-Up caught me like a whirlwind. The town filled with lean cowboys, tough rodeo riders, beautiful cowgirls, Indians from the Umatilla Reservation, fancy pickups pulling horse trailers.

Vern bought me a denim jacket at Hamley's, and I believed that cowboying was the best job in the world. He also bought me a twenty-five-foot lariat, and I spent September afternoons roping the ever-patient Thumper and stray cats in the alley.

When Round-Up events actually arrived, I gobbled candy thrown by the Westward-Ho Parade floats and cheered wildly during the rodeo events. Vern took me on a Thursday night and we sat in the cheap seats, but Vern said they were the best because of their location—close to the chutes.

After reveling in the pageantry of Happy Canyon, I visited the cowboys camped in their pickups and trailers on the fairgrounds. To this day, I can smell the hay and horses, beer and barbecue. I swaggered home with an oversized cowboy hat that one of the wranglers had given me when he saw I was bareheaded. Even now, I appreciate his generosity. "I got another hat in the truck," he said.

The next day, Vern took pictures of me dressed in Western attire, holding the lariat. We sent copies to my grandparents, my aunt Grace and uncle Oscar. Vern even sent one to his brother in Idaho, which was unusual, because they weren't very close.

Vern and I had to enjoy these activities by ourselves, because my mother's allergies grew even worse. I began to rely more and more on Vern, who claimed he'd never been sick a day in his life. For reasons I never understood, Vern's cowboy secrets ended in Pendleton.

I had felt important to Vern when he touched me and became confused when he stopped, because I thought I had displeased him in some way. My concern increased one day when he took me to a playground in a part of Pendleton I didn't know. As a practical joke, he drove away while I was playing. When I realized he and the car were missing, I became terrified and wandered the unfamiliar section of Pendleton for hours. Finally, I found the Umatilla River and followed it back to known territory. Our house was empty.

Both my mother and Vern were out searching for me along with a couple of police officers. My mother was frantic. After we were reunited, she remained furious at Vern, but he treated it all as one big joke.

"Don't be such a worrywart," he told my mother. "Craig was pretty smart at figuring out how to get home." He clapped me on the shoulder.

I glowed with his praise.

■ ■ ■

My stepfather kept a bottle of iodine in the bathroom medicine cabinet. The bottle bore a black skull and crossbones. No one was allowed to touch the bottle except for Vern.

Each morning, he stood in the bathroom shaving and putting on his Old Spice aftershave. He stood naked except for his boxer shorts, and I could see the distinct muscles on his arms and chest. He lifted weights four times a week—always including Sundays because he never went to church with us.

"Bring me a glass from the kitchen," he told me.

When I brought the glass, he filled it with tap water. After removing the bottle from the cabinet, he took out the dropper and carefully squeezed three drops of iodine into the water, then swirled it. The iodine spread out like dark blood.

He studied the water and iodine for a minute. "Don't you ever try this. It would kill you."

"I won't." For a long time I feared the iodine might kill him and I'd be held responsible somehow, because I'd brought him the glass. My fingerprints were all over it.

I believed wholeheartedly that Vern had some extraordinary power, because it didn't kill him. And he was quick to contribute to this belief.

"No one can kill me because I drink this," he told me. "It's an inoculation against death."

I knew what an inoculation was because I'd had to get shots before attending school.

The skull and crossbones made me afraid. Still, I asked, "When can I take some of the iodine?"

"I'll tell you when it's time," he said. "But you can't be a momma's boy."

"I won't be," I promised.

Sometimes when he was away working at Rieth and my mother was asleep, I went into the bathroom to study the bottle. Twice I carried in a glass and filled it from the tap, then squeezed iodine into the water, but I was nervous and clumsy. I couldn't get the drops to come out one, two, three the same way Vern could.

The death's-head made me too afraid to drink. Maybe I'd die in the middle of the night. Vern had taken me to see *DOA*, a movie where the hero is poisoned in a bar and spends the entire movie trying to track down his killer before he dies. In the process, the hero suffers terribly from the poisoning. "You have luminescent poisoning," the doctors tell him, but can't do a thing to help him.

Those two times I actually squeezed iodine into the glass, I eventually poured the water down the bathroom sink. The first time, I stared in alarm at the reddish brown stains it left. After getting some of my mother's cleanser, I scrubbed the sink until it was gleaming white again. The second time, I was more careful to pour the water straight down the drain hole.

I washed and rinsed the glasses twice but worried that some iodine trace remained. What if my mother drank from that glass and I poisoned her? I put both glasses into the garbage can and covered them with newspaper.

Vern found the second glass one morning when he salvaged the newspaper to read the sports page. "How the hell did this get in here? It's a perfectly good glass."

He didn't take the glass out himself, but just pointed to it.

My mother fished out the glass and set it on the counter to be washed. "I must be getting absentminded," she said.

"It's being pregnant," Vern said. "Pregnancy messes up your mind."

When my mother sat down at the table to drink her tea, I got up and began washing the glass. My plan was to put it far back in the cupboard where no one could drink out of it.

"What are you doing?" Vern asked.

"I'm washing this glass. It was in the garbage and it's dirty."

"He's trying to help out," my mother said.

"That's a switch," Vern said. "He never helps out around here."

"He helped you rake the leaves last weekend," she said.

Vern couldn't deny it, but he said, "Big help. I could have done it faster myself."

That was probably true. By the time he finished giving instructions and criticizing, I was too nervous to do a good job.

"I love the smell of burning leaves," she said. "It reminds me of fall in The Dalles when I was a girl."

"Well, you're not in The Dalles now," he said, putting down his coffee. He scowled at me. "Why don't you stick up for yourself, instead of letting her butt in?"

I didn't say anything.

My mother furrowed her brow. "Now let's just have a pleasant morning."

"I'm going to bed." Vern pointed at me. "If you're such a big help, go wash the bird shit off the car, why don't you? It got covered out at Rieth." He left the kitchen.

"Well, I guess you have a chore," my mother said. "You can take the radio outside to keep you company, but don't wake up Vern. He's a light sleeper."

"I won't," I said.

She washed the breakfast dishes, including the iodine glass. I

kept track of where she put it, determined to keep it out of circu-
lation.

"Why does Vern take iodine?" I asked.

She shook her head. "I wish he wouldn't. I'm afraid he's going
to harm himself." She looked at me. "Don't you ever take it.
Promise me."

"I won't ever take it," I said.

"It's got the skull and crossbones right on it, but there's no rea-
soning with Vern."

"He said it makes him invincible."

"That's not right," she said. "He was just teasing. He takes it
because he's afraid of getting a goiter."

"What's that?"

"It's a kind of tumor that grows on your neck. Right about
here." She showed me. "In the old days, people used to get goiters
from not having enough iodine in their diets. Would you like to
see a picture? Your great-aunt Stella had one."

Mom got out the photograph album from the bottom drawer
of her mahogany chest-on-chest. Stella's goiter was the size of a
peach. "That makes me sick," I said. "How could she even swallow?"

"It doesn't block your throat." She closed the album. "Now
don't worry. There's iodine in salt these days." She showed me the
blue Morton's container, which said "iodized." Then she added,
"And in ocean fish. That's one of the reasons Vern likes to eat
halibut."

I saw a chance to get on Vern's good side. "If I catch more fish,
maybe he'll quit taking the iodine. I could help him out."

"I think they have to be ocean fish, but I don't know why.
Maybe you can ask your teacher."

I did ask, but Mrs. Rumpel didn't know much science. She
knew nothing about iodine. Mostly, she just collected quarters
every morning for school lunches and took the count down to the
principal's office. Sometimes, she was gone a long time; a few of
the kids claimed she couldn't stand teaching us. I never ate school
lunches because Vern said lunch quarters added up to over five

dollars some months. Instead, I brought a sack lunch from home—usually bologna or sandwiches made from leftovers.

"I want to start having school lunches on Fridays," I announced one evening.

"What on earth for?" my mother asked.

"On Fridays, the Catholic kids always get fish sticks," I said. "They'll never get goiters." I thought of how the Catholics took their fish stick lunches to a far table and ate together.

"That's the dumbest thing I ever heard," Vern said. "And stay away from my iodine."

I had visions of watermelon-size goiters inflicting everyone but the Catholics. I secretly touched my neck, and it seemed swollen already. The more I touched, the worse it got. And in order to swallow, I had to gulp and gulp.

■ ■ ■

In Pendleton, my mother's allergies caused her enormous suffering. Also, she had a miscarriage there, the first of several, and her afflictions dampened her enthusiasm. When the opportunity came for Vern to bid on a telegrapher's job in Baker, he tried for it, even though he claimed he didn't have a "Chinaman's chance" because the job paid a lot more than working at Rieth.

My mother remained optimistic. "If you don't try for better opportunities, you won't get them," she said. To Vern's surprise and my mother's delight, they offered him the job.

I didn't want to leave Pendleton, but they both insisted Baker would be a fresh start. "I'm just positive I won't suffer from this horrible hay fever in Baker," my mother said. They talked about buying a house of their own and promised me a bedroom with a closet. In Pendleton, I slept on a roll-away bed in the front room.

"How about getting a dog like Thumper?" I asked.

"We'll see," they said.

6

THE LEPER

Vern and my mother purchased a small house in Baker, the only place she ever lived where she didn't pay rent. She slipped eagerly into the role of homemaker.

The basement held a wringer washer, and she hung the clothes out to dry on the backyard clothesline. Yellow towels because that was her favorite color, white sheets, my school clothes, Vern's white shirts—all hung out to dry in the Baker sunshine.

"I love the climate here," she said more than once. "It's so sunny. And I love the way the light shines on the hardwood floors." In Baker she was free of her hay fever.

Sunset, Good Housekeeping, and 1950s cookbooks contained recipes she found exciting to try. She cut out the magazine recipes and glued them to note cards kept in a file box. Beside each recipe, she wrote Vern's response and mine.

Rancho pork chops (cooked well) with ketchup, lemon, and onion
Vern and Craig both love these.

Hawaiian ham with pineapple and cloves (remove cloves before serving)
One of their favorites. Good for company.

Halibut au gratin.
Not Vern's favorite or Craig's either.

Pot roast
Can't go wrong—Vern likes potatoes but not carrots.

She made a pot of coffee around four in the afternoon, just when he was getting up, and she appreciated the fact that he always got dressed before coming to the dinner table. In summer, Vern drank iced tea with dinner, and in winter, he and my mother both drank hot tea. She took milk and sugar in hers while he stuck to lemon.

For special occasions, such as paydays and holidays, she made pineapple upside-down cake, which Vern and I both loved. She never baked pies. "I just can't get the crusts right, but my mother makes wonderful pies."

Grandma Lange did make tasty pies and always baked "dokeys" from the crust scraps. These she covered with sugar and cinnamon. I loved them so much, I burned my mouth because I couldn't wait for them to cool.

My mother remained a firm believer in not saying anything unless you could say something pleasant. During dinner, she discussed new recipes she might try, *Sunset* travel articles, neighbors she met downtown or in the grocery store.

I added to the conversation with a brief description of the school day, recess, upcoming sports events. I brought home tests and report cards showing good grades. My mother always stressed the importance of school, especially the sciences.

My second grade teacher had said that I was college material, prompting my mother to start saving a small amount each month for my education. She herself had graduated second in her class at The Dalles High School and attended Linfield College for a semester before leaving due to a lack of funds. However, she was determined that I would become the first person in our family to graduate from college.

Vern remained cooler about my schooling, but on occasion he'd say, "Of course he's smart. He's got me for an example."

My stepfather wasn't a talker, but he did outline plans to fix up the house. And he'd offer remarks about the railroad. Trucks were taking more of their shipping away and the railroads would have to cut back. He blamed Eisenhower and the interstate freeway system for damaging the railroad. If he got "bumped," we'd have to move out of Baker.

My mother noted that he was building seniority all the time and she was certain that wouldn't happen. Leaving Baker, the little house, my friends—it wouldn't come to that.

During the six years we lived in Baker, I don't remember anyone coming over for dinner, except relatives and a couple of my friends. Perhaps Mom invited the Lutheran minister. Vern attended church only on Easter and Christmas. "All the minister wants me to do is open my wallet and let the sunshine out," he said.

Baker had a wonderful old theater, the Eltrym, which had been named for the owner's wife. Spelled backward, Eltrym was Myrtle. Vern took me only to movies he liked. He refused to attend Saturday matinees or children's movies, although we did see *Son of Paleface* with Bob Hope and Jane Russell. "She got big whoppers," he commented after the movie. "I could go for those."

Some of the movies he liked gave me nightmares. In *It Came from Outer Space*, a spaceship from Mars landed in the desert near a small town and aliens gradually took over the citizens, turning them into mindless robots. "Something like that could happen around here," Vern said. "Who would know if aliens took over one of these hick towns? Who would even care?"

"Which town do you think they'd want?" I asked.

He sneered. "Any one of these jerkwater towns your mother is so crazy about seeing. Halfway, North Powder, Union, Haines."

He had named the places we'd visited. My mother wanted to see every small town; then she insisted on driving up and down every block. It drove Vern nuts.

"There's Lime, where you work when you're not in Baker," I said. "It's pretty small." I liked the idea of aliens getting my stepfather.

"Forget it," he said. "No alien is going to mess with me."

A lot of those movies gave me nightmares. But the leper movie was the worst. In the leper movie, Douglas Fairbanks Jr. falls in love with a beautiful woman played by Myrna Loy. Her husband has been diagnosed with leprosy and banished to a leper colony on an island off the coast of Louisiana. He has to live with other lepers and have no contact with normal society. When he finds out about his wife's new boyfriend, he becomes ferociously jealous, escapes by stowing away on a supply boat, then spends the entire movie trying to touch the lovers so they will get leprosy, too. As his disease progresses, parts of his face peel away and his fingers fall off.

The movie terrified me. I developed a phobia about leprosy and became convinced that a leper would touch me, and I'd have to leave behind all my friends in Baker.

Vern didn't help. "Leprosy is the worst disease on planet earth," he told me after the movie. "When I was in the navy, we saw a leper colony in the Philippines. The lepers didn't have fingers or toes. They just rotted away from the disease, joint by joint. Most of them were missing their noses, too. They couldn't pick their nose like you do all the time, you little bastard. I'd rather be dead than have leprosy."

He only called me "little bastard" when my mother wasn't around.

At home, I studied my face in the bathroom mirror, covering my nose with a folded washcloth. I didn't like the way I looked. I made fists and imagined my hands stopped at the knuckles. How could lepers even eat? I wondered. Or throw a baseball? No lepers could play baseball, I determined. They couldn't hold a bat with no fingers or run to first with no toes. At least not very fast.

. . .

At the school library, I looked up leprosy in the encyclopedia. They had grim pictures. The lepers looked as horrible as Vern had described them. The article said leprosy came from living in filthy conditions. There was no cure.

Living in filthy conditions described half the boys in my school, especially the Wagontire brothers. In kindergarten, they gave all the other boys scalp ringworm by wearing our hats. We had to shave our heads and paint the ringworm with iodine every morning. Each day the school nurse checked to make sure the iodine was covering the scaly patches.

Now I stopped going to the bathroom in case one of the Wagontires was in there spreading leprosy. On the playground, I avoided the Wagontire boys entirely.

In class, I imagined the pretty girls and how they might look with leprosy: Sandra Town, Gail Lawrence, Rhonda Hester, Priscilla Paugh—each one missing fingers and toes. How could you kiss a girl who was missing her nose?

During the daytime, I kept watch for lepers, but I realized how vulnerable I was whenever I slept. Five nights a week, Vern was away working in Lime, so that left just my mother and me in the house. And I worried that Vern might catch leprosy from one of the hobo jungles beside the tracks. If he got leprosy, I was sure he'd come back to touch us. He was mean like that.

At night, I barricaded my bedroom door with my dresser. I also opened my bedroom window, so I could leap out fast when the lepers came bumbling into the room. It would take them awhile to enter, especially since they had to turn the doorknob with only a few fingers. This would give me precious time to escape through the window.

This went on for weeks. I caught bronchitis from the cold—it often fell below zero in Baker—and I had painful ear infections, but these were better than leprosy, I figured.

One Sunday, our Lutheran minister, Reverend Gitzendeiner, introduced a special missionary who had worked with the lepers in India. He described their plight, showed slides of the suffering lepers, and took up a collection. Afterward, we were supposed to go up and shake his hand, but I didn't want to get near him. Complaining of a stomachache, I went downstairs to the bathroom, but then didn't go in, afraid the missionary might have used it. The next Sunday, after making sure the missionary was gone, I asked Reverend Gitzendeiner how it was that the missionary didn't catch leprosy. "Faith, my boy. Faith," he said. "In the Bible, Jesus cures the lepers. Jesus can do all things, if we believe."

I tried to have faith, but I believed Jesus might need a little help. My bedroom had twin beds, and I tied a rope between the legs closest to the door, so it stretched across the pathway a leper would take as he tried to touch me. This would trip the lepers, especially since they had no toes for balance. While they picked themselves up after tripping, I could be out the window.

In January, I had double ear infections. My mother put warm drops in each ear and plugged them with cotton. Her face was troubled because the doctor said my hearing was likely to be impaired.

One night, I awoke to a thud and muffled yelling. My bedroom door stood wide open, the dresser shoved to the side. A dark object lay prone, stretched along the floor between my twin beds.

An honest-to-God leper, I thought. Caught in my trap.

I started for the open window, taking care to crawl over the headboard so the leper couldn't reach out and touch me.

"I think I broke my fucking wrist!" the leper cried out just as I reached the window. He yelled so loudly, I could hear him through the cotton in my ears. I put my hands on the sill and was about to leap when I froze.

My mother appeared in the doorway. Wearing nothing but a flimsy nightgown and slippers, she was no match for a leper, even a wounded one.

"Mom, it's a leper. Get away!"

She turned in my direction and said something, but I couldn't hear, so I took the cotton out of my right ear.

"Honey, are you okay?" she asked.

I was ready to answer when the figure on the floor said, "No, damn it to hell."

To my amazement, the leper's voice sounded exactly like Vern's, now that the cotton was out.

"Let me help you up," my mother said, stepping toward the Vern-like leper.

"Don't touch him, Mom," I warned. "He might be an imposter."

She leaned forward, as if studying the figure's identity.

"I felt a draft out in the hall," the leper said. "I opened the door and saw the crazy little bastard has the window wide open. All the heat's getting sucked out."

This sounded like my stepfather, except for calling me "bastard" in front of my mother. He was always fretting about closing the windows and losing heat. But I remained skeptical and confused. Vern was scheduled to be in Lime for two more days. If this really was Vern, why was he now lying on the floor of my room, occupying the place of a leper?

"There's a goddamn rope tied between the beds," the leper said. "That's what tripped me."

My mother turned on the bedroom light and helped him sit. The way he held his damaged wrist, I could count all five fingers. Maybe this was Vern or maybe it was a leper in the early stages of the disease—dressed in Vern's clothing.

"Why is the window wide open, Craig?" my mother asked.

I looked at the window as though I hadn't noticed it before, which was difficult because my hands were clutching the sill. "Someone forgot to close it, I guess. Someone opened it, I guess, and then someone forgot to close it."

"Jesus H. Christ," the leper said. "Jesus H. Christ himself couldn't pay our heating bills."

My mother stiffened. "I wish you wouldn't swear like that. With the window wide open, the neighbors can hear every word. Especially the way the sound carries on these cold nights." Her voice was cool and controlled. "And never say *bastard* again in this house."

She turned to me. "Now, Craig, would you please close that window?" Under the circumstances, I closed the window, shutting off my escape route. I turned the latch with a flourish.

"I'm nailing that window shut," the leper said in a threatening

manner. "If I can swing a hammer with this wrist, I'm doing it tomorrow. When I'm finished, Houdini couldn't open it. I don't give
a damn if you bake all summer. You can roast to death for all I
care."

This sounded more and more like Vern. It had to be him.

"What's this rope doing here?" Mom asked. "Why is it tied between the two beds?"

"I was practicing for the Cub Scouts. You're looking at a clove
knot."

"That's not a clove knot," Vern said. "That's a double granny.
Hell's fire, it doesn't take a four-year hitch in the navy to know
that."

My stepfather stood and staggered to the door. He banged his
good hand against the wood. "For this, I'm killing myself in Lime.
Choking on dust all day." He waited for one of us to say something.

I decided the best course of action was to get back in bed. I half-
stumbled over to the bed and cupped my hand over my right ear.

"Don't fall. Are you all right?" My mother's forehead crinkled
with worry lines.

"Woozy," I said. "I'm just a little woozy."

"It's the ear infection—the doctor told us it could make you
dizzy."

Turning to Vern, she said, "We better take you to the hospital
and have some X rays."

"Get some ice," he told her. "I'm not paying any more doctor
bills." He glared at me. "Keeping that window open, no wonder
you're sick. All the time, I thought you were just a pansy."

My mother took his good arm. "Let's go to the kitchen. I have
ice in the freezer."

"I should have stayed in Lime," he said. "The main conveyor
broke down, so they can't load cars for two days. But I should have
stayed in Lime."

My bedroom door was still ajar, so I could hear her open the
freezer door, the crack of ice cubes in the tray. Then pounding. I

knew she had put the ice cubes in a clean dish towel and was breaking them up with the meat tenderizer.

I heard the furnace kick in and felt the heat rising through my bedroom register. The house was getting back to its routine. My forehead felt hot. I wondered how high your temperature went with leprosy.

In the kitchen, my mother talked to my stepfather in soothing tones. But he was quiet in a menacing way. I figured he'd go along for a while, then come take it out on me when my mother wasn't looking.

Later, my mother came in with a glass of ice and a straw. I pretended to be asleep until I felt her cool hand on my forehead.

"I want you to suck on some of this ice," she said. "I want that fever to come down." She took my shoulder. "What's all this nonsense about lepers?"

I sipped some of the ice, collecting my thoughts.

"Earlier, I was delirious, I guess," I said. "Maybe I was having a nightmare about that movie with the leper and that missionary at church."

"You have an overactive imagination," she said. "I'm going to have a talk with Vern about the movies he takes you to. But not tonight. He's still awfully worked up."

My mother stood and crossed to the window. In the pale moonlight, two tall pines cast their shadows across the frozen snow.

"What am I going to do?" she said. "You men will be the death of me."

The next morning, Vern went to the drugstore and returned with an elastic bandage to wrap his wrist. Then he went into the bedroom and nailed the window shut. The violent pounding made my ears throb. My mother stood at the ironing board, lifting her hand off the iron a couple of times to touch her throat. She went down to the basement to get more clothes from the line.

When Vern passed through the kitchen, he shook the hammer at me. "Try opening that window, you little bastard." He spoke quietly so my mother wouldn't hear.

I knew I wasn't a bastard, but Vern called me that to remind me my father had left.

He took a hunting knife and cut the rope into tiny pieces, then threw them into the garbage can. "A clove knot. If I ever see rope tied like that again, I'll strangle you with it."

After Vern went back to Lime, Mom took me to the doctor's again and he prescribed more powerful antibiotics. She had the doctor tell me about leprosy and he assured me there were were no lepers in Baker. I guess that included the Wagontire boys.

Throughout the winter, the fear of lepers and isolated colonies eventually faded. I had come to realize that I had more to fear from my stepfather than all the lepers in the world.

7

HOBOES

When I was eleven, once in a blue moon my stepfather would let me come to work with him on the graveyard shift. Knowing this event was coming up, I'd trade comic books with friends and check out adventure tales from the library so I had plenty to do during his eight-hour shift. We'd walk to the railroad depot, because Vern believed in staying in shape, even though smoking Chesterfields cut his wind. These night journeys struck me as adventures where exciting events might happen or Vern would say something profound. Once I pointed out a dog near the lumber mill where my friends and I begged scrap wood for building projects. Vern told me it wasn't a dog, but a coyote that came into town hunting a cat or small dog to kill.

"In Australia, a coyote will steal a baby," he said. "Over there, they call them dingoes."

This cunning and dangerous animal caught my attention. I had been wanting a .22 rifle and saw this as a possible reason for making the purchase. I could protect our home from marauding coyotes.

"Could I kill a coyote with a twenty-two?" I asked.

He stopped to light a cigarette. "With hollow points. But you'd need to be a darned good shot."

"You could teach me," I said. "I bet you're a good shot."

He squinted at me through the smoke he exhaled. "I don't want you shooting a toe off."

"I'd be careful. Danny Freeman and I shoot rifles out at the ranch." Danny was my closest friend.

"We'll see," he said, which was a little better than, "No."

As we approached the station, Vern spotted a hobo lurking behind a boxcar. "Wait here," he told me, and crossed two sets of tracks so the hobo knew he'd been spotted.

"Hey there, buddy!" Vern called out. "You can't loiter around here. Get it down the line."

"Who says?"

The voice sounded young and rough. I was scared for my stepfather.

"I work for the railroad, and I'm telling you to move on."

"You ain't a dick. There ain't a dick between Portland and Boise now."

Vern stripped off his jacket, revealing his white shirt glowing under the train yard lights. He took three quick steps toward the man, who suddenly held his arms out. In the light, you could see he was missing his right hand.

"Mister, I don't want to cause trouble. I just need to get to Spokane. My brother lives there."

Vern had stopped moving toward him. He considered the situation for a moment. "A freight comes along at three. You can catch it below the yard, down by the grain elevator. When it stops in Hinkle, switch to the Burlington Northern. You'll be in Spokane for lunch."

"I'm obliged." The man touched his shirt pocket with his hand. "Hey, I'm fresh out of smokes. You got an extra?"

Vern shook his head. "I just smoked my last one."

The man picked up his bag and started trudging down the track. "Anyway, I'm really obliged, mister."

After the hobo had walked a hundred feet, Vern retrieved his jacket and slipped it on. When he stood in front of me, he closed his fists and shadowboxed until his breath came out in quick puffs and a bright red spot appeared on both cheeks.

"How do you suppose he lost that hand?" I asked.

Vern shrugged. "Logging, mining, farm accident."

"It's a tough break," I said.

"Listen, kidaroo. A hobo will want an advantage. Give him an inch and he'll take a mile. You got that?"

I nodded.

"A Negro, too. He'll grin and nod, roll his eyeballs. And when your back is turned, he'll step right where you told him not to. Understand?"

"I understand. But how do you know?"

"You learn human nature in the service. In Baker, you don't have to worry much—just about hoboes—but in the navy, you got all kinds now. Uncle Sam's melting pot."

■ ■ ■

We stopped at the Union Cafe across from the railroad depot. A couple of brakemen in striped overalls and blue bandannas hunched over platefuls of pancakes and sausages.

Vern nodded at them and they returned the nod.

"Packing your bodyguard with you tonight?" one said.

"That's right," Vern said. "Craig's riding shotgun. He just helped me chase a hobo out of the train yard. Big sucker. At first I thought he'd give us trouble, but the old kidaroo here scared him off."

"He looks like a scrapper," the brakeman said. "Chip off the old block."

I felt proud, even if I wasn't Vern's real son. The men seemed to respect my stepfather.

Breen, the night cook, came out from the kitchen holding a spatula. "Shirley called in sick, so I'm running the whole shebang. What'll it be?"

Vern spread his hands on the countertop and leaned forward. "You aren't feeding the hoboes, are you? I just had to chase one out of the yard."

Breen lowered his gaze. "I don't feed nobody, unless they got money. Paying customers." He pointed the spatula at Vern. "That includes you."

"If you feed one, he tells ten others," Vern said. "Pretty soon it's nothing but big trouble."

"I'm strictly cash-and-carry," Breen said. "If you want something to eat, say it now. I got hash browns to turn."

"I'll take a coffee to go," Vern said. "Give the boy a hot chocolate."

"Just a second." Breen went back into the kitchen and turned the hash browns. Then he got the drinks. "Forty-five cents."

Vern tapped two quarters on the counter, spun one around, then laid both down. "Keep the change." He picked up his coffee. Maybe we'll see you for breakfast."

"Not me," Breen said. "With all this money, I'm heading to Florida."

"Take the bus," Vern said. "The train's too slow. You'll be dead by the time you get there."

We all laughed at that one.

I sat at the stationmaster's desk, reading comic books. Vern smoked cigarettes and operated the telegraph. *Click-clack, click, click, clack, clack, click, click.* When messages came to him, he wrote them down with sharp yellow pencils that had the name Union Pacific printed in red. The green visor that he wore cast an eerie light on his face. Every hour or so, he took off the visor, slipped on his coat, and walked around outside the station. He carried a heavy black flashlight.

I walked from window to window, watching him shine the light into dark corners looking for hoboes. I hoped he wouldn't find any.

Back inside, he hung his jacket on the coatrack and put on

the visor. Then he leaned back in his chair, resting his feet on the desk.

"Everything was okay out there?" I asked.

"Aye, aye, sir!" Vern gave the coatrack a mock salute. "All clear ashore and on deck." He chuckled, then leaned my way. "Do you know the worst thing about hoboes?"

I thought a moment. "They steal things?"

"They steal plenty all right, but that's not the worst thing." He paused. "They carry diseases. Hoboes are riddled with diseases."

Riddled was a peculiar word to me. One time, when Danny and I had shown his older brother Dave a beer can shot full of holes, he had said, "You really riddled that one." Now I imagined the hoboes walking around with gaping bullet holes. "What kind of diseases?"

"You name it," Vern said. "Tuberculosis and trichinosis, for starters." He looked at me. "Hoboes get trichinosis from eating bad pork. Most of them are too dumb to even know they have it. They think it's the flu or arthritis. It's tricky to diagnose. Doctors call trichinosis 'the chameleon of diseases.'"

"Is trichinosis the worst?"

"It'll kill you fast enough," Vern said. "That's why I eat my pork cooked all the way through. But the very worst is social disease. Do you know about social disease?"

"A little." I had heard the older boys talk about clap on the playground. If they wanted to taunt a girl, they said she had the clap, or crabs—I knew crabs meant lice. Some had gone to the principal's office for calling out those words.

"I've heard of clap," I said.

"Clap's just a nickname for gonorrhea," Vern said. "In the navy, sailors would go ashore and get clap from the whores. Then they'd come back on board and get the whole ship clapped up. The problem was they'd ignore being sick until they couldn't piss without screaming. That's how bad it burned. Then you'd have long lines on the ship—guys waiting in their shorts for penicillin shots. Some of them had bad sores on their puds."

It sounded awful. "That would cure them, the penicillin?" I asked.

"Most of the time. But if they didn't get treatment when they should, later on they'd go blind or crazy, maybe both. See, in the navy you had doctors and medicine. The trouble with hoboes is they don't get treatment. You never see doctors riding the rails. So like I say, the hoboes are riddled with disease."

I wondered whether it would be worse to be blind or crazy or both. If you were crazy, would you even know you were blind?

"Sometimes hoboes mess around with each other," Vern said. "Do you know what 'riding the caboose' means?"

"Like the brakemen? They jump on the caboose and signal all clear down the line with their lanterns."

"Not like that. Sometimes hoboes mess around with each other. They get sick and don't get treated. After awhile they go crazy. They might start messing around with kids—little girls. Even little boys. That's why I won't tolerate any hoboes hanging around the station or the yard."

A message started coming in on the telegraph and he leaned over to copy it down. His head bobbed as he wrote, the green visor moving up and down.

I was trying to make sense of what he said. I knew from school that you could get sick from messing around with girls, but I didn't know what eating pork had to do with it. And nobody had spoken about "riding the caboose."

I went into the men's room and inspected my pud. It seemed okay, but the light was dim. According to Vern, not being a hobo and taking penicillin seemed to be the best way to keep from being riddled, but I had an ice-cold fear I might have caught something when Vern touched me under my pajamas. He hadn't acted that way since he and my mother were married and we moved to Pendleton. He now slept in bed with my mother, and their wallpaper had yellow flowers.

When I came out of the men's room, Vern started sending a message in response to the telegram that had come in. I tried to read my comic book, but I couldn't focus. Maybe I was clapped up. Maybe I'd go blind or crazy.

The telegraph seemed to mock me.

click-clap, click-click, clap-clap-clap

I couldn't sit still. I jumped up and walked to the window. To prove to myself I wasn't going blind, I concentrated on reading objects in the early-morning light. I read the license plates of cars, the letters on the Chinese restaurant down the block. I went to another window to see if my sight was okay from there.

"Stop jumping around," Vern said. "I'm not going to bring you along if you keep me from doing my work."

"All right," I said, trying to control my agitation.

"Don't be a little bastard."

At eight, when he got off shift, Vern was in a better mood. "Let's see about some breakfast," he said, putting on his coat.

I gathered up my comic books.

The Union Cafe had a different cook, a gray-haired woman who watched four eggs sizzle as she smoked a cigarette. A young brunette waitress, one I'd never seen before, came over to take our order. She was pretty, in a "fast" way, wearing too much makeup and lipstick. I wondered if she slept with older boys and if she had the clap.

Vern took out two silver dollars and twirled them on the counter. "Sausage and eggs," he told the waitress before she could ask. "Cook the sausage dark, okay? Well done. You'll have to ask my sidekick what he wants."

"What'll it be, handsome?" she asked.

"I already told you," Vern said with a quick grin. "Weren't you listening?"

"You're lucky to have such a good-looking boy," the waitress told Vern. "In a couple of years, you'll have to chase the girls off with a broom."

"Yeah, I'm the luckiest guy in the world." He punched my shoulder, hard enough to hurt under the coat. "And he's the luckiest kid."

"He looks just like you," she said to Vern.

"Miracles happen every day," he said in that sarcastic tone he had.

She ignored him. "God sends a miracle every day, but we have to stay on our toes to recognize it." She turned to me. "So what's for breakfast?"

I knew I didn't want pork. She was looking directly at me and I saw her pink tongue dart over her small white teeth as she licked the pencil's tip. I glanced down at the menu, ashamed suddenly for thinking she might have the clap. "Pancakes, a short stack."

She wrote it down. "Anything else?"

"Coffee," I said. "Make it black."

She glanced at Vern.

"It's way past his bedtime," he said. "Bring him a tall glass of milk."

On the way home, Vern told me not to mention the hobo because that incident would worry my mother. I just told her about the trains heading east and west, breakfast at the café.

She smiled. "You're lucky to see so much at your age. There's a world out there beyond Baker, and you're just beginning to learn about it. I want you to learn about other people and cultures."

I'm sure she wasn't thinking about whores or social diseases.

The clap still worried me. But I remembered all the earaches I'd had every winter and the penicillin the doctor prescribed. We had some prescription medicine left over, even though the doctor recommended finishing the bottles.

However, when my ears had stopped hurting, Vern told my mother to stop giving me the pills. "Save some of that. This way, we won't have to go to the doctor all the time," he told her.

"That's not how they said to do it," she replied. "Look at the instructions."

"Figure it out," he said. "The doctor's got a sweet deal going with the pharmacist. They prescribe more than you actually need so the pharmacist makes more money and the doctor gets a kickback."

"They both go to the Lutheran church," my mother said.

"The Bible's full of hypocrites. Have you ever seen the doctor's home? It's a mansion. No one has a place like that unless they're crooked."

Now, when the bathroom was clear, I went in and closed the door. Opening the medicine cabinet quietly, I found the penicillin. Gray-and-pink pills. One hundred milligrams each. How much would it take to get rid of the clap? I wondered.

Someone knocked on the bathroom door and I closed the cabinet.

"Open up!" It was Vern.

"I'm having a stomachache," I said, unrolling some toilet paper loudly enough for him to hear.

"You ate too many pancakes," he said. "Five minutes and this door better be unlocked. Light some matches, too. I don't want it smelling foul."

I checked my penis. No sores. The light was better here than at the station. Everything seemed all clear. I pissed into the bowl. I guess it stung just a little but no burning. I didn't need to shout with pain like the sailors.

Opening the cabinet again, I took one of the small pills and washed it down with a palmful of water. What the heck. I took another. Tomorrow, I'd take two more. Who would know?

I closed the medicine cabinet door harder than I intended and it made a metallic click. When I opened the bathroom door, Vern glared at me. He was dressed in only his boxer shorts.

"Took you long enough." He sniffed. "I don't smell any matches."

"I forgot, but it was a false alarm."

Walking over to the sink, he looked at his reflection in the mirror. He slapped each cheek a couple times. "No jowls." He glanced at me. "How old do I look? Pretend you don't know me."

"Pretty young," I said. "Thirty, give or take a year."

He was actually thirty-eight.

He stuck out his chest. "I'm just hitting my best years. There's no fat on me."

"I can see that," I said.

"What the hell were you doing in the medicine cabinet?"

"Nothing. Just looking for an aspirin."

"If you didn't stay up all night, you wouldn't get a headache."

"Yeah," I said. I almost added, "Thanks for taking me," but that would have been too much.

Opening the cabinet, he scanned the shelves, then reached for the iodine bottle. As he unscrewed the dropper, the skull and crossbones waggled at me. I was relieved the iodine was right where he'd left it. I hadn't touched the bottle. And Vern didn't think to check the penicillin.

He held the dropper. It was two-thirds full of dark red fluid. "Don't ever go messing with this iodine," he said.

"I won't."

"Well, don't just stand there. Get me a goddamned glass."

"Sure thing," I said, heading for the kitchen.

8

RONNA AND RAZZLE-DAZZLE

"I've told them I don't want a pink room at the hospital," my mother said. "I prefer any color but pink."

"You might have a girl," Vern said. "Pink is a girl's color."

"I like yellow," she said. "Yellow rooms are so cheerful and bright."

"Well, you might get pink anyway." Vern touched her stomach. "Patients can't be too choosy. If it's Vern Junior, I'll try to find you a blue room."

"Blue's okay," she said. "It's my favorite color on Craig. So soft. When he wears blue, his skin looks just like velvet."

Vern acted as if were going to say something smartass about my skin—like velvet was for pansies—but instead, he came over and put his hand on my shoulder. "If I'm in Lime when she starts to have the baby, I'm counting on you. Call the taxi; help your mother into the back seat."

"I will."

He squeezed a little. "Don't forget the suitcase."

The suitcase contained clean underwear, a hair brush, comb,

mirror, and toothbrush. Ivory soap. My mother didn't like scents of any kind, including perfume and scented soaps, so she took a bar of Ivory everywhere she went.

"Don't worry. I won't forget."

He patted my shoulder. "That's the old sox, the old bean, the old fight, the old kidaroo."

I grinned because Vern always said that when he wanted me to do something.

"Do you think it will be a boy or a girl?" he asked. "Which do you want?"

"I don't care," I said. "Either one would be great."

"Any baby is a miracle," my mother said. "All babies are flowers in God's flower garden."

"But Craig has to have a preference," he insisted. "Which one is it?"

The tone of his voice had changed, and I suspected a trick question. If I said "a girl," I'd be going against his desire for Vern Junior. And if I said "a boy," he'd say I wasn't considerate of my mother. I hesitated.

My mother might have noticed the edge in Vern's voice and helped me out. "After all I've been through, I'm just looking forward to the miracle of a new life. As long as it's all there with ten fingers and ten toes."

She had had five miscarriages. Finally, a new doctor had prescribed thyroid tablets, making it possible for her to keep this one.

All of us agreed on the name "Ronna" for a girl. At first, my mother favored Rebecca Ellen after one of the neighbor girls she liked. However, when she read a *Ladies Home Journal* article by a woman named Ronna, she changed her mind.

"Grab the suitcase and call the cab," Vern told me.

"What for? It's not time."

"Practice. I want to see how long it takes you." He checked his watch. "You've already wasted eight seconds."

I hurried into my parents' bedroom and grabbed the suitcase. It was light, so I carried it to the front room door fast. Then I went to the phone and looked up the Baker Taxi number.

"Forty-six seconds," Vern said. "Speed it up."

I fumbled with the phone book, losing the page.

"Slow as molasses."

"Here it is. What should I do?"

"Order a taxi. Give them the address and wait for them to write it down. After they read it back, tell them you've changed your mind and hang up."

I didn't want to call and then cancel a taxi. "What if they come anyway?"

"Do it right and they won't."

When the man answered the phone, I gave him the address. He read it back to me. "That's right," I said. "Thank you very much but I've decided to wait until later."

"You're canceling the cab?"

"Just until later."

"Get off the line," he said. "This is a business phone." I heard him mutter "fucking kid" before I hung up. I flushed with embarrassment.

"Not bad," Vern said. "Now carry the suitcase out to the curb, so you can flag down the taxi."

"He's not coming."

Vern scowled. "Practice makes perfect."

I carried the suitcase out and set it on the curb. I jumped up and down to keep warm. This was the dead of winter.

Byron Brinton, the newspaper publisher and our neighbor, drove down the street in his new car. After seeing me, he stopped and rolled down the window. "Is your mother having her baby? I can give her a ride to the hospital."

"I'm just practicing in case Vern's in Lime when it happens."

He nodded. "Next time, practice with your coat on or you'll be going to the hospital yourself."

"Okay."

"Let me know as soon as she has the baby. We'll announce it in the paper."

"Sure thing."

Vern whistled and signaled for me to come in. I started back without the suitcase then hurried to retrieve it. On the porch, I asked, "How long did it take?"

"Numbskull. Don't forget your coat. I'm not paying for any more doctor bills." Inside the house, he shook his head. "Over three minutes."

"That's too long, huh?"

"In the navy, guys bled to death in two. You've got to shake a leg."

"Let me try it again." I knew I could do better.

"Maybe you're not cut out for this responsibility." He frowned. "Maybe I'll have to take vacation hours and stay here. Of course, we couldn't go anywhere this summer if I take all of my hours now."

"Don't do that." My mother came in from the kitchen. "Write the taxi number in the front of the phonebook. That should speed things up."

"You should have thought of that," Vern told me.

On the second try, I held the button down and pretended to talk with the cab driver. Vern acted as if he didn't notice. My mother smiled while I raced through the drill. I didn't make any mistakes and was standing on the curb with the suitcase in short time. After zipping my coat, I turned and waved at Vern and my mother.

She waved back excitedly and Vern raised his arm halfway. Grinning, I carried the suitcase back into the house.

"Eighty-five seconds," my mother said proudly. She turned to Vern. "See, we can handle this, if you're in Lime."

"The kid is fast," Vern said. "I taught him good." As I carried the suitcase toward the bedroom, he added, "You win the diamond-studded stomach pump."

Coming from him, that was the highest praise.

While Vern was in Lime, Mom went into labor, and we made it to the hospital without a hitch. My baby sister, Ronna, was born

February 10, and my mother glowed with happiness. After the delivery, she turned to the baby lying beside her. "She has an adorable heart-shaped face. She's just perfect."

The nurses transferred them to a yellow room. "They couldn't have been any nicer," my mother said. "I'm so fortunate."

■ ■ ■

That summer I turned twelve, and we received a call from a California social worker who was about to place a fourteen-year-old girl in juvenile hall. Lola, the girl, had been arrested for shoplifting. A background check revealed that her mother had been arrested for loitering and creating a public disturbance. Now about to enter a mental institution, the mother was declared an unfit parent. The mother's boyfriend, a Lompoc penitentiary guard, had no interest in the child. Both Lola and her mother asserted that Vern was her father. Now the social worker wanted to know if Vern and his family were willing to take Lola in and give her another chance.

I don't remember discussing the options, the pros and cons, as families sometimes do. Nor do I recall anyone ever raising the question of whether or not the girl was actually his. I imagine both my mother and Vern agreed that she was. Still, my mother had never heard about this girl until the social worker called. At times, she grew agitated. "I hope this is the right thing to do," she said to herself a couple of times, but I overheard.

When Vern was at work, she called my grandmother. From their conversations, I'd say my grandmother had her doubts.

"The girl needs a second chance," my mother said over the phone. "I'm doing it to keep peace in the family." She convinced herself but not her mother.

I also believe my mother was in a particularly generous mood because she was so happy to have my sister Ronna after her miscarriages. "I feel so blessed," she said frequently.

I do remember my mother and Vern sitting at the kitchen table when they told me about the decision to take Lola for a trial period.

Mom's sewing machine and ironing board would remain in the small room they were going to fix up for the baby. Ronna's crib would stay in their bedroom until Vern could frame a room for Lola in the basement. After that project, Lola would occupy the basement room and mom's old sewing room would be converted to the baby's room.

"We'll have a lot of fixing up to do." Vern rolled the toothpick with his tongue. "You can be my carpenter's assistant, my number-one tool packer. The old sox, the old bean, the old fight, the old kidaroo."

I helped him carry his tools and lumber to the basement. "It gets awful cold down here in the winter," I said.

He scowled. "I'll have the electric baseboard installed by then. It'll be warm as toast."

I looked at the wringer washer, which was always breaking down. He'd tried to fix it half a dozen times. Still, I liked the idea of learning a little carpentry. Vern frequently told us that next to the telegrapher, the ship's carpenter was the most important job on the ship.

The first glitch occurred when the California authorities bought Lola a bus ticket only as far as Portland. Probably they didn't realize Baker was another three hundred miles east.

She could have waited for another bus, but Vern said the city offered too many temptations. He drove to Portland to pick her up. Mom suggested that he take the train, but he laughed and said the train was too unreliable.

They were three hours late getting back because a heater hose broke near The Dalles. They got it fixed at the Texaco station and hung out in Johnny's Cafe, where it was air-conditioned. Vern had let the car's engine cool for a couple of hours.

Lola dropped onto the family with the force of an atomic bomb. At first, she dressed entirely in pink; even her suitcases were pink. She was by turns boisterous, moody, sullen, expansive. Around the boys, she flaunted her budding sexuality with tight skirts, tighter blouses, and gobs of makeup, including bright lipstick.

She refused to tone down her act in spite of suggestions from my mother. All her clothes were bright and skimpy. "Don't you think you should cover up a little more?" my mother asked.

"You're just not used to California," Lola said. "This is nothing. You should see L.A."

"But this is Baker," my mother said. "It's nothing like California."

All my friends were fascinated with Lola and a little afraid of her, because she was unlike any of the Baker girls. "I guess they grow up wild like that in California," Danny said.

"I guess."

"I'm going there to college," he said. "My brother Riley says it's unbelievable."

"The way she dresses, boys are going to get the wrong idea about her," my mother told Vern.

"She just has to get used to Baker," he said. "And Baker has to get used to her."

Lola pretended to be bored to death with Baker. "Main Street is nothing but a dumping ground for old miners," she said after we walked downtown. "And forget about the shopping. I don't have gray hair yet." She paused. "Oh my God! Where am I going to get my hair cut?"

"There's a school for beauticians in Pendleton," I said, because I'd heard about it from Danny's older sister. "After the girls graduate, some come back here."

She looked at me as if I'd stepped off a spaceship. "You are kidding, right? I saw Pendleton when we drove through. Nothing but hicks and cowboys."

She insisted on going in all the clothing stores, even if she just made fun of the styles. I went with her because Vern instructed me to show her the town. In the department stores, I hung around the men's section, looking at the cowboy boots and western shirts until I got bored. Then I waited outside. I don't know exactly what Lola did, but she seemed to take a long time. If a store carried cosmetics, she lingered in that section. I prayed she wouldn't shoplift anything and hurt my reputation, but the saleswomen kept a pretty close eye on her. They could tell straight off she wasn't from Baker.

Once she bought some especially bright lipstick and applied it thick. "How do you like this?" she asked when she came out of the store.

"It's okay."

"Razzle-Dazzle. That's what they call it. How about letting me kiss your cheek so I can see how it will look on my boyfriends?"

I moved away.

"Scaredy-cat. I'll bet you're afraid your girlfriend will see."

"I don't have a girlfriend," I said, even though I had a crush on Rhonda Hester.

"I'll find out, you know. I won't let you have any secrets."

On hot days, Lola liked to go swimming at the natatorium. This gave her a chance to show off her body and her swimming skills. She must have swum a lot in California, because she swam faster than any of the Baker girls. She made aggressive, clean dives from the high diving board, and all the older boys flocked around to help her out of the water or hand her towels.

I could see how they looked at her, and it made me uncomfortable.

"Show-off," I heard Betty Lawrence say as Lola knifed into the pool.

"She thinks she's pretty hot stuff," Karen Jasa replied.

Judging from the boys' reactions, she *was* pretty hot stuff. After showing off in the pool, she paraded around the poolside, teasing boys, laughing at their jokes, scuffling to the point that the lifeguard threatened to throw her out. But behind his sunglasses, he was looking just as hard as he could at the cleavage exposed by her deep red bathing suit, the white crescents on her upper thighs where the tan line ended.

In the pool, she horsed around with the boys until the lifeguard left his chair to discipline them. Then she swam away, holding her breath and staying underwater longer than I thought was possible.

Day after day, the routine was the same. I'd take her and she'd chat about California and the interesting boys down there. She flattered me, saying I was a good guy and she appreciated my showing her around. However, once we reached the pool and she got around older guys, she ignored me almost completely.

I stayed with my own friends: Danny Freeman, Bobby Connell, Greg Holden, even Donald Lanning, who was deaf in one ear and always cocked his head at a peculiar angle.

Danny watched her a lot. "My brother Dave says he could dive straight into that."

I slugged his shoulder. "Knock it off. She's my sister." Even so, I knew what he meant. "Anyway, Dave's going steady."

"He's thinking about playing the field." Danny nodded at Lola. "That field."

After she had enough of swimming, she dried off carefully at poolside, taking a long time to towel between her thighs and breasts, all the time sneaking glances to see who was watching. Satisfied she had a good audience, she lay in the sun while the boys hovered and made passes.

Eventually, she went into the dressing room to shower, and then she emerged again, make-up in place—right down to the Razzle-Dazzle. She had a way of not drying off completely so her damp blouse clung to her skin in places.

In the last couple of hours before the nat closed and we needed to go home, she went on rides with some of the older boys. When they came back, she was more mussed, and I could see traces of lipstick on the boys' cheeks and necks. If the dressing room was already closed, she fixed herself in the park, making pouty lips at the compact mirror.

On the way back to the house, she'd ask me not to say anything about driving around with the older boys. "Don't be a tattletale," she warned.

Lola even had a little ditty:

Tattletale, tattletale,
Hanging on a bull's tail;
When the bull begins to pee,
You will drink a cup of tea.

"Tell that to your mother," she said and laughed.

Lola thought she was pretty clever, but Danny Freeman and I had already heard that one from Dave. He loved smoking cigarettes in the hay barn, shooting pheasants on the neighbors' ranches, tearing down the back roads in his father's pickup. Still, we never tattled on Dave. In Baker, none of my friends tattled on anyone. That was the code.

One day as we were walking back, Lola asked, "Do you know Waylon Clowers?"

"I've heard of him," I said.

"He drives so fast, it scares me. My heart's still pounding." She stopped walking and grabbed my hand, then pulled it to her chest. "Feel here how it's racing. Thump, thump, thump. It's never pounded like this before."

I felt the firmness of her breast, and a few heartbeats, before I pulled my hand free. I became hot and tingly all over.

"Did you feel that?"

"I felt it."

She studied me with her steady blue eyes. "Do you think I'm going to be okay?"

I nodded, catching my breath. "Next time, tell him not to drive so fast."

"Maybe I will, but I've got to admit, it's damned exciting!"

That night, my stepfather was a in a foul mood because he had to pay a twenty-five-dollar fine for a traffic ticket. He was drinking his second highball when I got home.

"That cop was a little turd, just throwing his weight around. I know I wasn't speeding."

"Maybe the speedometer is off," my mother said.

"You don't know anything about cars," he said. "If I run into that cop again, I'll give him a piece of my mind. If he ever rides the train, I'll have them turn off the heat in his car. His balls can turn blue."

"Vern Hecker!" my mother said.

"They've heard worse," he said. "The way kids talk nowadays." He pointed at me. "Haven't you heard worse?"

"I've heard worse," I said, thinking of all the swearwords we practiced out at Danny's. Dave had a couple new ones every time.

"I haven't," Lola said, and then she laughed. "Now I've got to go wash out my ears."

Vern laughed, too. "What's the worst you've heard, the very worst?"

"That's quite enough from all of you," my mother said.

"You should have been in the navy," Vern said. "That's it, Hazel! You should have been a Wave."

In late summer, my mother packed a picnic lunch and we drove out to Radium Hot Springs. Every August, the Gypsies passed through Eastern Oregon and camped at the hot springs. I liked the dark-eyed Gypsy girls with their bright swimsuits and colorful jewelry. The year before, I'd bought a knife from Ramone, an older Gypsy boy, who took me out behind the trailer caravan and unwrapped the knife from its goatskin covering. It had a wicked curved blade and a bone handle.

"My uncle stabbed a Basque man with this knife," Ramone explained. "He gave it to me so the police wouldn't catch him with it. We just heard the man died, and now I'm afraid to keep it." He held up two fingers. "Only two dollars. They can't trace it to you."

A knife that had killed a man excited me. I would smuggle it out to Danny's on the school bus. I didn't have two dollars on me, but I borrowed it from my mother. I told her I was buying some agates. She had high hopes for me to become a scientist, perhaps a geologist, so she went for the agate story. I borrowed some agates from Don Lanning and showed them to her just to cover my butt.

. . .

Radium Hot Springs lacked a high diving board, so Lola used the low board for her performance that day. She tried all her tricks on those Gypsy boys, and they gathered around her just as fast as the Baker boys at the nat. She flirted, splashed water and giggled, played tag around the pool. She wore a new two-tone lavender swimsuit she had bought in Boise when Vern took her there to shop, and it showed everything she had and a little more. "Marilyn Monroe wears a padded swimsuit all the time," she had said. "Even she can use a little help."

Lola had brought some Coppertone tanning oil, and the boys wrestled with one another and horsed around, trying to determine which ones would help her apply it. Finally, she chose two of the older boys. They were tall, dark, and muscular. One had a mustache and a gold tooth.

The Gypsy girls clustered in small groups and glared at Lola, but she wasn't afraid of them. She walked straight up to them, tried on a few bracelets, complimented them on their hairstyles. They were fascinated by her swimsuit, and, turning her back to everyone else, she showed them exactly how it worked. Before long, she had them gossiping and laughing.

Lola was on a roll: queen of the pool.

Vern had staked a baby blanket so Ronna stayed in the shade. She had terribly pale skin, and Mom didn't want her exposed to too much sun. My mother wore a straw sunhat with yellow ribbons that tied around her neck. She seldom wore a hat, and I thought she looked good in it, like an actress on the Riviera or something. A few times people had said my mother resembled Grace Kelly, except that her nose was a little sharp.

"What a wonderful day for a picnic," Mom said. "After that hard winter, it feels so good to have some real heat. I just love Baker. It's so beautiful here, but the winters are a little long."

She spread out the picnic and called everyone to eat, but Lola stayed in the pool. She was teaching some of the girls how to dive. "Don't you think you should eat something?" my mother asked.

"I'm not hungry yet," Lola said.

"Swimming always made me hungry." My mother got out the deviled ham sandwiches. "Why doesn't she come out of the pool? Vern, you should tell her."

"Hazel, relax. She's having fun," Vern said.

We ate the sandwiches, celery with pimento spread, and black olives. Watermelon chunks and pineapple upside-down cake were dessert.

"This melon came from Hermiston," my mother said. "We used to get them in The Dalles. Nothing tastes as good as a Hermiston melon in August."

She sprinkled salt on her melon and Vern wrinkled his nose. "How can you treat a good melon that way?" he said. "A melon is supposed to be sweet."

"When I was growing up in The Dalles, we always put salt on them."

"That's how they'd treat a watermelon in The Dalles, all right." He shook his head. "They make them ditsy in The Dalles."

After eating dessert, I wanted to go back in the pool, but my mother insisted that I stay out. "You have to wait an hour so you don't get cramps. When I was a girl, a schoolmate drowned in the Columbia swimming down by Klindt's farm. She went right back in after eating."

"Look at this pool," I said. "Even with a cramp, I could float to the side. Anyway, there's twenty people around."

"Hey!" Vern said sharply. "Listen to your mother."

Some of the Gypsy boys were shooting off fireworks behind a line of trees, so I went to see what was going on.

They had caught crayfish from the creek and were racing them along a small raked area. They threw firecrackers at the crayfish to make them scuttle faster. Every so often, they'd blow off a couple legs or a claw. When the crayfish were too crippled to compete, they were dropped into a cooking pot.

As I went back to the pool, I was surprised to see Vern swimming. He wore tan trunks and swam with steady, even strokes. After swimming a few laps, he stood, shaking the water from his head.

"Put on your swimsuit, Hazel," he called to my mother. "Craig can watch Ronna."

She shook her head. "I want the kids to have fun. Anyway, I'm enjoying just watching her sleep."

"Suit yourself, then."

I started to get back in the pool, but Vern checked the clock hanging over the concession stand. "It's not time yet."

"Almost," I said.

"I'll tell you when you can get back in."

Lola came over and splashed me with some water. Sitting on the side of the pool, I had a difficult time not looking down the front of her suit. I tried to focus on her eyes and smile. Even without the Razzle-Dazzle, she had good lips.

She splashed me again. "Hop in. The water's great."

"I have to wait until Vern says it's okay."

"Do you want me to ask him for you?"

I nodded. "You can try. We won't get a chance to come back again this summer."

She swam over and said something to Vern but he shook his head. Then she said something else and pointed at the clock. After swimming back, she said, "Okeydokey."

"Hey, thanks." I slid into the pool.

She smiled and snapped her fingers. "I'm magic. I made fifteen minutes disappear just like that."

Suddenly, she tried dunking me. She was strong, and catching me by surprise, she managed to get my head underwater for a moment, but I was able to straighten up and break free.

She laughed. "You're pretty strong for a skinny guy."

She grew excited. "I've got a great idea. Let's play Kings and Crowns. I'll bet Daddy and I can whip anybody." She started yelling to the other swimmers. "Hey, everybody. Kings and Crowns. Daddy and I can beat all comers. Who wants to bet a dollar?"

We chose up pairs then. Looking at some of the broad-shouldered boys, I figured we could take Lola and Vern, no sweat. "Let's make it two dollars," I said. "Easy money."

"No gambling," my mother called from the picnic area. She didn't believe in gambling, and even disapproved when Vern lost money on the punchboards in the restaurants and bars.

"Your mother would make a dandy truant officer," Lola said. "Well, no money then. Just winners and sore losers. I'll bet none of you can stand losing to a girl."

She climbed on Vern's shoulders with an easy kind of confidence, and seeing her perched there made me realize how much they looked alike. Her strong shoulders and solid upper arms came from swimming, while his were from lifting weights. They had the same hairline, but I'd never noticed it before because of her style. And their eyes and lips matched.

"Well, let's get started," she said.

"Rules first," Vern said. "All's fair in love and war. Except for the following: no hair pulling, ear biting, eye gouging, or hitting below the belt." He waggled his finger. "And no titty grabbing."

The boys grinned at this and nudged one another.

My mother turned red.

"We'll start on my whistle," Vern said. "It's every man and woman for themselves."

I paired with Ramone, the boy who had sold me the knife the year before, and I figured our stiffest competition was the two boys who had helped Lola spread her tanning lotion. The rest, I thought, we could take with a little luck.

When Vern whistled, the pool erupted into a wild grapple of arms, shoulders, heads, and necks. Two large boys tried to pull me down from behind, but Ramone held me steady while he turned to face them. I got the upper boy in a headlock and Ramone surged past them, using the strength in his legs to give me more leverage. I shifted my right arm back and forth, rubbing the captured boy's ear until he gave up and fell into the water. I let go and he came up, splashing and coughing. Touching his tender ear, he said, "Hey, man. You got a wicked style."

But I didn't pay any attention. We were on to another round of Kings and Crowns. We beat this pair, too, and the struggles continued another ten minutes, until only Lola and Vern and Ramone and I remained undefeated. To my surprise, the two biggest boys had lost to Vern and Lola. The one with the mustache stood in an odd way and there was pain in his smile.

"You can knock her off easy," Ramone said. "We'll make the losers buy us Cokes."

I didn't want to hurt Lola with a headlock, so I tried grabbing her shoulders and pulling her down, but she knocked my arms away with her elbows. Then I got her around the middle, but she gripped Vern's neck and shoulders with her thighs and I couldn't loosen her. She banged on my head and ears with her palms, so I let go.

"Stop messing around and pull her off," Ramone said.

I grabbed her upper arm and tried to twist her off, but that didn't work, either.

"Let's take these pansies," Vern said, and Lola war-whooped. She grabbed a handful of my hair and jerked my head down and to the side.

"No hair pulling!" I grabbed her wrist with both my hands and twisted in opposite ways until she let go.

"That hurt, damn it!" Her eyes showed her pain.

"You pulled my hair," I said.

Vern shoved into Ramone, trying to knock him off his feet, but Ramone was too strong.

Lola grabbed me around the shoulders and tried to pull me off, but she couldn't. I got her shoulders and we wrestled back and forth, evenly deadlocked. Ramone's firm grip on my legs held me steady.

Lola gripped me so tightly, her fingernails dug into my shoulder. It hurt, but I just struggled harder to unseat her.

Ramone gasped and bent his knees slightly.

Lola released my shoulders and threw a forearm into my Adam's apple. I saw a red flash and felt a fist punching into my crotch. I gritted my teeth.

She grabbed my neck and fought like a crazed badger.

My legs were sliding away as Ramone loosened his grip, then let go altogether.

The fist and Lola's strength were more than I could withstand. I fell into the pool, water gurgling up my nose.

"We won! Hey, everybody, we won!" Lola stood on Vern's shoulders, waving her arms back and forth.

"The winners and still champeens!" Vern shouted.

Ramone acted embarrassed, as if he couldn't believe we'd lost. I was glad none of my Baker friends had been around to see the defeat.

"Hey, man. I'm sorry," he said.

"We did pretty good." I touched the tenderness of my Adam's apple. My crotch hurt, too.

"I let go," he said. "After I got smacked in the nuts, I couldn't hang on. It really hurts."

Thinking of the fist in my crotch, I said, "Somebody punched me, too."

"It might have been her," he said. "She might have kicked me."

"Aren't you going to congratulate us?" Vern asked.

"Ramone got hit in the privates," I said. "Hit or kicked. You didn't win fair."

"Don't be a sore loser," Vern said. "All's fair in love and war."

"You said no hitting below the belt."

"Maybe it was an accident. Or the luck of the draw." Vern's face grew darker. "Take it like a man."

I took a breath. "Congratulations," I said.

I got out of the pool and bought a ten-cent bag of popcorn at the concession stand. After the exertion, the popcorn tasted good. But I was in a bad mood. I hated cheaters and I hated losing.

Ramone came over and shared the popcorn. "How you feeling?" I asked.

He shrugged. "I been kicked in the balls before. Losing to a girl, though. That's bad." He ate some more of the popcorn. "Have yours dropped yet?"

I knew what he meant. "Not yet." We talked about it when Coach Piedmont, our PE teacher, wasn't listening. Bart Shumway's had dropped, and one of Danny's. He kept waiting for the other.

I checked myself every morning. "Pretty soon, I think."

"Getting kicked in the nuts hurts more when they've dropped," Ramone said.

Still in the pool, Vern and Lola started splashing each other. He cupped his hands and scooped waves of water at her. After she'd had enough, she giggled and swam away from him. Reaching the ladder, she tried climbing out, but he was right behind her. He grabbed her leg and yanked her back into the pool. She shrieked as he dunked her.

He held her under for what seemed like a long time. When he let her up, she coughed hard and spat out water.

"Got your breath?" he asked, and when she nodded, he dunked her again.

This time, she was angry when she came up. "Stop it," she cried. "Stop it right now."

"Who's going to make me?" he said. He had her around the head and used his size and strength to force her underwater again.

I could see her struggling.

"You going to help your sister?" Ramone asked.

I stood. "Hey, maybe that's enough dunking for now. She's tired."

Vern pushed her down farther. "Losers don't get any say."

I didn't know what to do. I was afraid that by interfering, I would only make things worse.

"Do you want me to let her up?" He had a goofy grin on his face. "That's right."

I noticed the man coming out of the concession booth. "Let her up, please," I said.

Vern's grin had faded. "Get in here, Lippy, and you can take some of it."

"Shit, man," Ramone said.

My mother strode to the pool. She had been focused on Ronna, but now she realized something was amiss.

"Vern, that's enough horseplay. Let her up this instant! Someone's likely to get hurt!"

"Some people can't stand a little fun," he said, and let Lola go.

He swam to the deep end with easy, effortless strokes, then floated on his back, eyes closed.

We all looked at him but no one said anything.

Lola held on to the side of the pool, catching her breath. She seemed shaken. After a while, she asked my mother, "Hazel, why didn't you stop him earlier?"

"I just didn't see it soon enough."

We both helped Lola out of the pool. I handed her a towel.

"Sometimes, Vern doesn't know when to stop," my mother said.

Lola wiped herself off without bothering to see if anyone was watching her. Ramone bought another bag of popcorn and the three of us shared it. Lola shivered in the breeze and her hand shook a little when she reached for the paper sack.

Most of the Gypsies had wandered back to their tents and trailers. Smoke rose from campfires and I could smell crayfish cooking.

"It's time for my dinner," Ramone said. He shook hands with both of us. "See you next year."

After he was gone, Lola patted her toweled hair. "I must look terrible. I must look downright ugly."

I shook my head. "You look okay."

She tried to smile. "That's pretty damned weak." Her face was somber.

"You look good," I said. The truth was that without her makeup and Razzle-Dazzle she looked a lot like Vern.

My stepfather swam back and forth, back and forth. He had the pool entirely to himself, and he wasn't likely to get out until he was good and ready.

9

BABY STEPS

During the fall, Lola wiggled to get on Vern's good side. Time and again, she kept bringing up their victory in Kings and Crowns, flattering Vern about his strength. One morning when she came out of the bathroom all razzle-dazzle, she gave him a big hug and kiss, leaving a smear of lipstick on his cheek.

"We really showed up those boys, didn't we?" Lola said. "None of them were as strong as you are, not by a long way."

Vern smiled as he wiped off the lipstick. "I keep in good shape."

My mother thumped Vern's plate of toast and eggs in front of him. She dropped the frying pan into the sink.

Vern slid his eyes her way, but didn't say anything.

"How much can you lift, anyway?" Lola poured some Cheerios into her bowl. She never had anything but cold cereal and orange juice in the morning. She sprinkled on the sugar.

"In the navy, I could bench-press twice my weight. No one else on my ship could do that."

"I'll bet you're even stronger now." She took a drink of orange juice.

What a little suckup, I thought. Still, I was in a good mood because I thought Vern was going to be gone for five days. However, to my disappointment, Vern came home from Lime on Wednesday evening. The main conveyer line had broken at the lime plant and they had to wait on parts from Denver.

While I was disappointed, Vern was elated because he was still getting paid. "Nothing like the good old railroad," he said, although he always cursed it violently those times he got bumped.

"I'm really glad you're home," Lola told him. "I've got a math test Friday and you can help me study."

For some reason, she had never learned the multiplication tables in California, and that really held her back. When Vern wasn't around she whined until I helped her, but even though I worked with her, using flash cards—stuff I'd learned in the fourth grade—she never seemed to get it. Instead of concentrating on the problems, she put on fingernail and toenail polish or twisted her hair. Eventually, I just gave her the answers to save time. Having Vern help her was actually a relief.

Lola could have asked my mother for help, because she was good at math, but Lola never approached her. My mother occasionally asked me how Lola's studies were coming along.

"She's not too quick to grasp things," I said. I really tried to help, because if her teacher held Lola back, she'd be in my class, and I didn't want all my friends teasing me about her.

Vern got the flash cards and Lola sat on the floor in front of his easy chair. If she couldn't get an answer, her mouth turned pouty and Vern gave it to her right away. Each time, he sounded like a big shot.

He's acting like a king with his subject, I thought. At this rate, she's never going to catch on. I was keeping an eye on Ronna as she crawled around the room.

My mother went out to the kitchen and got a big yellow broom. After coming back into the front room, she began catching spiderwebs in the broom straws. She stretched out, raising the broom to get the corners of the ceiling, the places near the lights. Sometimes the broom didn't catch the cobweb, but pushed it flat against the ceiling, leaving a dark line. When that happened, my mother said, "Oh no."

Vern looked up from the flash cards. "Get a vacuum and do that in the morning, when you can see something."

"I just can't stand to see these cobwebs floating around."

When my mother wasn't looking, Vern made circles by his temple with his forefinger, indicating she was nuts. Lola nodded and laughed.

Suddenly, I saw Ronna pull herself up, hanging on to a green chair, take a couple of steps still holding on to the chair, then walk toward Mom. She took three more small steps before falling on her butt, cushioned by the big diaper.

Mom exclaimed, "Look! Look, she's walking all by herself. My baby is walking!"

And then Ronna walked again, this time toward Vern. He picked her up and held her way over his head. "Look at this kid."

"She really walked right up to you," Lola said. "That was so neat." Her voice hit a false note and I knew she was miffed because she didn't have his attention anymore.

He set Ronna down, and sure enough, she walked again.

"Just over nine months," my mother said. "This little baby was getting ready to walk." She made cooing noises and held Ronna to her.

Vern touched Mom's shoulder. "Hazel, let her walk."

My mother stepped back. "Barely nine months. She's smart as a whip."

"Of course." Vern squatted and held out his arms. "She takes after me."

Ronna laughed and walked to him again. He grabbed her before she could fall and lifted her high.

"Let me try." Lola knelt in Vern's place, but Ronna didn't walk to her. Instead, she walked to my mother.

"She's got to get to know you a little better," Mom said. "Don't feel bad."

Lola tried again. "Come here, baby. Come here, Ronna. Walk to sister."

But she wouldn't.

I got caught up in the mood. "Here, let me try."

Squatting in Lola's place, I held out my arms. After hesitating, Ronna took two steps toward me, then tumbled down.

"She was trying," Mom said. "Baby was really trying to walk to her big brother."

Just then I thought Lola might get sore or say something sarcastic, but she didn't. All she said was, "She'll know me better after awhile."

"That's right," my mother said. "She heard Craig's voice all the time she was in my stomach."

Vern got the Brownie camera and took four pictures, but Ronna wasn't walking anymore, just standing and holding on to the chair. "We'll get her another time and say it's the first," he said. "Who will know?" He set the hot blue flashbulbs on the table so Ronna couldn't grab them and burn her hand.

"I'm so glad she's wearing that yellow sleeper for the pictures," my mother said. Yellow was Mom's favorite color. "Does anyone remember who gave her that sleeper?"

No one said anything.

"Danny Freeman's mother, Wilma," she said. "When I first saw it, I thought, Ronna will never be able to wear that sleeper because she's just so teeny wee. But Wilma knew she'd grow into it. She knew babies grow so fast at first, it's a good idea to give them clothes they can wear after several months."

Vern took two more pictures. "Might as well shoot up the roll."

Pretty soon Ronna grew tired from the exertion and started getting fussy. Mom gave her a bottle and set her in the playpen. When Ronna was settled, making sucking noises on the bottle, Mom called her parents in The Dalles. Her voice rose with excitement. She described every detail, and then some.

When she finally hung up, Mom called her sister Grace and went through it all again. After Grace, she started dialing Oscar, but Vern came and put his hand on the phone.

"That's enough," he said. "This is really costing."

"I know it costs a king's ransom," Mom said, "but she'll never take her first steps again. And Oscar's girls will be so excited."

"Oscar reads," Vern said. "Send him a letter."

10

POLKA DOT

The next weekend Vern brought home a two-pound box of chocolates he had won playing the punchboards at the railroad café in Huntington. Before dinner, we all ate a few chocolates because they were a treat, and Vern encouraged us to celebrate his winnings.

"I'll bet this box is worth three bucks at drugstore prices." He offered candy to Lola. "And I won it on my third nickel."

My mother was still trying to lose weight after having the baby, but that didn't stop her from eating chocolates. "My spirit's willing to diet, but my flesh is weak." She opened one of the chocolates wrapped in gold foil. "This has hazelnuts," she said. "Just like my name."

She tried another, maple cream this time. "Once I went to Victoria and ate maple creams. They made the candy right on the premises."

"'On the premises,'" Vern repeated in a mocking tone. "You mean they made it right there."

She ignored his remark. "That was the best chocolate I ever ate, although I'll go for anything chocolate."

It was true. While pregnant with Ronna, my mother had consumed at least two Hershey bars a day. She preferred them plain, without nuts. Sometimes she'd send me to the store to get them, because she didn't want the grocery clerks to know she was eating two bars or more a day. "Carrying this baby is hard work; I'm just keeping up my strength," she had said.

Vern studied the printing on the box. "These were made on the premises in Cincinnati," he said.

"That's better than on the premises in Huntington," Lola said, and he laughed. She selected another. "I wish they had chocolate-covered cherries. Next time, win some of those."

"I'll do it just for you," he said. "Nothing's too good for my very own flesh and blood."

"Daddy, what I really want is a horse," she said.

Vern had taken her out to Lime to see where he worked, and on the way back, they had stopped in Durkee at Benson Fivecoat's ranch, where she rode a quarter horse she liked. Now she was pressing him to buy her a horse. As far as I was concerned, that was her pipe dream, because we didn't have any extra money. Each month Mom and Vern argued about the payments they already had.

After a meal of Rancho pork chops—made with catsup, onions, and lemon rinds—and broccoli and mashed potatoes, Lola and I went into the front room while Mom "slicked up the dishes."

"I'm taking Ronna over to see Daisy Wicks," she told us. "Daisy just loves seeing her. Does anyone want to come with me?"

I liked Daisy because she was always good for buying a subscription or sponsoring laps around the school for sports teams, but I didn't want to go that night. I was reading *Dave Dawson at Dunkirk*, a book about the Royal Air Force heroes of World War II, and I figured Vern would take out the chocolates again.

"I've got a pineapple upside-down cake in the oven," Mom said. "Don't spoil your appetites."

Vern sat in his favorite chair, reading *The Caine Mutiny*. He had taken me to see the movie with Humphrey Bogart. Vern saw every Bogart movie at least twice. The way Vern combed his hair and smoked his cigarettes were poor imitations of Bogart's style.

Lola threw a sofa pillow on the floor, then lay on her stomach, elbows propped. She had two teen magazines, but seemed to have trouble getting comfortable. She squirmed and shifted from side to side. As she moved against the pillow, the contact pushed up her breasts, making them seem bigger. I kept peeking.

After a while, Vern got out the chocolates again. He put one in his mouth, then held out the box to Lola. "How about it, sweetheart?" He was trying to do Bogart.

Lola shook her head. "I don't want to get fat," she said. She turned to me as I glanced away quickly. "Do I look fat to you?"

"No." I looked at her face.

She reached back, patting her rump. "What about here? Do I look okay from behind—or do I look fat?"

"Your caboose is fine," Vern said. "Anyway, most cultures think a little meat on a woman is a sign of beauty. Skinny is considered ugly in many parts of the world."

"What cultures?" She seemed interested.

"Well, the Philippines, for one. Some of the Filipino women I saw out of the Subic naval station were a little heavy, but they were plenty attractive. Lots of navy men married them and brought them back to the U.S."

"I go for chocolate," she said. "Maybe I should move to the Philippines."

"I liked the Philippines." Vern rattled the box and selected another chocolate. "We'll have to go there sometime. All the Filipino men are crazy about blondes. You'd be a big hit when you get older."

"Well, if I'm going to the Philippines, I guess I can eat another chocolate." She leaned forward, reaching for the box, and I could see the red lace of her bra and most of one breast.

She bit into the candy and some of the filling dribbled onto her chin. She licked it with her bright pink tongue. When she bit into another, a section of chocolate fell onto her chest. Moistening her finger, she dabbed at it, then put her finger in her mouth. "I'm making a big mess," she said.

"What are you staring at, Owl Eyes?" Vern's lips were thin with annoyance. He was talking to me.

"Nothing," I said.

"Don't lie to me," he said. "You were staring. Why were you staring at your sister? Is there something wrong with you? Something weird?"

"I was just looking. I wasn't staring." I tried to concentrate on my book.

"When I talk to you, look at me!" Vern sprang out of his chair and grabbed my shoulders, jerking me to my feet. "Don't lie to me, you little bastard!"

I tried twisting away, but he got me in a headlock and squeezed tight. "I want you to apologize to your sister." When I didn't say anything, he told her, "Let's see how he likes the old Dutch rub."

I tried pushing his arm away, but he was too strong. I could have kicked him, but I was afraid of his reaction.

He made his free hand into a fist and began knuckle-rubbing the side of my head, just above the ear. "The old Dutch rub gets them every time." He knuckled me harder. "Apologize."

The side of my head burned with the rubbing and he squeezed tighter. Then he stopped rubbing and pounded the top of my head with his palm—until red orbs flashed behind my eyes.

I almost managed to free my head but my ear wouldn't clear his grasp. He continued rubbing my head until I felt it must be bleeding. Then he started rubbing the ear until it was blazing hot. I was starting to cry and snot ran out of my nose and onto the floor.

"Do you want to give him some?" Vern asked Lola. "He was staring down your blouse."

"No, you're teaching him a good-enough lesson," she said. "But he should apologize."

"We can do this all night, tough guy," he said. "If you want any skin left on your scalp, you'd better say you're sorry."

I didn't see any point in holding out any longer. "All right, I apologize."

"Louder," he said. "I want you to say, 'I'm sorry for being a Peeping Tom.'" He thumped my head again. "Do it!"

I felt ashamed and furious with myself for not being able to escape or whip him. "I apologize for being a Peeping Tom."

"Now we know exactly what you are," he said. "A weird little bastard."

I expected him to let me go then, but he didn't. "Bring me the bathroom soap," he said to Lola. "Make sure it's good and wet." When she had left for the bathroom, he said, "Maybe this will teach you a lesson."

"You'd better stop it," I said. "I already apologized."

"Are you going to go crying to your mommy?" he asked. "Peeping Toms need to be punished."

Lola came back with the soap. "Are you going to wash out his mouth?"

"Let me go!" I demanded. "I already apologized. Lola, you heard me."

"I want you to wash out his eyes," Vern said in a low, menacing voice. "That's what we did to guys in the navy when they looked at you queer in the showers. We held them down and washed out their eyes. After that, they never looked."

Desperate, I tried to pull free.

She hesitated. "He doesn't deserve that. Even if he was looking."

"Give me the soap then." When she handed it to him, his grip loosened just a little, and I kicked him on the side of the shin as hard as I could.

He cried out in pain, dropped the soap, and released his grip enough so I could slide my head free. "You little shit-tail pansy!"

Racing to the front door, I flung it open and was on the porch and down the steps before he could grab me. I ran around the side of the house and into the alley. I tore down the dark alley, across the side street, and into the next alley.

I paused, looking back, and when I saw a pair of headlights swing out of our garage, I cut through a yard and didn't stop running until I was two streets over. By then, my chest was burning as much as my scalp.

I didn't know what to do. Danny Freeman's ranch was too far and the night was cold. Bobby Connell lived across town with his grandparents, but they went to bed early. I decided to stay put until Vern got tired of looking for me and my mother came home.

Three cars drove by, and I stayed hidden behind some small pines in a vacant lot. I was about to leave when I saw a fourth car coming very slowly. I tried to melt into the trees.

Vern had his window rolled down and was staring hard into the semidarkness. I gasped when I realized he had a flashlight with a powerful beam and was shining it into the dark corners. Quickly, I scrambled up one of the taller trees until I was about six feet off the ground, concealed in the thick branches. I held my breath as he played the beam around the trunk of the trees where I had been standing earlier.

"Do you see him?" I heard him say.

I was astounded to hear Lola's voice answer. She was with him. "He'd better not tattle," she said, "or you're in big trouble."

Vern snorted, said something I couldn't hear, and then they were past. When I came down from the tree five minutes later, my legs were shaking and my teeth chattered.

Keeping to the back alley, I made my way to Daisy Wicks's house. She had the shades pulled down, so I couldn't tell if my mother was still there or not. I hunched under the kitchen window, listening, but I didn't hear any voices.

I got scared, thinking someone might report me as a Peeping Tom for real, so I snuck back into Daisy's alley and began moving cautiously toward home. It was only two blocks. Then I remembered the pineapple upside-down cake. Mom would have gone home to take it out of the oven and poke in a toothpick to see if it was done. I felt a rush of relief. Vern wasn't likely to get any revenge when Mom was around.

Approaching the back of our house from the alley, I was surprised to see the car wasn't in the garage. Were they still looking for me?

"Where on God's green earth have you been?" my mother asked when I entered through the back door. "And where is your coat? You'll catch your death out there. It's November. Don't you have a lick of sense?"

The pineapple upside-down cake was cooling on some metal racks. The top of the stove felt barely warm when I touched it. I'd been out a long time.

"I went to Bobby Connell's," I said. "He's putting together a model battleship. The time kind of slipped by."

"What about Vern and Lola?"

I shrugged. "They were here when I left." I tried to change the subject. "Can I have a piece of that cake?"

I got the milk out of the refrigerator while she cut the cake and started talking. "Daisy couldn't believe how Ronna's walking." Then she noticed the scrapes. "My God! What happened to the side of your head? It's all raw and there's some dried blood."

I touched the side of my head. "Bobby and I were just wrestling. He got me in a headlock."

"You boys better stop horsing around, before one of you winds up in the hospital."

"I'll put something on it before I go to bed."

The car pulled into the alley and parked in the garage.

"Here they are," my mother said. "It's about time."

Vern limped a little when he came into the kitchen. Lola carried a box of chocolate-covered cherries.

"There you are," Vern said to me. "We were looking all over for you. Where the hell have you been?"

The way he was full of bluster, I could tell he didn't know how much I had told. Let him sweat, I thought, and took another bite of cake.

"One minute he was here and the next he was gone. Isn't that right?" Vern looked at Lola.

"That's right," she said.

My mother glared at me. "Didn't you tell Vern you were going to Bobby Connell's?"

"I guess I didn't."

"Look what Bobby did to the side of his head," my mother said. "They were wrestling and he got all skinned up."

"That does look a little raw," Vern said. "But it makes him tough."

I figured he was relieved I hadn't tattled on him, but I never did. "Bobby and I are putting together a model of the *Arizona*. Didn't you say you saw the *Arizona* when you were in the navy?"

"I saw where the Japs sank it," he said. "I was on a destroyer," he explained to Lola. "We blasted those Jap subs with depth charges."

"I wish you wouldn't use that word," my mother said. Hood River and The Dalles were filled with very nice Japanese people.

"A Jap's a Jap," he said.

"I won't have you talking like that. You're setting a very poor example."

"You must have been brave to go against those submarines," Lola said. "My mom's boyfriend was in the navy, but he never got out of San Diego."

"Shore duty is for pansies," Vern said.

Lola nodded and took one of the chocolate-covered cherries from the box. "He was a pansy all right."

I wondered if there was a difference between a pansy and a shit-tailed pansy as far as Vern was concerned.

"I noticed one strange thing," my mother said. "I found a bar of soap lying on the floor in the front room. How did that get there?"

No one answered her.

"I'm about ready for bed," I said, and headed for the bathroom. The bar of soap was in its usual place. After washing my hands, I applied Unguentine to the raw patches on my head. I winced as my fingertips touched my skin.

I went to bed thinking it had been a terrible night, but it could have been worse. At least I hadn't had my eyes washed out with soap. Vern was heading back to Lime soon, and I was convinced he'd cool down. In a strange way, kicking him might have been a good action. Sometimes he was easier to get along with when I wouldn't take his guff.

When I lay down, I kept the Unguentine side off the pillow. I heard Vern drive the car out of the garage. I figured he was going to the Hoot-Owl tavern to wet his whistle and thank his lucky stars I wasn't a squealer.

In the kitchen, Lola spoke to my mother, something about a horse.

"Why are you talking about a horse again? A horse is out of the question."

Lola's voice rose. "It's not your decision. My daddy makes the money in this house. You don't control the purse strings."

"Get out of my kitchen!"

Glass shattered. Then more glass. Ronna woke up crying.

"You've broken my mother's china, you tart!"

Lola stomped down the hall and flung open my bedroom door. "You've been listening, you little bastard. The next time, I'll soap your eyes good." She clumped into the basement and started throwing things against the walls of her room.

My mother managed to get Ronna quiet.

I knew I should come out of my room, but I didn't. I switched on the light and started reading *Dave Dawson at Dunkirk*. While the British tried desperately to evacuate their troops, Dave Dawson, the intrepid Spitfire pilot, and his squadron provided air cover, dogfighting with every Messerschmitt the Germans threw their way.

I wondered what a tart was.

■ ■ ■

When I woke up the next morning, fantasies about the RAF had vanished. A part of me wanted to kill Vern, or cripple him up real bad, or even throw acid in his face. I slipped my pocketknife into my jeans. If he made any kind of move at breakfast, I decided I'd slice him.

I slid into my chair with a curt "Morning." Only my mother acknowledged me. Vern was listening to Lola go on about the horse she wanted. Her words came tumbling out.

"I talked with Jimmy Fivecoats and he said they had the perfect horse for a girl—it's an Appaloosa mare. Jimmy said his dad would sell it for a good price. Right now is the time to get it."

"We just don't have the money," my mother said.

"I can get a job," Lola said. "Mr. Fivecoats will take payments." Turning to Vern, she asked, "He'll agree to take payments, won't he, Daddy? He'll do it for you, since you're friends and all."

"He'll do whatever I want him to," Vern said. "You don't need to worry about that."

"I can't wait to see it," Lola said. "I'm telling you, I can't wait."

"Where are we going to keep a horse?" my mother asked. "A horse is totally impractical."

"Have some sense of adventure, Hazel." Vern drank his coffee. "Didn't you ever want something so bad you could taste it?"

"I never wanted a horse," she said. "I grew up in town."

"Give us a little slack," Vern said. "Think of all the ranch kids with their sheep and their cattle and their horses. Think of all the Four-H kids and Future Farmers of America around here. Raising livestock teaches responsibility and good citizenship."

My mother's mouth became a thin line.

"We can keep the horse at Fivecoats's ranch," Lola said. "I'll figure out a way to get back and forth—I'm good at getting rides."

"Girls shouldn't hitchhike." My mother turned to Vern. "You shouldn't allow her to have such crazy notions."

"Craig can get in on it, too." Vern looked at me. "Ask Danny Freeman about keeping the horse at his place. They have horses, don't they?"

"Four," I said. I didn't plan on asking the Freemans about keeping a horse for Lola or helping out in any way.

Vern spread his hands and smiled. "Four or five. What's the goddamn difference? They still have to throw hay and shovel shit."

Vern and Lola made a plan. She was going to skip school and drive with Vern to Lime. He'd drop her at Fivecoats's when he went on shift and pick her up after. When the weekend came, they'd return to Baker and discuss the horse's purchase.

"Lola can't skip school," my mother said. "She's way behind in math."

"We'll take the damned flash cards," Vern said. "Anyway, I'm smarter than those junior high school teachers."

"I just won't have a horse," my mother said.

"She'll win ribbons and prizes. Money, too."

"I'll beat all those snotty ranch girls that think they're so high-and-mighty." Lola's face showed determination. "I'm tougher than they are, and I'll train my horse better, too."

"You can be a champeen barrel racer," Vern said.

She clapped her hands with excitement. "I've even got a name picked out. Polka Dot."

I thought that name sounded dumb. Blaze would be better.

"That's great." Vern put his hands behind his head and leaned back. "Polka Dot. Doesn't that sound great, Hazel?"

"I don't know anything about horses." She made her hands into tiny fists. "But I pay the bills and I know we don't have any money."

"Well, we've got a little in the bank," he said.

She struck the table with her fists. "That's Craig's college money and you're not touching it."

"It costs a lot to go to college," I said.

"I don't see why not. After all, I'm the one who earned it."

My mother gave him a withering look; then she turned the look on Lola.

"I promise it won't cost you anything." Lola tried to touch my mother's arm, but Mom jerked it back. "I'm going to get a job after school," Lola said.

"With your grades? You're barely making it now."

My mother had a good point there.

"You can bitch about this later," Vern told my mother. "No school today." He turned to Lola. "Throw your things in a suitcase. I've got to leave in half an hour."

When she left the table, Lola seemed pleased, as if she had won already.

"Listen." Vern gripped my arm and I tensed. "Old sox, old bean, old pal, old kidaroo—talk to your pal Danny, okay?"

Big fat chance, I thought.

"If you do that, I'll tell you what. I'll make sure you get a twenty-two this Christmas."

"A twenty-two?" This was a new possibility. I wanted a .22 so bad I could taste it.

Vern picked up a toothpick and rolled it in his mouth. "That's right. Not a lousy single-shot, either. How would you like a Remington bolt-action that shoots shorts, longs, and long rifles?"

My mother glared at me, and I knew what I was supposed to say. But a repeating .22 was more than I had dreamed of. I had been ready to settle for a single shot when I was fourteen. "You promise, right?"

My mother sucked in a short breath.

He made an X over his heart. "Cross my heart and hope to die."

Vern wasn't reliable with his promises, like showing up at my ball games or taking me fishing, but I was convinced he was on the level this time. A .22 rifle was too serious to lie about, even for Vern.

He scooted back in his chair and stared at my mother, but she wouldn't look at him. "So both kids are happy, Hazel. What more could you want?"

"I'm not speaking to you until you apologize for saying 'bitch.'"

"You're talking right now," he said. "Right this very minute."

She looked at me as if she could slit my throat because she thought I had betrayed her. "Get ready for school, right this instant."

I raced to the bathroom, but Lola had locked the door. "Hurry up." Just thinking of the .22 made my head feel better.

When she came out of the bathroom, Lola was all made up razzle-dazzle. I figured the look was for Jimmy Fivecoats, who was working on the ranch with his father. Jimmy had gone to Oregon State, but partied so much he flunked out. On weekends, he sat on the tailgate of his red four-wheel-drive pickup outside the Eltrym Theater and offered rides to all the high school girls. Some of the loose ones went for it.

"Jimmy goes for those dirty legs," Danny told me once. "He's so wild, he makes my brother Dave seem like a preacher."

Lola carried her pink suitcase to the car and Vern tossed in his suitcase and shaving kit. Mom followed him out to the backyard and threw the package of flash cards at him. Some scattered at his feet, but he didn't pick them up. He drove off and she came back inside the house, looking like she'd chewed iron. The flash cards remained in the driveway.

"I'm really disappointed in you," she said in a way that made my ears burn.

"I don't want to be late for school," I said, knowing she'd cool down by the time I got home.

"You come straight home from school. Don't lollygag. I need some support around here, damn it all to hell."

■ ■ ■

Danny was impressed with the news about the .22, but more interested in my raw head. "He really nailed you good." Danny touched the patch above my ear. "Does that hurt much?"

"Only when I think."

"Then you got no problems."

"I kicked Vern so hard, he dropped the soap and called me a 'shit-tailed pansy.'"

"My dad doesn't cuss at us. It's the Lutheran in him." Danny rubbed the seat of his pants. "He whips us, but not Riley. Riley can take him. Dave's almost big enough. I've got awhile to go."

I looked forward to the day I'd be too strong for Vern. "I'll take him down and rub his nose in dog shit."

"That's too good for him," Danny said. "Hey, come out to the place this weekend. I'll square it with my folks."

"Good deal." When I told Danny about the horse Lola wanted, he said, "Lola better be careful around Jimmy Fivecoats." Danny made an O with his thumb and forefinger, then pushed his other forefinger back and forth through the O. "Jimmy knocked up a girl at Oregon State."

"What happened?"

"Dave said the rubber broke. If I had a rubber break, I'd kill the guy that sold it to me."

"You don't have a rubber."

"I do, too."

"Let's see it, then."

"I'll bring it tomorrow."

"Listen," I said. "My sister's pretty wild, but she's not doing anything like that." I was surprised to find myself sticking up for her.

11

THE PORTLAND ROSE

I had always been excited about going to Danny Freeman's ranch. Even though I was a town kid, for the weekend I was a wild and free cowboy and hunter. We rode untamed, wild-eyed calves that threw us off until we were giddy, shot up tin cans with .22s, hunted quail and rabbits. We trespassed on the neighbors' ranches, poached their game, fished out their ponds. Danny's older brother Dave taught us to smoke cigarettes, and we talked late in the night, swapping dirty jokes, tall tales, ghost stories, and exaggerated plans.

A trip to Danny Freeman's ranch roused the envy of all the sixth-grade boys and stirred the curiosity of the girls. Since my stepfather usually had the car in Lime, I always packed my suitcase and carried it to school, so the other students knew that I was the chosen friend for the weekend. I stayed jumpy and excited all day, anticipating the next day's school bus ride, the weekend's shenanigans. This weekend was promising to be even better than the others. Riley had purchased some pheasant chicks from the Fish and Game Department the year before, and we planned to shoot a few roosters for dinner.

"Maybe we'll shoot a couple hens by mistake," Danny had said. "If we bury the feathers, what's the difference?"

Danny's ranch had always been a great escape from Vern and the weekend tensions, but now that Lola had come, it felt good to be away from both of them. If I had to stay home, I suffered headaches and a sick stomach.

Preoccupied with thinking about all the fun I'd have at Danny's, I hardly noticed the moving van on our block. As I drew closer to the house, it seemed curious that the van was backed onto our lawn and the loading platform lowered to our porch.

I thought Mom must be getting a new wringer washer because the old one was always "on the fritz," as she called it. Vern had tried fixing it himself half a dozen times, but the rollers always came loose, so Mom had to wring the clothes out by hand, and in winter, they took a long time to dry on the basement clothesline.

However, the two men in gray jackets and matching caps weren't carrying anything into the house. They were hauling furniture outside to the van. As I watched, they carried out my mother's mahogany chest-on-chest. When I stepped onto the porch and looked into the van, I saw the blue love seat, leather-topped drum table, needlepoint chair, and my grandfather's old rocker.

"Hey, what's going on?" I asked the stocky man near me. The name tag on his jacket said JIM.

"You got eyes. We're moving these people."

"I live here," I said.

"Then we're moving you."

"That's wrong," I said, and went inside to see about the mistake.

My mother was feeding Ronna in the kitchen, but the room was empty except for the high chair.

"Where's the table?" I asked. "Two guys are carrying out our furniture."

Ronna cooed in delight at the sound of my voice and spit out her food onto the highchair's tray. Apricots.

I gave Ronna a kiss. I wasn't alarmed because the house had

become cramped with the addition of two sisters. Maybe we were moving to a bigger place.

"What in cripes is going on?" I asked my mother.

"Go to your room and finish packing." She wore a wool sweater and skirt, the kind of clothes she used to wear to work, not for around the house. As she fed Ronna, she kept dropping the spoon. "I wouldn't let them touch your fishing gear or the valuables on your dresser. But you need to hurry. Thank heavens you came home straight from school."

"I'm going to Danny's tomorrow. I've got to pack for that."

"I'm sorry, Craig, but you won't be able to go this weekend. I need you to help me move. You and Danny will have to get together another time." She took a small washcloth and wiped off Ronna's mouth.

The baby gurgled and slapped her hands against the tray.

Suddenly, it struck me that we were moving to Durkee or Lime, closer to Lola's damn horse or Vern's work. He frequently complained about the long drive. "We're not moving to Lime, are we?" Lime was too small to have a school, and I didn't want to go to school in Huntington, away from my Baker friends.

"Of course not." She took off Ronna's soiled bib. "I'd never raise a child in Lime. I'm not that desperate."

"Well, that's a relief," I said. "Cripes, who wants to go to school in Huntington? The Bulldogs beat them every year."

"Oh, son." She gave me a long hug. When she stepped back, her eyes were troubled. "We're moving back to The Dalles."

I couldn't believe it. "I don't want to move."

She touched my arm. "What's your last name?"

I didn't answer, but I knew what she meant. Vern had never wanted to adopt me.

"That's right. You're my child, not his." She lowered her voice. "I'm not talking in front of these moving men, but we have to leave. It's imperative."

"Is it the horse?" I asked, even though I knew it wasn't.

"Of course not. Now get ready."

"Vern?"

"I'm not saying anything right now."

I didn't want to go back to The Dalles. "I could live with Danny Freeman. Dave and Danny and I are all blood brothers. We cut our thumbs and took an oath."

"I need you to help me. I'm serious. Please get packed."

Ronna rubbed her eyes.

"She's so tired," my mother said. "She can't go to sleep with all the commotion."

I turned and slouched toward my bedroom.

"You'll want to wrap your breakables carefully. That collie dog your aunt Grace gave you is made from real china."

The bedroom was almost empty. They had taken down the posters of Gene Autry, Hopalong Cassidy, and the Cisco Kid, as well as the autographed picture from Rex Allen that he'd signed at the Eltrym Theater. Dust curls indicated the places where the twin beds and the leper trap had been. Even the yellow curtains were gone. Mom had worked hard sewing them, and I figured she wasn't going to leave them behind.

My chair and nightstand were gone. Nothing remained in the closet except for my fishing equipment and BB gun. My baseball glove, basketball, and shoes were in an open box. I picked up the wooden totem pole from my dresser and wrapped it in a T-shirt. I did the same with the china collie dog, the yellow piggy bank with one pink ear. Then I opened the top drawer and stuffed in the wrapped items, along with assorted pieces of petrified wood and a small thunder egg. Looking at my bare dresser top made me feel empty and terribly alone.

"We're waiting on you," Jim said. He and his partner stood in the doorway, ready to carry out the dresser and box.

I picked up the BB gun, disappointed that Vern wasn't going to buy me the .22 bolt-action.

"I'll wrap that BB gun up good for you," Jim said. "My boy's got one just like it."

"I was thinking of taking it with me."

Jim shook his head. "They might mistake you for Jesse James

fixing to rob the Portland Rose." He held out his hand. "I'll treat it right. Most likely, we'll beat you to The Dalles."

"Okay." I handed him the rifle.

After they'd carried everything out, I left the room quickly so I wouldn't cry.

In the kitchen, the refrigerator hummed away. When I opened the door, all the food remained, just as if we still planned on living there. I jerked open the drawer at the bottom of the stove. All the pots and pans were gone, packed in the van along with my grandmother's incomplete china set, the silverware, the cheap everyday plates.

Outside, my mother was giving the men final instructions. "One twenty-one West Ninth," she said. "It's a two-story gray house. You can put the furniture and our other belongings in the basement. My parents will show you where."

She called into the house. "Hurry, Craig. We've got to get to the depot. Daisy's waiting in the car."

At the last minute, I went down into the basement and grabbed Vern's boxing gloves and helmets. The truth was, I felt like pounding the shit out of someone. Since there wasn't anybody to hit, I kicked the washing machine a few times, until my toes hurt as much as the rest of me.

■ ■ ■

Daisy Wicks drove us to the train station. Ordinarily, I liked driving with her, but not today. A good-hearted Mormon woman, Daisy could always be counted on to buy lemonade or give me fifty cents for a school raffle. Usually, she entertained us with jokes she picked up waitressing, but she wasn't humorous today.

"I don't know what I'm going to do without you," she told my mother. "And Ronna's a ray of sunshine in my life. Who told you she was ready to walk? Aunt Daisy, that's who, and I was exactly right."

"You can come see us in The Dalles," my mother said. She sounded convincing.

"I wish you were a Mormon," Daisy said. "If anything happened to you, the Church would provide for your children. I don't know what I'd do without the Church."

It seemed odd to arrive at the train station without Vern. Before he got bumped and was forced to start working in Lime, Vern had been the Baker telegrapher on the graveyard shift. During stopovers, the conductors, engineers, and brakemen would come into the station to smoke, chew tobacco, and tell jokes. The waiting room smelled like oak benches, furniture polish, brass spittoons, and tobacco smoke.

Mom bought round-trip tickets from Ralph Meldo, the ticket agent, and for a moment my heart soared, thinking we might come back to Baker somehow. But the hollowness in my heart as I thought about the moving men carrying my stuff into the van made me realize I held a false hope. She simply bought round-trip tickets to keep Ralph from suspecting anything. And to keep up appearances.

"Going to see your folks again?" Ralph asked her.

"Ronna just walked," she said. "Mom and Dad are anxious to see her."

"Walking already! Isn't she a doll? Look at all that fine blond hair."

"She's my pride and joy. I feel so fortunate to have everything in two children. Boy and girl, light and dark, brown eyes and blue."

"They grow so fast." He handed her the tickets. "She'll be riding a trike by the time you come back."

"She is growing up fast." My mom nudged Ronna's chin with her forefinger. "Aren't you, sweetie?"

Ronna reached for Ralph's glasses but he just chuckled and leaned away from her.

"Good thing Vern's out in Lime," Ralph said. "Sounds like he'll be batching for a while, and I don't want to hear him bellyaching about his own cooking."

"I expect he'll get by," my mother said.

• • •

As usual, the Portland Rose was late coming out of Boise. We waited in the station almost an hour. Several people stopped by to admire Ronna, and Mom talked with them about her walking, the clothes my grandmother had sewn, the touch of colic the baby had at the hospital. She tried acting natural, but I could sense she was anxious for the train to arrive.

This would be a good time to clear out, I thought. Just leave for Danny Freeman's. But I'll help Mom and Ronna get to The Dalles, I decided. Then after a week, maybe two, once they're good and settled, I'll come back on my own.

While we waited, the Wagontire boys passed by, hitting each other with sticks. Since the ringworm incident at school, they had both gotten soup-bowl haircuts. The Wagontires continued down the street, shouting, throwing rocks at each other and jabbing each other's butts with the sticks.

Even though I never played with the Wagontires, somehow it was good to see them. The boys reminded me I was still in Baker. Maybe the train wouldn't come after all.

When the Portland Rose finally arrived, half a dozen people got off. They all looked normal, I thought. None of them seemed to be running away from home.

"Well, I guess this is it," my mother said, gathering up my sister and her baby blankets. I grabbed a small suitcase we hadn't checked and the diaper bag.

"Watch your step, missus," the conductor said as my mother stepped on the small metal stool, then onto the train steps. Malcolm, give these folks a hand," he said to the black porter.

"I'd prefer to sit on the right side," my mother told the porter. "That way, I can see the Columbia later on."

A bald man in a white shirt occupied the seat in front of us. He turned around as we settled into the seats. "Cute baby," he said. After eyeing me a minute, he asked, "You the brother?"

"I sure am."

"You got yourself a towhead sister."

• • •

As the train began moving slowly away from the station, I refused to look at Baker passing by. Instead, I focused on the bald man's head. His ears were small and he had a wart on the right side of his neck. I remember because Joe Freeman, Danny's father, had a wart in the same place.

When we were five miles out of town, I moved to the left side of the car because I knew the Freeman Angus Ranch would be there. And I glimpsed it all for a moment, the old red barn where we smoked cigarettes and shot holes in the roof while aiming at flitting sparrows, Lady's doghouse, the corral where we rode calves until we were giddy, the house itself, a two-story white clapboard with a wide porch.

I saw Danny's father walking bowlegged toward the barn, and I realized he'd already eaten supper and was going to check on the cattle before night fell. I placed my hand on the cool window glass, feeling as if I could reach out and pull the entire farm toward me and hold it close. But the train had picked up speed and the Freeman place was already gone, left behind with the rest of Baker.

I wondered what Vern and Lola were doing at that very minute. They could be at the Fivecoats's place with the horse, or maybe they had gone to Huntington for dinner and were sitting in a café right now, never suspecting for a moment that the house on Valley Street was cleaned out.

What would Lola think? She had moved up from California for a more stable life, but that change hadn't lasted a year. Would the authorities put her in a home, or let her stay with Vern? Something wasn't right between them. I knew that much. Still, I felt sorry for Lola, even though she wore revealing clothes and way too much makeup, and even though she talked too loudly and laughed too hard. When I came back, I'd look her up and tell her I would still be her brother.

The conductor came through and punched our tickets, placing the blue tags under the metal strip above our seats. "Going with us as far as The Dalles. You sure got a doll there."

Ronna reached toward him and he handed her the shiny ticket punch. "You can be the conductor." She moved it toward her mouth but my mother stopped her. "It probably has a lot of germs," she said.

"I never thought of that." He seemed a little embarrassed. "What is she? About a year?"

"Ten months." My mother took the ticket punch from her and Ronna squalled. "There now, baby, there." She held Ronna against her shoulder, patting her back. "She just started walking."

"I love kids," the conductor said. "I've got two grandkids."

My mother nodded. "We're going to see her grandparents now."

"Well, they're in for a treat," he said.

"Yes, they are." She changed the subject. "Can you please tell me if you're still serving dinner?"

The conductor snapped open his gold pocket watch. "Twenty more minutes. It's the next car." He moved down the aisle.

Turning to me, Mom asked, "Are you hungry? You must be after all the moving."

A part of me didn't want to eat, but I was hungry. Anyway, I always liked the dining car. When I traveled on my own, my mother normally fixed sandwiches rather than pay train prices for food, but Vern had worked out a couple deals with the waiters where I ate cheeseburgers for free. "I'm hungry," I said.

"I brought along some money. Let's splurge. We can celebrate a fresh start."

My look must have dampened her enthusiasm. She touched me on the shoulder. "Listen, honey, I know this is very difficult for you, but it's going to be much better in the long run. You'll see." She handed me the diaper bag. "Please go ahead. I have trouble opening those doors while carrying Ronna."

I did go ahead, feeling important as I opened the pneumatic doors between the train cars. Usually, I was pretty good at matching my gait with the train's swaying.

My mother paused before entering the dining car. "Just wait a second."

The doors closed so we were sealed off. She touched my shoulder. "Momma's smart about people, but I'm not. I thought she was wrong about Vern."

I felt angry at my grandmother, as if she had caused our hasty departure. But only one word came out of my mouth: "Lola?"

My mother didn't answer.

The train swayed and I lurched against the metal door, feeling my balance slip.

The dining car door opened and a man in a brown suit hesitated a moment as we moved to the side. He nodded as we passed.

The dining car host led us to a clean table beside the window. A single red rose in a slim vase decorated the table. Ronna took a spoon from the place setting and began hitting the knife.

"I think she's going to be a drummer." The waiter dazzled his smile, showing a gold tooth.

Since she was busy with Ronna, the waiter asked Mom if he could fill out her service card. "I'll have the lamb chops well done and a cup of tea, very hot. And milk for the tea, please. And could I have an extra serving of the spearmint jelly?"

"Of course," the waiter said. "And for you, young man?"

"I'll have a cheeseburger," I said, handing him my marked card. "And a Coke."

Mom raised her eyebrow. "Wouldn't you like to have a steak? I said we could splurge."

The Freemans would be having steak Friday night. Usually it was from an old bull, tough and stringy. They sold the good steer meat for profit.

"A cheeseburger will be fine," I said.

When our drinks came, I held Ronna, because Mom didn't want her close to the hot tea. I had to keep my Coke halfway across the table.

The food arrived and Mom took Ronna back, because she wanted me to "eat in peace," as she put it. Although Mom had some difficulty eating her own dinner, she seemed to enjoy every bite. She cut the lamb chops in small pieces and ate them with the spearmint jelly.

"I love lamb chops," she said. "But I never fix them at home because they're so expensive."

The waiter brought more hot water and another tea bag. My mother made certain the hot teapot was a safe distance from the baby. Somehow, the waiter produced a rattle and Ronna focused on shaking it.

"You don't get good service like this in Baker," Mom said. "I could get used to it." She used her second tea bag. "I feel absolutely extravagant."

We had passed through La Grande and were winding through the Blue Mountains. Ahead, I saw a small cluster of lights. "I'll bet that's Meacham."

The waiter brought the bill. Ronna thumped the table with her rattle, and he grinned at her as he cleared away Mom's plate.

Past Meacham, a solitary light, perhaps from a ranch, caught my attention. Suddenly, out the window, I saw a forked-horn buck hanging twisted in a barbed-wire fence. It appeared that while the deer had been trying to leap the fence, one of his hind legs caught between strands, and his struggles entangled him further. The deer's head hung on the side of the fence closer to the tracks, and I could see where his antlers had scoured the snow down to the bare ground. Dark bloodstains and hunks of hide littered the snow, revealing where coyotes had gutted and eaten most of the helpless deer.

I couldn't swallow the meat in my mouth. Setting down the cheeseburger, I reached for my linen napkin and spit out the half-chewed meat. When I looked out the window again, the deer was gone. We were winding through dark woods. Black trees crowded the track and an occasional telegraph pole flicked by.

"Craig, you look pale." My mother placed a ten-dollar bill on the table. Apparently she hadn't seen the deer.

My mouth was dry, so I drank a few sips of my Coke. "I saw a dead deer hanging from the fence."

"Perhaps a train hit it." She seemed thoughtful. "Those poor deer don't stand a chance against a train. I'm certain the bright lights and noise are frightening and confusing."

"Headlight, Mom. A train has just one light."

"I suppose so."

I blinked a couple times, trying to clear the horrible image of the deer. I looked at the crisp ten-dollar bill. She must have gone to the bank.

The waiter took the money and brought her back two dollars.

"You're good at math," Mom said. "What's twenty percent of eight dollars?"

"A dollar sixty," I said.

"Well, he was most pleasant and accommodating. I'm going to leave the whole two dollars."

■ ■ ■

My mother and Ronna fell asleep back in the coach. I decided to check out the lounge car attached to the men's rest room. Vern had told me if I hung around in lounge cars, I could learn a lot about life by listening to men's conversations.

When I pulled aside the heavy brown curtains, the conductor sat in one of the upholstered chairs. His hat occupied the seat beside him. He was balding and seemed shorter and older without the hat.

In the next seat, a man in a cowboy shirt was drinking bourbon on ice and bragging about Alaska. "The country down here is all used up," he said. "In Alaska, you can still breathe. And I can make three times as much money as I make down here."

"That's fine for you," the conductor said. "The Union Pacific doesn't operate in Alaska."

"Not my problem," the man said.

He lifted the bottle and nodded at the conductor. "Snort?"

"Not on the job," the conductor said.

"What about you, kid?" The man winked at the conductor. "In Alaska, I see boys younger than him stepping up to the bar. They get served, too."

"Not on this train," the conductor said.

The man laughed and splashed some more bourbon into his glass. "There I go—contributing to the delinquency of a minor."

The waiter stuck his head through the curtains. "We're closing the kitchen. Do you gentlemens want anything?"

"Bring me a Squirt, would you, Doc?" the conductor said. He glanced at me. "You want a Squirt, son?"

"Sure," I said.

"I need some ice," the Alaska man said. "I'm down to slivers."

Doc came back with two Squirts, already opened, three glasses, and lots of fresh ice. "You gentlemens want your Squirt over ice?"

"That's right. On the rocks," the conductor said.

"Me, too," I said.

Doc used a pair of silver tongs to put the ice cubes in all three glasses. He poured the Squirt in two and handed the glasses to us. He set coasters with Union Pacific crests beside each of us and handed the third glass to the Alaska man. "I got you a fresh one, in case you want it."

The man slugged down the rest of his drink and set the glass on the tray Doc held. Then he took the fresh glass and poured bourbon over the ice.

When Doc had left, the conductor said, "That's a damn good waiter; in fact, he's the best this line's ever seen. I suppose he'll retire pretty soon and I'll have to break in a new man. Doc's been with the UP longer than me."

"They make good waiters," the Alaska man said. "I'll give them that." He took another drink. "You know what's funny? Indians. You can't make an Indian into a waiter. I don't know why that is. I used to live in Pendleton but I never saw an Indian waiter. How about you?"

The conductor drank a sip of Squirt, then shook his head. "I've never seen one, either, come to think about it."

The man turned to me. "What about you, kid?"

"I've seen Chinese waiters," I said. "In Baker, we've got a Chinese restaurant."

"We've got three in Fairbanks," the man said. "Yeah, Chinese make good waiters and waitresses even. I kind of like the way the women wear chopsticks in their hair. What's your favorite Chinese food, anyway?"

"Fried shrimp," I said. "Or maybe sweet-and-sour pork."

"I like the duck with lichee nuts," the man said. "Ever had it?"

"No," I said. In fact, I had never seen it on a menu.

"It's like Chinese women," the man said. "Sweet, but an acquired taste."

The conductor rose and put on his hat. "Pendleton," he said. "Some of us have to go to work, fellas."

The Alaska man got to his feet, but he swayed a bit. "I'm getting some fresh air."

"Don't be too long," the conductor said. "We'll only have about ten minutes."

The man saluted the conductor. "I won't let you leave without me."

I decided to get some air, too, so I went onto the platform. Seeing Pendleton made me sadder, because we'd once left it for a fresh start.

The Alaska man walked off the platform and started across the street to the Golden Dragon. "Don't let them leave without me, kid," he called over his shoulder.

That made me anxious. I was always anxious when I got off the train someplace just to stretch my legs. I was afraid of being left behind. I decided to keep an eye on the conductor and make sure he knew when the man got back.

After ten minutes passed, the conductor called out, "Train time!"

The brakeman signaled all clear.

"All aboard!"

I climbed the steps. "The guy from Alaska's not back."

The conductor checked his watch. "Then he's out of luck." He picked up the stool.

The train began to move. Across the street, the Golden Dragon's door opened and the man stepped out. He was carrying a sack.

The train began to move faster, and the man picked up his pace but didn't run.

"You'd think he had all day," the conductor said.

"Come on," I called. "They won't hold the train."

He ran and caught the car by the time we reached the end of the platform. When he hopped aboard, I smelled deep-fried shrimp.

"You sure took a chance," the conductor said.

"Don't I know it," the man said. "I used to live here and my ex-wife is around somewhere."

After the three of us returned to the lounge car, the man poured himself a drink. Once again, the conductor refused a snort, so the man took two ginger ales out of the paper sack along with the container of shrimp. "I come prepared," he said. "But they were out of Squirt."

"Thanks a lot," I said when he handed me my ginger ale and the shrimp.

"You're a polite kid," he said. "I don't like sullen kids. Dig into those shrimp now. You're a growing boy."

I tried the shrimp—very hot and delicious. I took a swig of ginger ale to avoid burning my mouth. "Good shrimp."

He nodded. "They were fresh out of lichee duck, but you try it sometime and remember me when you do."

"You bet." I handed him the shrimp container.

"Don't you wonder how they get shrimp in Pendleton? Maybe they're not shrimp at all."

"What else would they be?"

He shrugged. "Snails. Sheep tails. I don't dare ask the cook." He took another slug of whiskey. "Once I ordered a seafood cocktail in Rock Springs, Wyoming." He spread his hands. "Canned tuna fish with mayonnaise and relish."

After a while, I saw lights ahead and hundreds of boxcars lined along side tracks. "That's Hinkle coming up."

The conductor shifted in his seat. "You know Hinkle? You must come from a railroad family. Who works for UP?"

"Vern Hecker. He's a telegrapher."

"Hell, I know Vern. So he's your dad?"

"Stepdad." I didn't know what Vern was anymore.

He peered at me. "You must favor your mother. Vern's stocky and blue-eyed."

"I look like my real father," I said.

The Alaska man laughed. "You got lucky, kid. You don't look like a railroader." He took another drink. "No offense," he said to the conductor.

"Vern still in Biggs?" the conductor asked.

I shook my head. "Lime."

"Lime now? Huh." He was trying to sound like it wasn't a send down to be in Lime. "So you live in Huntington?"

"I live in Baker," I said, even though we'd just left. Baker was a big deal compared to Huntington.

"The Baker Bulldogs. Purple and gold."

"We have good teams," I said, pleased the conductor knew the school colors.

"Jeez, what a sorry-ass place!" the Alaska man said, peering out the window at Hinkle. "And I'll bet it looks worse in the daylight. Just like some of the women I know." He laughed.

The conductor bristled. "It's a railroad town. A lot of good people live here."

"They deserve better," the Alaska man said. "Do they ever!"

The conductor rose. "I don't have to listen to you insult the railroad."

"Don't get sore. I was just making an observation."

The conductor ignored him. "Tell Vern hello for me. James Lee. I'm kind of surprised. Vern never mentioned having a son. A chip off the old block."

"James Lee. I'll tell him." I wasn't too surprised Vern hadn't mentioned me.

After the conductor left, the man looked at me. "He was rude, don't you think? Kind of abrupt?"

"He was upset about the railroad, I guess."

"Hinkle. Dinkle. Pinkle. It sounds like a bad nursery rhyme." He poured himself another drink. "The thing to remember is that people don't have to be stuck." He waggled a finger at me. "It's a free country, right? If you're stuck, get unstuck. That's my motto. I was stuck in Pendleton with a bad marriage and a lousy job. Now

I'm in Fairbanks with my own auto-body shop. Kepler's. You ask. Everybody knows it."

"I'd like to see Alaska," I said.

He tapped the side of his head. "Now you're hitting all the cylinders. Alaska's the best place in the world for a fresh start. You come up and I'll put you to work. Alaska winters just eat up the cars. I got more customers than a whore in a mining camp."

"I'll remember. Kepler's."

He reached for my hand. "Tom Kepler. I own the place."

"Craig Lesley," I said.

"Craig Lesley." He thought for a moment. "What happened to your real father? Death or divorce?"

"My mom and dad got divorced."

"No shame in that," he said. "I've been divorced three times. And I been a stepdad twice. Nothing worked out like we planned, so we got unstuck." He scowled at his drink. "Hey, it's a free country, right?"

"That's right." I wondered what he'd be like as a stepdad.

"It's a free country, but divorce isn't free. That's the good thing about Alaska. It's hard to collect alimony in Alaska."

After a few minutes, the man began to nod. His body rocked slightly with the motion of the train. Now that he was asleep, not animated with stories and liquor, he appeared older. His face looked troubled. I could see spikes of gray stubble on his chin and under his jawline.

Outside the window, the Columbia River shimmered in moonlight. The train picked up speed, thundering by Arlington. My life is running backward fast, I thought, like one of those comic train scenes in the Saturday matinee. Rufus next, then Biggs, and then our stop in The Dalles.

What was I going to do in The Dalles? When I was little, I enjoyed having my grandfather show me off to his coworkers at the *Chronicle*, but I was too old for that now. I wanted rowdy weekends out at Danny's. Once, I had picked bachelor's buttons for my mother and grandmother, but now the flowers were for girls who stirred my emotions—Rhonda Hester and Gail Lawrence. Maybe even Lola.

I felt so low that I didn't want to see my grandparents. I could predict our arrival: my grandfather standing on the platform, wearing his wool vest and smoking his crook-stem pipe. Him kissing my mother and Ronna on their foreheads, then tousling my hair and saying I looked exactly like my uncle Oscar.

My grandmother kissing me on the cheek. Then Mom handing her the baby and saying, "Momma, she's already walking. Can you believe that?" My grandmother cuddling the baby, and saying something bad about Vern. All of us piling into my grandfather's two-toned Chevrolet and driving up Union Street to 121 West Ninth. My grandfather chuckling and tapping his pipe on the hula-girl ashtray my uncle had brought back from Hawaii. The girl's skirt swaying in a risqué way and my grandfather muttering, "Ain't that something."

Now, out the train window, I looked for the old Biggs where Vern had once worked, but it was gone, flooded along with Celilo Falls by the backwaters of The Dalles Dam. Vern and Lola were as good as gone, too.

Maybe The Dalles would be a fresh start for my mother and baby sister, but not for me. Those years with Vern had changed me. I wanted things to be different, to be innocent again, but this was how it was.

On the outskirts of town, the train slowed. I smelled the creosote plant where they treated the railroad ties against weather and age.

Creosote didn't work on people, I thought. Nothing stopped the weathering or the rot.

"The Dalles!" the conductor called. "This stop. The Dalles!"

I saw a shadow against a fence and realized a black dog was digging a hole to the other side. I remembered the small buck tangled in the barbed-wire fence. He hadn't crossed cleanly to the other side, and I realized that I never could either. A part of me would remain behind, forever tangled in Vern's harsh and unrelenting grasp.

12

THE FREEMAN RANCH

I never saw Vern again. Or Lola. My impulse on the train to tell her I would still be her brother remained nothing but a delusion. From then on, my mother, Ronna, and I formed a small family and we were on our own. After eight months of staying with my grandparents in The Dalles, the three of us moved to Madras, where my mother found a job working on the Warm Springs Indian Reservation nearby.

Another fresh start.

Forty years after the three of us took the Portland Rose, fleeing Baker like Gypsies in the night, a chance encounter led to news about Vern. On a long drive home to Portland from Seattle with our two young daughters, my wife, Kathy, and I stopped to get dinner at Cousins, a family-style restaurant off the freeway in Centralia, Washington. Kira and Elena jumped out of the car, racing each other to see who would reach the door first and open it, causing the cow replica to moo loudly. Inside, a hostess greeted us with a hearty "Howdy, Cousins!" and the waitress used the same moniker at every opportunity. The girls drank from plastic cups with orange cow heads for lids, a souvenir item they insisted on buying to take home.

As I waited to pay the bill, an old man in railroad garb also waited to pay his. We exchanged pleasantries, and I asked him what job he had had on the railroad.

"I was a telegrapher," he said.

"Really! Did you ever know a telegrapher named Vern Hecker?"

"Sure. I knew Vern when we worked out of Tacoma. He was short and tough and mean."

I had to laugh. Those words summed him up so well.

"Is he still alive?"

The man shook his head. "Vern died a couple years back. You a railroader? How did you know him?"

"I was his stepson."

The man's face flushed at his earlier comment and he tried backtracking. "You know, Vern never forgot Christmas. I remember the great cookies he always brought down to the station. His wife baked them. You could count on those good cookies every Christmas. . . ."

He kept rattling on about the cookies, attempting to make up for his earlier remark.

"It's okay," I told him. "Vern and I were never that close. I haven't seen him in years."

When I told Kathy the news, she asked how I felt.

"A little cheated. I always thought we'd meet up and I'd pound on him awhile." Of course, when I thought of Vern, I remembered him as he had been, not as some gimpy senior citizen.

"Are you going to tell Ronna her father's dead?"

The question caught me off guard. I didn't know the better thing to do. "What do you think?"

"I think she'd want to know."

Ronna said it was good to get the news. Even so, I wondered how she felt about never knowing her father. My sister had accom-

plished what my mother had always desired: a home of her own
and a loving husband who was also a good father to his son.

Except for health problems, my mother was in a good spot. She
lived with my sister and her husband, doting on their son as she
had doted on my daughters, and as my grandparents had on me.
Unconditional love.

On hearing the news of Vern, my mother's only remark was,
"Well." She spoke firmly, as if satisfied to know that he was gone
and she had outlasted him. So was I.

As for my pal Danny Freeman, I didn't see him for twenty years
following that last ride on the Portland Rose. Still, I often
thought of him, especially when I borrowed his first name for my
Indian rodeo rider, Danny Kachiah.

When Kathy, the girls, and I traveled to Baker (now Baker
City) for a reading and book signing, Danny and Dave, along with
their wives, Sue and Twila, put on a picnic in one of the meadows
where we had hunted as boys. Wildflowers bloomed in profusion
and Sutton Creek burbled nearby.

Danny and Dave hauled the picnic equipment by all-
terrain vehicles and trap wagons. Modernization had come to
the ranch. Horses were reserved for rodeo and jackpot roping
events.

They set up picnic tables, sun covers, a propane barbeque, ice
chests. We ate like lords and ladies, feasting on Freeman certified-
Angus steaks, hamburgers, hot dogs, potato salad, green salad,
macaroni salad, carrot and raisin salad, Jell-O salad, baked beans,
pork and beans, green beans, corn on the cob, sliced tomatoes and
cucumbers, apple pie, chocolate cake, rhubarb cobbler. . . . I can't
remember the rest.

As we sat under the trees, Kathy heard a beautiful birdsong
and asked Dave what it was. Dave tilted his head and touched the
red bandanna around his neck. "It's a robin."

"We've got robins in the city," Kathy said. "I've never heard
one sing like that."

Dave leaned back in his chair and grinned. "It was probably

sad to be in the city. These are happy robins because they're out in the wide-open spaces."

Danny and Dave took Elena and Kira on ATV rides, and the girls sat on their laps, laughing and half-steering the iron horses. Kira, the wilder of the two, shouted, "Faster, Danny, faster!" from her four-year-old lungs, while Kathy and I yelled for her to hold on.

Smiling, Danny went faster.

Before we packed up, we took a group picture with an automatic camera. Country folk and city slickers glowing after a good time together. Dave wore a rakish cowboy hat and a sly look. At any moment he might start "educating" Danny and me about things our parents would disapprove of.

On that wonderful day, things settled exactly right.

II

BACK TO MONUMENT

■ ■ ■

13

NEWTON AND ANNA

The gold bug bit my grandfather Newton Jasper Lesley, Rudell's father. As a result, he spent much of his early life in Idaho, prospecting for gold and silver. Eventually, he discovered that gold was easier to get by excavating the miners' pockets rather than poking around the creek beds, so he ran a tavern near Coeur d'Alene. He was a big man, capable of handling most rowdies and toughs who frequented the bar. The money was good and the lifestyle was exciting.

Newton let a young gambler run a table in the tavern for a quarter of the man's earnings. This worked out well until, eventually, one of the rowdies accused the young man of cheating. Although no firm proof existed, the accuser held a grudge.

At that time, the law meant nothing, so when Newton learned that the rowdy belonged to a group of vigilantes, he thought it best for the young man to hide. He spirited the card dealer away to a trapline shack he knew high in the mountains near one of his diggings. After warning the gambler to stay put and keep a watchful eye, Newton left, promising to bring food and clothing the next day. The gambler requested a woman, too.

As he had promised, Newton returned with supplies the next day. However, before he reached the cabin, he found the gambler facedown in a creek. Bullet holes riddled his body. Someone had cut off his hands.

Keeping a hawk's eye for intruders, Newton buried the gambler, digging the hole with a rusty pick he found inside the shack.

Hoping he had seen the end of violence, Newton returned to the bar, only to discover one of the young man's friends hanging from a noose on the porch.

Without stopping to pack, my grandfather rode his horse across a high railroad trestle and kept following the tracks in case the vigilantes were watching the highways. He had the food and clothing he had taken for the gambler, and he traveled all the way to his brother's place near Tillamook, Oregon, on the coast, where he decided to rest and hole up until any danger passed. He was afraid to go back to his father's ranch in Monument because it was too close to Idaho. Still cautious, he got a job cruising timber, work that would keep him out of sight of any suspicious eyes in Tillamook. On one job up the Nehalem River, twenty miles from town, he met a young girl named Anna Jackson.

In her diary, Anna recorded, *Newton Lesley was the first man I ever saw other than my own relatives and a few married men.*

He must have appeared to be a savior to her, because her life was so difficult. Her mother divorced her father for another man; then her mother and stepfather had six children of their own, as well as his two older boys.

Anna described her life:

My stepfather didn't work and we never knew how we lived. Daisy my youngest sister which was born directly after my mother remarried, was a tiny baby when my mother went hunting with my stepfather and was gone for five days. During the time they were gone the dogs which my stepfather always had around got into the cabin and eat all our food. Leaving me, 8 years old, with his two children and my baby sister for 4 days without any food. I was so sick that I couldn't eat when they came back. They didn't

*get any meat and I don't remember what we did live on during the
period right after that.*

*My stepfather was too lazy to even keep us in wood so that
was his oldest boys and my job, during winter and summer.*

Anna lived with her mother and stepfather under these circumstances until she turned twelve. At that time, they moved
even farther up the river. Although several of the children had
reached school age by then, none of them was allowed to attend.

*They sold the Homestead for practically nothing and bought
several head of cattle, which we took to our new home. We put up
a little hay and the folks would leave us children and be gone for
days at a time and leaving us feeding the cattle during the winter.
We eat bread and bacon grease which was given to us during several of these absences. The stock all died before the winter was
over, from starvation.*

Newton appeared to be a man who could rescue her from this
life. After they had known each other for two years, they married.
She was fifteen and he was forty.

Anna and Newton stayed near the coast at a place called Lost
Creek and homesteaded for six years. During that time, they had
seven children: Huston (who always went by Hoot), Manila, Dora
(who later died, leaving three more children for Anna to mother),
Elvira, Martin, Clarissa, and Julia (Judy). Searching for a better
life, they packed their sparse belongings and moved inland to
Monument where they planned to work on Newton's father's
place.

*When Newton and I and the children started to Eastern Ore-
gon we just had our clothes and a few other belongings, and no
money except for the $60 I had saved in several months previous.
We left Tillamook and went to Garibaldi by team and wagon, and
then from Garibaldi to Astoria on the boat Vosburg. As we were
going over the bar in Astoria, a swell hit the boat and knocked it*

*on our side. I was laying down when the boat turned on its side.
Huston, Dora, Manila, and I were all laying down because we
were sick. Huston was 8 yrs. old at the time. There was a lot of
cowhides and other trading skins, and they were all lost overboard.*

*We went from Astoria up the Columbia 100 miles to Portland
on a river boat, passenger boat. The State Fair was on now but
we didn't get to go. I wasn't able anyhow. We went from there to
Heppner on a train and then to Monument on the stage. Heppner
to Parker's Mill, Scott Place to Monument. We changed horses at
these places. When we got to Monument we started living in
Grandma Lesley's old house. Newt started working for his sister,
Sarah, at her livery stable. He worked there all winter, and than
later on the next year we moved to the Monument Homestead,
where it was too rocky to grow much. We were all sick.*

Anna wouldn't see Tillamook or any of her own relatives again
for over thirty years. In Monument, she had five more children:
Donald, Rudell Newton (my father), Sarah (Sally), Lela, and
Robert (Bob).

I've often wondered how young Anna felt when she first traveled to that Monument country. Compared to Tillamook's dense
forest and lush meadows and the ocean's magnificent views, Monument has a dry, rocky, and barren landscape. Remote, too. She
must have had a thousand second thoughts, but for her, there was
no turning back.

Newton hardly proved to be a perfect husband. The allure of
gold never left him, and at various times, he set out to find gold in
Idaho, Oregon, and Alaska. He'd disappear for five or six months
at a time, leaving the farm work and child care to Anna and the
older children.

At times, former companions from prospecting days would
stop by to tell spellbinding tales of lost mines, rich veins,
overnight wealth. Newton always proved eager to light out on another adventure. Surely, he thought this to be far more exciting
than working and taking care of twelve children. Fascinated by
the strangers' stories, the children listened intently, savoring each

word but fearing their father would take off again, leaving them with less money and more chores.

All the burdens rested on my grandmother's small shoulders. She worked like a mule in harsh conditions and wrote of one task:

> *I never had a very easy time during this period of selling milk. It was real cold at Monument during the winter and I didn't have the proper clothing to keep myself warm. Usually I had to take one or two of the small children with me and try to keep them warm also as I was delivering the milk. During this time I raised a big garden and canned all of the food we had for the winter months. I churned butter in a barrel churn and sold butter also.*

For his part, Newton did little. Aunt Sally told me, "Dad never worked except during harvest time, and then he'd be mad."

Anna made up for him, and then some. When her daughter Dora died, my grandmother took in her three children and raised them as her own.

Only in a few rare instances did my grandmother acknowledge her hard life. She instructed all the children to sing while they worked, and she taught them "Billy Boy," "You Are My Sunshine," "The Strawberry Roan," and "The Sinking of the Maine," among others. She insisted that they sing. "You can't cry if you're singing."

When Newton died, she was a widow for six years. She remarried but found little love in it:

> *I never knew what real love is. Each of my marriages was a marriage of convenience. First to get away from my family and the next for someone to help me with my family and heavier responsibilities. . . . For twenty-nine years straight, I always had a baby in the house.*

14

MADRAS

I spent two years in the late 1950s making America safe for democracy by keeping a vigilant eye out for enemy planes—North Korean and Russian-piloted MiGs that might be threatening Oregon's interior near Madras. My mother, Ronna, and I moved to Madras, a town of seventeen hundred people in the sunny interior of Oregon, so my Aunt Mac could help with Ronna. During those days, my father and Monument were far from my thoughts and I had word of him only when Grandma Lesley visited. Watching for enemy planes was first and foremost on my mind. Tuesdays and Thursdays after school, my friend Tub Hobson and I stood on the flat roof of the Madras Fire Department, scanning the horizon for hostiles.

With the naked eye, and a single pair of cloudy binoculars traded back and forth, we repeatedly swept all four quadrants, taking no chances enemy planes would sneak by us to attack Culver, Gateway, or, God help us, open fire on Madras itself. Our Boy Scout leader had warned that even seemingly harmless places like Metolius were prime targets, given the fact that they grew and stored potatoes there. He told of starvation during the Irish potato famines and how Stalin had starved the Ukrainians by taking away their potatoes. Now our enemies threatened Central Oregon's spuds. I was convinced by the leader's speech, but Hobson was more skeptical.

"Hairballs," he whispered.

In spite of our best intentions, strict discipline faltered in about an hour. By that time, my eyes stung from staring over Mount Jefferson, Mount Bachelor, Three-Fingered Jack, and the Three Sisters, roughly the directions of North Korea and Russia, if you drew a line toward infinity.

Tub slugged me hard in the shoulder. "Don't rub it," he challenged.

His fists were bigger than mine and he had already grown the beginnings of a mustache.

"I think I felt a mosquito," I said but didn't rub it, even though my shoulder hurt like hell.

"I can throw farther than you can," Tub said.

"Not unless the bears come out of the woods."

"Betcha I can."

Dozens of rocks, some large as apples, mysteriously appeared on the flat composition roof before we manned each shift. We figured other high schoolers, probably the "hoods," threw them up in a night ritual. Our task was to throw them off—aiming for the city fire department's pumper truck parked in a gravel back lot half a block away.

My shoulder remained sore after Tub's slug, but I limbered up and selected a baseball-sized rock. To gain momentum, I ran toward the roof's edge, then flung the rock hard and high. It clanged off the truck's water tank.

Imitating the voice of a baseball announcer, I spoke. "Tub Hobson rounds third and Lesley makes the throw from deep center field. It's going to be awfully close, folks, but he's called out at the plate. What a major-league throw!"

"Pure blind luck, you throwing that far." Tub spit on his right palm, wound up, and threw with a mighty oomph.

The rock fell short.

Cupping my hand behind my ear, I asked, "Did you hear a clunk, Tub? Maybe I'm getting deaf."

Disgusted, he thrust his hands in his pockets and shrugged. "Hey, no kidding. How come you always outthrow me, Lesley? You got smaller arms and skinnier shoulders." He seemed genuinely puzzled.

"Physics," I said.

"Physics?"

"Remember, you got a C in Mr. Johnson's physics class and I got an A. Momentum and thrust, Tub. Angle of trajectory. Keep that in mind."

"Weenie Arm!"

In that five minutes or so while we goofed off, I suppose a plane or two could have snuck by unnoticed, but fortunately, they didn't.

What did fly across the Madras skies during our watch? A yellow biplane crop duster, numerous magpies, a confused pheasant that wandered into town and dodged sparse traffic. Closer to the earth, we also spotted a few wobbly drunks escorted by the police from the Shangrila Bar to the city lockup, where they idled until their red-faced wives reclaimed them.

Thank heavens no enemy planes threatened Madras on our watch. In those days, the city police car had no radio (tight budget), so if an emergency occurred, Madge Frudgett, the dispatcher, lit a red beacon on top of the firehouse. The light was visible from anywhere in Madras—except the dark, smoky bars. When he saw the light, Herb Vibbert, the officer on duty, would stop at a house, ask to borrow their phone, and call in to see what was happening. All of this took time.

While Tub and I were freezing in the winter, baking in the summer, the light flashed only a few emergencies, but most were routine: stolen bicycles, cows breaking through fences, pregnant women going into early labor. Whoever spotted the flashing light first got to punch the other volunteer squarely in the shoulder and say, "Don't rub it," then add, "Do you see any enemy planes, Horse Face?"

Most shifts were uneventful outside of the throwing and punching. For the last hour of the shift, I gazed toward the snow-capped beauty of the Cascades—the jagged crest of Three-Fingered Jack, the rugged beauty of Broken Top—and I'd dream of catching brook trout later in the summer and hiking alpine meadows filled with wildflowers.

Shifting my eyes, I'd watch the sunlight glinting off the tin potato-shed roofs at Metolius and realize they did make ideal targets. Strengthened by my resolve to complete my duty, I'd stare hard at the sky another twenty minutes until black dots danced before my eyes. But even so, my mind wandered to my uncle Oscar's sporting-goods store and all the equipment I planned to buy with summer earnings.

Finally, Madge would crunch out onto the gravel parking lot to announce that our shift was over and invite us for cookies and Kool-Aid in the dispatch room. We descended the shaky ladder while two more eager Civil Air Patrol volunteers headed for the roof.

After scarfing the drinks and sticking extra Snickerdoodles into our pockets, Tub and I made our way toward separate homes, confident we had kept Madras safe for another three hours. We parted at the county jail, where sad-eyed men gestured out the bars, begging smokes.

"See you tomorrow, Bacteria Breath," Tub said.

"Same to you but more of it," I answered. I sauntered home, secretly pleased with his friendship and confident that any major-league scouts visiting Madras would covet my throwing arm. Once again, Tub and I had guaranteed that Central Oregon was safe from invaders.

Many years later, when the Metolius potato sheds finally did collapse, no one could discern a reason. Old age, gravity, saboteurs. No potatoes had inhabited the sheds for years, but a few transients had been reported taking up residency.

Earl Cordes, Jefferson County Fire Chief, drove out the five miles in response to a call from the sheriff's office. According to the story featured in the Madras *Pioneer*, Cordes yelled into the collapsed building (a dangerous mess) but got no response. "So far I've received no reply," he told the paper. "So they're either unconscious, dead, or not there."

I wonder what became of the so-called "transients." Perhaps they were saboteurs, following sinister orders from a foreign power. Were they agents from Cuba, North Korea, the former USSR?

Maybe Cordes is right. "Unconscious," "dead," or "not there" implies no one is threatening Central Oregon, but I'm not so easily convinced. Growing up with full knowledge of the Red menace, I know how sneaky those Commies can be. Even now, they could be hiding in the seed carrots, the bluegrass fields, or lurking in the mint, just waiting for us to lower our guard.

■ ■ ■

Oscar's Sporting Goods was my favorite Madras haunt. Owned by my mother's younger brother, Oscar's sold hunting and fishing equipment, athletic gear, bicycles, and boats. Advertised by a giant neon rainbow trout, the store was frequented by townspeople, Indians from the nearby reservation, pipeline workers, and tourists.

Oscar himself attracted customers like a magnet. Outgoing and humorous, he was the kind of straightforward, stand-up guy a small town relies on. Before going into the sporting goods and guide business, he had edited the weekly newspaper and worked at the liquor store, so he knew the codes and conduct of the town, both its light sides and dark corners. As a volunteer, he drove ambulance and fought fires. Oscar played trombone in the town band, marching in Fourth of July and Veteran's Day parades; he served four terms on the city council.

In short, he was everything my father and stepfather were not.

The summer my mother, sister, and I moved to Madras, Oscar put me to work in his store. I wrote out licenses, packaged worms, fetched twenty-pound blocks of ice (to cool beer and fish), and assembled bicycles. I watched Oscar carefully and learned the trade.

At first, he paid only seventy-five cents an hour, a quarter less than I could make doing field work such as hoeing mint or picking rock. However, I loved the store so much, I probably would have worked for free.

Lively characters gathered at Oscar's: coaches and crop dusters, realtors and radio promoters, avid fishermen (bait, lure, and fly), hunters and gun nuts, bakers and bankers, ranchers and rock hounds. In my novel *The Sky Fisherman*, I based the "back room boys" on these colorful characters who drank coffee, ate pastries, recounted wild stories, and frequently downed shots of whiskey in the store's back room. I modeled a couple on Oscar's old cronies from Burns, where he had worked as a newspaperman before moving to Madras.

When the store opened at seven, I had to wheel the bicycles from the aisles to the sidewalk outside. By clearing the aisles, I made a path to the worms, which were kept in a large refrigerator at the back of the store. It took fifteen minutes or so to clear the two dozen bicycles we kept on hand. During that time, the customers couldn't reach the worms, and they would browse for hooks, sinkers, nets, lures, hats, and sunglasses. We only broke even on the thousands of worms we sold, but the fishing tackle had a nice mark-up.

"Don't hurry with the bikes, Nephew," Oscar said. "Let the good people graze."

Around 7:30 A.M. Howard Maw, the baker next door, delivered a tray of pastries and doughnuts. Like most bakers, he got up around 3:00 A.M. so he could be to work by four; he was fond of pointing out that by the time we got started, he was halfway to quitting time. Oscar nailed an old wicker creel to the wall by the coffeepot, and people tossed in nickels for coffee, dimes for bakery goods. Once a week, Oscar took out enough cash to buy another five-pound can of Folger's. The rest he gave to Howard.

For at least an hour each morning, I packaged worms. In those days, a person could use bait everywhere, even on the Deschutes, and we sold thousands of worms each week in summer. Memorial Day, Fourth of July, and Labor Day weekends, I grew rummy from counting worms.

As the years passed and Oscar spent more and more days guiding on the river, I ran the store, along with Doris Vibbert, the
woman everyone assumed was Oscar's wife because she knew the
trade so well. On her days off, I was "chief cook and bottle
washer" as Oscar said, handling the store from seven until well after ten some nights. I remember those hot summer nights, the
smell of mint during the peppermint harvest, the sounds of
teenagers muscling their cars up and down the street, the deep
sense of satisfaction that came with wheeling in the last bicycle
and locking the door.

Oscar trusted me with the business, and I took the responsibility seriously. In all the years I worked for him, I never pocketed a
dime, although I took free Pepsis from the pop machine (he did
too) and bought my fishing and hunting gear at cost—"the relative's discount," Oscar said.

Loaning money, the activity that confused me most at first, came
with the territory. Oscar's didn't have a pawn shop license, but no
one else in town did either, and pawning was a vital activity. In
those days, Madras had no car title loan outfits or payday advance
places. When people were strapped for cash, they came to Oscar's
bearing boats, motors, Indian jewelry and beadwork, musical in-
struments, chain saws, war medals, fishing equipment, pistols and
rifles. They wanted anywhere from ten to a hundred dollars to buy
gasoline, keep the power on, or slide off the wagon.

If Oscar wasn't around, much of the time I was stumped. How
does a fourteen-year-old figure what a pair of beaded moccasins is
worth or a balky, five horsepower Evinrude? I didn't make too
many mistakes because I usually loaned low. People shook their
heads and grumbled about Oscar's absence, but they never refused
the money. And as the summer progressed, I began to catch on.

The most popular pawn item by far was a .30–.30 lever action
Winchester or Marlin deer rifle. In any kind of decent condition,
these rifles were good for twenty bucks. I always checked the actions to make certain they weren't jammed or frozen, and eye-
balled the walnut stocks for cracks. Once in a while, a drunk

would bring in a loaded rifle with a live round in the chamber. These occasions called for delicacy. Oscar kept a loaded Smith & Wesson .38 Special in a holster just under the cash register. Sometimes, I sidled close to the pistol, until I could get the belligerent customer to understand he needed to unload his weapon.

Always in demand, a second-hand deer rifle would bring thirty or forty dollars, especially as deer season drew near and families were still strapped from overspending on summer vacations and buying school clothes. Frequently, we got top dollar for unredeemed used rifles, because the buyer still paid only two-thirds the price of a new one.

One time I loaned twenty dollars on a bad pistol two Bend fellows brought in. They had long, slicked-back hair and hard expressions, not the usual affluent Bend types. The men seemed jittery and kept pressuring me to loan them the money. Even though my instinct said "No," I figured any used pistol was worth twenty dollars. Our cheapest .22 sold for sixty.

When Oscar got back from the river, he gave the hocked pistol a sorrowful look and told me I'd been snookered by a "gas station special," good for one stickup between Madras and Klamath Falls. He claimed the special, stamped from cheap Italian metal, was just as likely to blow up, blinding or maiming the shooter, as it was to wound or kill the gas station attendant.

He let me keep the pistol and deducted twenty dollars from my wages. I thought I had learned my lesson. The next week, a dirty, champagne-colored Buick pulled into the parking lot. The driver wore crumpled clothes, as if he'd slept in the car, and thin-soled peculiar-looking shoes with tassels. When he came in the store, he smelled of bourbon and cigar smoke.

"The Paper Boy is here!" he announced. "Come on out, Oscar!"

"Oscar's on the river," I said.

"Who's running the joint?"

"Today, I'm the chief cook and bottle washer."

The Paper Boy seemed skeptical. He surveyed the racks of shotguns and rifles, the shiny pistols in their glass case, the outboard motors. "The whole shebang?"

I nodded.

"Well, if you're the chief cook and bottle washer, I'm dealing with you."

His long, rambling story included knowing Oscar when he was flying P-38s in Hawaii. In addition, the Paper Boy bragged about managing showgirls in Reno, running a high stakes card room in Burns, winning a fortune by backing Evel Knievel.

"Me and Oscar go way back," he insisted. "The two of us were playing cards at the Ponderosa Lounge in Burns when we heard the banker shoot himself. See, kid, the auditor had come over from Portland to check on irregularities. Two hundred thousand dollars to be exact. When the auditor left for lunch, the banker made things right. Kablooey! As soon as he heard the shot, Oscar looked at me, and his eyes got big. He said, 'I figure I know where that money went' and he hustled off to the newspaper to write the story."

Now, the Paper Boy wanted fifty dollars for gas and a stake. He told me that the police had raided his card room, because he was having an affair with one of the officer's wives. The Paper Boy had been out buying bourbon and cigars, so they didn't nab him. As soon as he saw the police cars, he jumped in his Buick and took off. Now on the lam, he planned to head for Portland until things cooled down.

Offering collateral, he showed me a gold-plated cigarette lighter with embedded diamonds forming the Big Dipper. "Twenty-four carat gold, kid. The diamonds are real, too. I gave three hundred for it when I was in Vegas."

I steeled myself against getting snookered. Oscar wasn't going to deduct my wages again and make me "buy" a cigarette lighter. Anyway, I didn't smoke. The Paper Boy blustered and bellowed, but I refused to budge. Finally he left, threatening to come back in a week to get me fired.

Proud of my resolve, I told Oscar the story when he came off the river. During my recounting, he grew slack-jawed and mournful. I could feel the flush rising in my neck and cheeks. My mouth turned dry.

My uncle sat down wearily on an Igloo cooler. "I can't believe you treated the Paper Boy like that," he said. "He and I go all the way back to Hawaii."

"But he was a gambler from Burns with a fishy story and a flashy lighter."

"Nephew, you got a lot to learn. Anybody from Burns that stops by, you got my okay to give them a hundred dollars. All those gamblers have is their word, and they'll make it good. How do you think he got that moniker? The Paper Boy always delivers on his debts. The same for the wranglers, the road workers, even the Basque sheepherders who smell like shit. If they're from Burns, I'll back them."

"Okay. If you say so."

"Here's the ones to watch out for: Cowboys with hundred dollar felt hats and two hundred dollar belt buckles that say 'champion this or that.' They're wearing all their money.

"Doctors and lawyers especially. What have they done with all their money? Why do they need to hock something in the first place? Anyone from Bend. If I could buy those city dudes for what they're worth and sell them for what they think they're worth, I'd be a rich man."

"I'll try to remember," I said.

When the Paper Boy came back, he and Oscar went in the back room and broke out the Seagram's. After several Seven and Sevens, they grew mellow and nostalgic, talking about the war and Burns, the dark-eyed Basque girls they had dated. When they staggered out of the back, the Paper Boy waggled his finger at me. "You're a downright obdurate kid," he said. "Just like your uncle."

The Paper Boy made it to his car but not before knocking over two bicycles. He picked them up and put them back in line. "Straight as soldiers," he said.

After he had driven off, Oscar told me I better make out the night deposit. As I was calculating the sums, my uncle said, "When we were talking, he called you 'obdurate' three times. Do you know what I told him?"

"No."

"I said you were 'stubborn as hell,' too!" My uncle grinned and rolled his eyes. "Sort of like your mother."

Mom loved Madras and so did I. In retrospect, those were some of the happiest days of my life. And in spite of the tight money situation, she was relieved to be on her own. Oscar and Aunt Mac provided a kind of safety net. If I could have chosen a father, it would have been Oscar. He took me hunting and fishing, gave me all the time he could, considering how busy he was with the store and guiding—as well as with his own three daughters.

I admired him as a self-made man. And he could be stubborn as hell, just like my mother. Obdurate. I guess we were all stuck with stubbornness or we couldn't have kept going.

15

THE OLD MAN

Rudell was supposed to send fifty dollars a month child support, but he never did. Even so, my mother remained optimistic about the possibility. Each month, shortly after the first, she'd have me look in the post office box to see if the check had arrived.

She was too nervous to do it herself. Her hands trembled so much she couldn't work the combination for the box. I remember her look of anticipation fading when I handed her the bills, the occasional letters, the *Good Housekeeping* magazine, one luxury she allowed.

After a moment, she'd reset her face and state brightly, "Well, we're doing just fine by ourselves," or "Better times are right around the corner."

We needed the money, and sometimes she'd speculate on what we might buy if it came: a good used stove, two new tires for the car (she always bought recaps one at a time), a new school jacket for me, a winter coat for her. "But we'll get along, by hook or crook."

From all my aunt Sally said, Rudell wasn't doing so peachy himself. Some months, he never had fifty dollars. What he had was a fifteen-year-old wife and a baby girl, with more children coming rapid-fire—strangely like his own father, Newton. He'd tacked a lean-to onto a banged-up trailer in Monument and was catching coyotes and poaching deer.

Although I would have liked a pair of blue suede shoes and a decent baseball glove, in a way I was relieved the old man's shadow didn't follow me around like a rawboned hound. He was a loser, and I didn't need his presence darkening my path.

In all those years growing up, I saw him only three times. The first was when I was fifteen, lying in the hospital after I'd been mangled by a peppermint chopper and dragged almost to death over rugged field corrugations and swathed mint. After hours of intensive surgery in a one-horse hospital, the nurses numbed me with morphine round the clock.

For weeks, I gained consciousness only long enough to groan with pain for fifteen minutes before the next shot. In that daze, I learned to recognize small distinctions among my caregivers. One's breath smelled like birdseed; another had a turquoise bracelet; a third wore hooped earrings. I couldn't remember the rest.

Opening my eyes one day, I squinted at the tall, lean man sitting in the bedside chair. My father looked exactly like he did in his army photos, except his hair was thinner and his gray eyes glowed. At first I thought I was dead, and this was the bad place. Then he took out a yellow stick of gum and unwrapped it. I smelled Juicy Fruit, not brimstone, so it wasn't the afterlife. I must still be stuck in this one, I thought.

"I heard you was playing 'Chicken' with a mint chopper. I'd say you lost."

"I'm getting better." The truth was I hurt every second from a crushed pelvis and two broken legs, but I wasn't going to admit it.

"I'm staying with your aunt Manila. You know she's got that used-book store." He took a maroon book out of a sack: *Famous Oratories*. "Manila figures while you're in here, you can study up on your speechifying."

"Hard to turn the pages." I held up my damaged right hand. All the fingertips had been cut off during the accident. Each finger was severely swollen and covered with thick black stitches.

He grabbed my wrist and studied the hand. "You'll be a southpaw like your old man. Always stuck at first base."

And that was the encounter. As he was holding my wrist, the birdseed nurse came into the room and pricked my hip with another shot of morphine. I drifted into unconsciousness with an image of my father throwing me a baseball. When I tried to catch it, my hand was gone—chopped at the wrist. The white baseball rolled far away into a green field, and my father winked and pointed at the amputated hand.

Several days later, when I could stay awake for an hour or more, I asked the turquoise-jewelry nurse, "Was my father here, or did I dream him up?"

Her lips thinned. "That darned fool almost killed you. Nobody here knew you'd never laid eyes on him before. You went into deep shock and we practically lost you. The nurses' station has orders not to let him in again."

"So he was here. I'll be damned."

She fumbled open the night stand drawer. "He left you a note—sort of." She handed me a slip of paper and a greasy five-dollar bill. The paper read: "Buy some cegars when you can light them."

Six months later, while still recovering in our Madras apartment, I was sitting in a wheelchair staring out the window, when a '51 Oldsmobile with one blue door pulled up in front. Out piled my old man, his cradle-robbed second wife, and four stair-step kids.

My mother had just gotten home from her job at the Warm Springs Indian Reservation and was in the kitchen frying hamburgers. Ronna was staying with my aunt Mac.

When she heard the doorbell ring, my mother hurried into the front room and headed for the door. "A visitor. Maybe it's your friend Brian Stevenson."

"Wait, Mom!"

She stopped.

"Hand me my crutches—please." Somehow, I didn't want to be sitting down when that troop came through the door.

My mother opened the door and recognized Rudell. Her face blanched and her chin dropped. She stepped back, stiffening.

"Hello, Hazel, you're keeping good," my father said. "I don't believe you've met Raylene."

I crutched to the door and invited them in because my mother hadn't found her voice. After a long moment, she stepped back so they could pass.

"Pleased to meet you," Raylene said, stepping in and grabbing my mom's limp hand. Then she introduced each child so rapid-fire, I had trouble following: Yuba-Jean, Ormand, Opal, and Huston.

"This here's your brother Craig," she concluded.

They all smiled and shook my hand except Yuba-Jean. She kissed my cheek. The kids smelled like new clothes from JCPenney, cheap perfume, and Brylcreem.

The two tires I could see on the Oldsmobile looked new. I figured my father was bucks-up for once or he had put Raylene to work.

"You're not looking so puny," he said. "When you going to throw the sticks away?"

"Before long," I said, remembering how pleased the doctor was with my progress.

"Surefire."

"He'll be up and chasing girls in no time," Raylene said. "Not that he'd have to. He looks like you, Rudell—spitting image."

"He looks like my brother Oscar," my mother said tartly. She had found her voice. "In some pictures you can't tell them apart."

"Then Oscar's mighty handsome, too," Raylene said.

To my surprise, Rudell's second wife was a looker. She seemed barely older than some of the cheerleaders at Madras High School.

"I think we kind of took you by surprise," Rudell said to my mother. "You look like a rabbit caught in headlights."

My mother's hands smoothed her apron. "I was just fixing dinner," she said.

"Don't let us stop you, Hazel," Rudell said. "We were visiting Manila over in Prineville and wondering how Craig was doing. Still a little gimpy."

"I can fry some more hamburgers for the children," my mother said, nodding toward the kitchen. She seemed anxious to leave the room.

"Let me help," Raylene said. "You children go out back and play. I noticed a swing set. Come on now. Let the men stay and talk."

My father sat on my mother's yellow love seat, comfortable as pie. He resembled a man who was accustomed to stopping by his ex-wife's place at dinnertime every night of the week. I expected him to be edgy or nervous about seeing my mother after so many years, but he just leaned back and studied me.

"You in any pain?" he asked.

"Not too bad." In fact, the pain had grown prolonged and dull. Mostly, I was restless and bored. We couldn't afford a television.

"You was in a bad way up to the hospital. The nurses said sometimes you woke up yelling like you was gut-shot."

"Maybe I did. I don't remember."

"Well, everything's better now." He pulled out a pack of gum from his snap-button shirt pocket. Black Jack. "My mouth's a little dry." When he offered a piece, I took it.

Mom and Raylene were talking in the kitchen. I heard banging pots and the faucets turning off and on, off and on. Mom was shutting them off so hard the pipes rattled in the walls.

"I don't suppose you'll do much hunting this year."

"Not with these." I tapped the crutches.

"You ever kill an elk?"

"No. No elk." I had shot pheasants and ducks.

"I thought maybe Oscar took you up to camp."

"Not yet." I had been hoping to go, but the accident had ruined any chance this season.

"I killed my first elk when I was twelve. February, cold as hell, and we needed table meat."

"February's not hunting season."

"I hunt for meat. People get hungry year-round." He smiled slowly. "Hunting season is anytime I'm driving the car or carrying a rifle."

I couldn't argue that people got hungry year-round. Even Oscar fudged the law a little.

"Anyway, I took our horse Baldy and rode up into some sheltered valleys on Johnnycake Mountain. The elk moved down for the winter. After two days' hard hunting, I shot a spike. That's all the horse could pack. Field-dressed and quartered that elk, so I worked me an appetite and ate half the liver. I had this bad toothache, but the hunger was worse than the tooth. Still, it hurt to move my jaw."

I tried to picture it. I'd learned something about pain, far more than he'd felt from the toothache, I figured.

"It started snowing like hell, so I headed home, hunching forward in the saddle and resting my cheek on that warm elk carcass for a little relief. I had to swim Baldy across the swollen North Fork. I was froze near to death by the time I found the home place. Mom sliced the heart and we ate it with sweet onions. She boiled buckshot in milk, and when I drank it, the toothache quit.

"My dad finally came back from John Day and saw that elk meat hanging in the shed. When I told him the story, he said, 'God Almighty! You went all the way to Johnnycake for a damn spike!' But I could tell he was pleased, under the gruff."

"That's quite a story."

Rudell smiled. "I learned some things. A man's job is to put meat on the table. A good elk steak tops beef. I've killed thirty-seven elk. Maybe you should learn."

I resented the implication and didn't say anything. A man's job went a lot further than putting meat on the table, and as far as I was concerned, my father had been piss-poor at all of it.

"Your uncle Hoot and I always hunt together. We could prop you against a tree and herd some elk your way. Looks to me like you've got enough trigger finger left. Barely."

I was pretty sensitive about the hand. The black stitches had been removed, but my fingers remained swollen—resembling sausages. I was uncomfortable with it and usually hid the damaged hand when women were around. "Maybe next year. I'll be walking okay by then." I wasn't planning on going with him, but I thought saying "maybe" could move us off the subject.

"Surefire." He seemed pleased. "Hoot and I will show you the ropes next year."

Raylene came out of the kitchen. "You men can come and eat."

My father stood. "Let's put on the feed bag." He stepped toward me. "I don't suppose you need any help."

I waved him off. "I can make it all right."

That night after they were gone, my mother left the dirty dishes in the sink and turned on the teakettle. "I feel like having a drink," she said. "Too bad I don't drink."

"I've seen you order a Brandy Alexander." I felt like having a drink myself, even though I hadn't tasted anything but a little red wine at Thanksgiving.

"Only when I'm in a restaurant and want to splurge. Tonight, I sure don't feel like splurging."

"That was a dirty deal, him showing up like that."

She nodded. "It's typical of your father to land here at mealtime. When we were married, he always showed up unannounced just as people were cooking supper. I was so embarrassed. In my family, we were taught to call ahead."

I thought that if Rudell had called ahead, we could have made a getaway. Instead, six of them showed up unannounced. It seemed odd to have four half brothers and sisters I had just met.

"I feel sorry for Raylene. That poor little girl doesn't know sickum. Do you know he's got her cooking on a woodstove? Your aunt Sally told me. No electricity, either. Imagine. In this day and age, with four kids—a woodstove. Hell, they might as well be pioneers stumbling along the Oregon Trail.

"After the war, when he was shell-shocked, maybe he had an excuse for being so backwoods and wanting to get away to a simpler life—but not any longer." Anger flickered in her gray-green eyes. "He was just supposed to pay child support—that's all. But he never did. Now he's gone and hoodwinked a fifteen-year-old girl into marrying him and living like the Joads. Why couldn't he at least pick on someone his own age?"

"It's pretty unusual," I said, wondering how old Raylene was now. Close to twenty-five, I figured.

The teakettle whistled and she took it off the burner, pouring some into a thin china cup, then adding a bag of Constant Comment, her favorite.

"Do you want some?"

"No." I didn't like tea or coffee.

"He was different once. Before Rudell shipped overseas, we lived in Hattiesburg, Mississippi. In those days, we made a lot of plans."

My mother shook her head. "Your father gave me a couple of surprises—first running off, abandoning us, and then marrying Raylene. You never know, I guess."

"Look here, Mom, you're better off without him."

She squeezed my hand. "*We're* better off without him. But sometimes I think of those days in Hattiesburg, before he shipped out. We saw the sights and danced on Saturdays like Sunday wouldn't come. Some miserable weather. There's no humidity up here compared with the South. Sometimes I was so hot and sticky, I couldn't get my dress over my head. It clung like a peach skin. When I learned I was pregnant with you, I made such big plans."

Her voice slid, quiet with disappointment, and I realized how she must have loved him once and how it brought her hard sorrow.

"Something happened to him in the war. He was in the Battle of the Bulge and then fought the Germans all the way to Berlin.

"After the war, he was different." She sipped her tea. "I remember him coming into The Dalles on the ten-forty night train. It was still hot that late because the rocks hold the heat, but it wasn't humid. The train was five minutes early, and I was already there, holding you up in my arms for him to see." She paused. "I wrote it all down, every detail, so I could remember later and tell you."

"Okay, I'm listening."

"Like I say, he had changed. His back wasn't as straight. At first, I thought it was the three-day train ride. Anyone would be exhausted. But he was exhausted in a different way. He didn't want any responsibility—at least it seemed that way to me. He didn't even want you at first. Imagine that. His beautiful son. 'I might drop the little fella, Hazel.' That's what he said. But I made him hold you, right there on the platform, and he still looked handsome in his uniform, but rumpled and tired after the trip.

"Later that night, sometime in the early morning really, you started crying, and I said, 'Rudell, get up and quiet your son,' so he rolled out of bed. I saw his expression in the moonlight—completely bewildered. He turned this way and that, holding you gingerly while you kept crying. Then he set you on the bed. 'Hazel, I don't know.' Those were his exact words. In only a few months, he ran off, back to Monument, rather than stay and take some responsibility. All the gumption leaked out of him and he ran off like a deserter."

She shook her head. "Why on God's green earth did I marry that man?"

"I suppose you were in love," I said, even though I didn't know anything about it.

"In love," she repeated. "Yes. He had such a straight back at first, just like yours. Excellent posture. And he never became angry or flustered. My father always worried and fretted and stewed about everything—money, relatives, his job, anything mechanical. But not Rudell. I remember once when we were driving back to The Dalles along the Rowena Loop highway. We'd been up to see the wildflowers—grass widows and yellowbells. Suddenly the car started making a funny noise. Turns out we had a flat tire."

"A flat's nasty along that stretch of curves," I said.

"Flat as a pancake. And do you know what your father did?"

"Did he change it?"

She clapped her hands. "That's exactly right. He changed the tire. No cursing or worrying or fretting like my dad always did. He just got out and changed it. Simple. It made me feel so free. So absolutely free." She lifted her hands from the table, then let them drop with a thud. "Can you imagine how foolish I was? I married your father because he had a straight back and changed a tire without grumbling. And he had that slow way of talking. I found it attractive. No question, he looked good in a uniform." She tapped the teacup with her forefinger. "Maybe that's love, but I doubt it."

I didn't say anything. I didn't know about love. I watched the girls at school and imagined what their breasts looked like, how their damp thighs might feel. And I felt lonely and frustrated now that I was stuck with crutches and a mangled hand.

"Now that I think about it, I didn't know sickum, either. Marrying a man who ducks his responsibility, then ups and marries a fifteen-year-old. They have four kids and think they're all going to live off the land—fence building and poaching. Let Hollywood get ahold of that one! Throw in a little gold mining just to keep the dream of big money alive. There's a story for the Old West."

Reaching across the table, she gripped my wrist. "Craig, I want you to promise me one thing."

"Sure. What is it?"

"If anything happens to me, promise you won't get too close to your father. For instance, don't go hunting with him. If you want to go hunting, go with your uncle Oscar, but I don't want you to ever go with Rudell Newton Lesley. He never had a hand in raising you, bringing you along this far. After all my work, I don't want you to backslide."

It seemed an easy-enough promise to make at the time. "Sure. Anyway, I don't want to go hunting with him. I'll go with Oscar or Brian Stevenson."

She gripped my wrist tighter. "Fishing, too. You must not go fishing with him."

"All right. No fishing."

"Your father's not a mean man; I don't believe there's a mean bone in his body, but he's weak as water. No gumption. He was in the service four years and still came out a private. Your uncle Oscar made lieutenant in the air force. I'm certain that branch is more difficult than the regular army."

I tried to assess what effect my father's lack of gumption might have on me someday. I was determined to get ahead, succeed in high school and go on to college. I didn't want to inherit my father's weakness in any way. My mother's tone was more disappointed than angry, and I understood that she was fighting a solitary battle.

"Even after I'm dead, promise me you won't go to him."

"You're going to live a long time, Mom."

"Promise now. Don't backslide."

"Okay. I won't backslide. Cross my heart." And I crossed my heart with bold strokes of my crippled hand.

I knew that backsliding meant participating in any activity my father did: bass fishing, coyote trapping, elk hunting, fence building, even woodcutting. From my mother's point of view, he was a backslider not only because he had abandoned us, but also because he chose not to live in town and keep a job in a hardware store or newspaper office as her own father had done.

My father, Raylene, and their kids lived in a trailer backed up against wilderness. No phone or electricity. No street address, just a PO box in Monument.

My mother had other plans for me—college and a good job where I could wear a necktie or stethoscope, a job earned with gumption. And I intended to follow that path as well. I understood that living next to wilderness meant danger in a sense similar to working on a farm, where one fell victim to mint choppers and hay balers and tip-over tractors.

Still, in spite of best intentions, life is filled with unexpected compromises. In my youth, I overestimated my abilities and underestimated the terrible pull of my father's blood. Although my resolve was iron, he drew me like a lodestone toward the mountains.

16

UMATILLA ARMY DEPOT

I wanted to stay in Madras, but my aunt Mac went back to teaching art at the junior high school, and Mom couldn't find inexpensive, reliable child care for Ronna. After several failed attempts, we moved to Woodland, Washington, the summer following my sophomore year. There, my mother's older sister Grace could take care of Ronna.

Moving yet another time, especially in the middle of high school, angered me. Although I became president of the student body and graduated as valedictorian, I never felt as close to the Woodland school or town as I did in Madras. No doubt, a part of that was leaving Oscar.

My Woodland High School physics teacher, Leon Stroud, encouraged me to attend Whitman College, his old alma mater. With his guidance and strong recommendation, I was awarded a full scholarship by the George F. Baker Foundation. As a small-town boy, at first I felt intimidated by the students from high-octane schools in Seattle, Portland, and the Bay Area. But after the first year, I began to flourish.

One day during my sophomore year, I cut out of biology lab early and headed for the Delt house. The next day I had a big test in psychology. I planned to eat a quick dinner, wash dishes (my job in exchange for eating at the fraternity), then study.

As I passed one of the Delts on his way to campus, he said, "Hey, Craig. Your father's waiting to see you."

"What?"

"Your father's here to see you. He's got a young woman with him."

"Thanks." I knew it couldn't be my father—not at college. A campus was the last place for him to set foot. Somehow, the message got garbled. Maybe my uncle Oscar and cousin Annette had come by to see me. They had probably been scouting possible elk camps up in the Wallowas and decided to drive over to Walla Walla to say hello.

At the Clinton Street apartments, someone belted out "Frankie and Johnny," accompanied by a twelve-string guitar. "He was her man, but he was doing her wrong." I sang along with the music. The Beach Boys' "Fun, Fun, Fun" blasted from upstairs speakers in the Delt house. I knew Charley Budens, a Beach Boy fan from Southern California, would be dancing inside and admiring himself in the mirror.

I almost dropped my books when I saw the '51 Oldsmobile parked in front of the house. My father had parked the same car in front of my mother's apartment in Madras four years earlier, when I was recovering. What was he doing here? Did he have all those kids with him?

Rudell and Raylene sat on the couch drinking coffee and talking to Dennis and Tobin about deer hunting. "I saw two bucks across the canyon, and I put the sneak on them," my father said. After recognizing me as I came through the door, he grinned. "There he is, yessir. My oldest son. I see you finally got back to walking."

Raylene flashed a smile. "It's so good to see you up and around, Craig. Gee, you sure look like Rudell." Turning to the boys, she said, "Craig was run over and nearly kilt by a big old chopper. It's God's own miracle he's alive."

"It took him forever to heal," my father said. "He doesn't mend fast. We had fellas in the army like that—slow healers."

Dennis and Tobin studied me with curiosity. I was playing intramural football, and except for the damaged hand, seemed pretty healthy.

"What are you doing here?" I asked

"I came over to sell some coyote pelts. Three bobcats. I saved the hides from last spring, waiting for the price to go up."

"He's been feeling puny, too." Raylene looked worried. "I made him go to the Veteran's and get checked out."

"Are you okay?"

"They say I'm firing on all eight cylinders."

"That's good." I had a concern that my father might need to be admitted, then expect me to come see him regularly, so I was relieved.

"We want to take you out to dinner," Raylene said. "Some place dress-up."

If anything, I thought she was oddly dressed, like a slutty buckle bunny hanging around a rodeo. Her leather skirt was too short and her bright blouse too tight. She wore turquoise blue cowgirl boots, matched by fake turquoise jewelry. Still, she was pretty in a flashy way.

My father wore stiff jeans, a brown western shirt with snap buttons, and a Levi vest. Neither one of them even slightly resembled Whitman parents—middle-aged professional types from Seattle and Portland, dressed by Nordstrom.

"We figured you'd know where to put on the feed bag," Rudell said.

I didn't want to go. "I've got to wash dishes tonight. It's my job."

"Raylene can wash the dishes when we get back."

She flashed him a look. "That's all I do. Wash dishes, cook, drag kids helter-skelter, and drive a school bus full of brats."

A group of guys had started to form and they were getting an earful. Maybe it's just better to get them out of here, I thought.

This dinner will be ninety minutes, tops. They'll hit the road and I could come back and study.

"I'll get someone to cover for me," I said.

Bill Kelso, the kitchen steward, bustled around holding a spatula. "You'd better hurry and eat," he told me. "We've got to serve in fifteen minutes."

"I need a favor. Can you cover for me? I've got some relatives who want to take me out to dinner."

"Why don't they eat here? We're having pork chops."

Was he serious? "We're going out."

"Is that your sister? She can sit on my lap. She's a lot younger than he is." He smirked. "Your old man must have a little steam left in the pipe."

"Don't give me any shit. Cover for me, okay?"

Grinning, he pointed the spatula at me. "Only if you promise to fill me in on all the juicy details. She's my type. Young, but with some experience. How old is she anyway?"

"Fuck off," I said, but I couldn't shout, because they'd hear it in the front room. "I don't know how old she is. I only saw her once before."

"Is it a promise? I'm not washing dishes unless you promise and say 'pretty please.'" He glanced at his watch. "Too late to get anybody else."

My father's voice, then Raylene's, came from the front room. Something about poaching. I had to get them out.

"All right." After hesitating, I added, "Pretty please."

"Now that's a good dishwasher." Kelso slapped the spatula against his thigh. "The three of you have a wonderful time. And don't forget to find out how old she is."

A dozen Delts had gathered while waiting for the dinner bell. Tobin and Dennis, small-town guys who liked to hunt, were talking shotgun gauges with Rudell. The Seattle and Portland suburb guys were hanging back.

"I've got a sixteen-gauge pump," my father said. "Once I got a full house with it. Five birds, five shots. Of course, I don't put a plug in it."

"Aren't you afraid of getting caught?" Dennis asked.

"I hunt in Monument. The nearest cops are seventy miles away."

"Paradise," Tobin said.

"Let's go. Everything's set." I could see the other guys glancing at Raylene's legs and tight blouse.

"Sure good talking with you boys," she said on the way out.

Walking toward the Olds, my father asked, "Why are you washing dishes?"

Before I could answer, Raylene said, "More men should wash dishes. They might learn not to dirty so many."

"More women should learn to cook."

"Not everyone cooks exactly like your mama. If you like her cooking so much, move back with her."

"I can't." Rudell grinned at me. "She sold the place."

The car smelled like cheap cigars, wild animals, and the skunk-shaped deodorizer.

Raylene sat in back, arms folded. She was pouting.

"Where shall we go?" He started the car. "American food."

"Someplace dress-up."

They seemed wrong for the Marcus Whitman, and I never ate there because it cost too much. The Chinese place where I went with friends after studying late would have students I didn't want to run into.

"Let's go to the Red Apple." It wasn't dress-up, but I thought it was the least likely place we'd see professors or other Whitman students. They called it the "Road Apple" and stayed away.

Inside the restaurant, I steered us toward a rear booth. Two farmers in caps and field jackets were eating hamburgers.

Raylene's lips thinned and she slid into the Naugahyde booth. "This doesn't look too fancy."

"We're just early," I said. "Most people come later."

"Looks good to me. They got banana cream pie in the cooler." My father patted the seat next to him and I slid in.

Raylene brightened. "I get to look at two handsome men."

The waitress, a woman about Raylene's age, gave us menus and ice water.

We studied the menus and sipped the water. My father said, "These prices aren't too bad. . . ."

Raylene shushed him. "Money's not the point. We're here with Craig. It's our treat."

He nudged me. "She's got a champagne appetite and I've got a beer budget."

"I'm going to have a T-bone," she said. "Rare. I'm getting tired of venison."

"I wouldn't be surprised if she ordered those spendy fish eggs."

I attempted to shift the subject away from money. "How are the kids liking school?"

"I just had parent-teacher conferences," she said. "Yuba-Jean and Opal are doing okay, but Huston's a little behind." She twisted her napkin. "It's Ormand that's got me worried. How is he supposed to keep up in the hospital?"

"Darn kid went and got himself hit by a car. Knocked him halfway across Irrigon."

"And he's in the hospital?" I was trying to figure just how far halfway across Irrigon might be. Taking the bus to college, I'd passed through Irrigon—a few watermelon stands along the road, a tavern, a Baptist church, scattered houses with dusty, weed-filled yards. I'd been raised in small towns all my life. Still, I couldn't picture living in any place that desolate.

"Both legs broke. One shattered." She shook her head. "The doctors already operated three times. That old bastard had a suspended license. We should sue for his eyeteeth."

"No sir! I'm not paying for any lawyers."

"What happened exactly?"

"When the car smacked Ormand, somehow his feet got locked under the bumper," she said. "The car pushed him backwards a hundred feet. Wrecked up his legs."

"Not quite," my father said. "The policeman came and measured it. Exactly eighty-six feet."

"What's the difference? His legs got wrecked up."

"Fourteen feet. In the hospital, I looked at his shoes. The soles

had practically ground clear off. I just jabbed at them with my finger and poked holes straight through."

"He needed different shoes anyway. His feet are way bigger
than Rudell's."

"I'm sorry," I said. "I'm really sorry."

Our waitress took the orders, letting us know that the special was
baked stuffed heart. Rudell asked her, "Beef or elk?"

"Cow's heart."

"That's okay. Just bring it."

Raylene ordered the T-bone rare and I got a chicken-fried
steak, my utility meal when I didn't know or care what I wanted.

"I handled the accident emergency all by myself." Raylene
seemed proud of her accomplishment. "The nearest ambulance is
in Hermiston and we couldn't wait. A couple men rushed over
and one had plywood in his pickup, so we rolled Ormand real gentle onto a sheet and slid that into the bed. I stayed back there
holding Ormand's hand while that man drove ninety miles an
hour all the way to the Hermiston hospital. The wind just kept
whipping my hair in my face all that time."

Rudell reached across the table and took her hand. "She did
fine. I was stuck way out at work."

"I had to be brave for Ormand's sake. We go to see him just
about every day, but not today, because we're here."

"Maybe I can go see him." I didn't have a car, so I'd have to go by
bus. However, going anywhere from Walla Walla was inconvenient.

"He'd just love that. Your father can't go too much because
he's got an important job working security at the Umatilla Army
Depot, where they keep all kinds of gas and bombs."

"Hey. You remember people aren't supposed to know all the
stuff we got stored there. It's just like they said during the war.
'Loose lips sink ships.'"

She lowered her voice. "Sometimes he checks identification to
make sure no foreigners sneak in. Even the commanding colonel
has to show your father proper ID."

• • •

The Umatilla Army Depot stored chemical weapons, nerve and mustard gas, and tons of explosives in hundreds of concrete bunkers out in the Oregon desert. When you drove the stretch of Interstate 84 from Boardman to Hermiston, the depot lay between the highway and the Columbia River. The bunkers were separated so if the munitions in one exploded, that force wouldn't set off the contents of another, at least in theory. Over the years, the earth that covered the bunkers to conceal them from airplanes had grown desert vegetation. The casual traveler might not notice the bunkers at all or would assume they were Indian burial mounds until becoming aware of their sheer numbers. Mile after mile of stored weapons slumbering until the next war made the depot seem ominous and eerie.

Occasionally, you'd hear of an accident in which a bunker blew up, killing a few depot workers or army personnel. My great-uncle Farrell had worked there when one of those explosions occurred. He had immediately called Pendleton to report the accident.

"I heard that explosion twice," Farrell told me. "Once at the army depot when it killed those three men, and I heard it again over the phone when I was talking to the police in Pendleton. That's how long it took the sound to travel fifty-two miles.

"I thought it seemed strange. Those men were blasted to smithereens already, but in Pendleton they didn't know anything had happened until they heard the explosion."

After World War II, Farrell and his wife, Rena, lived in cramped government housing units directly across from the depot headquarters. They worked making ammunition crates to store bombs and rockets in the bunkers.

Later, their place was converted to housing for pigs after a crafty state senator obtained title to the land. Drivers could smell the pig farm stench for miles away, then see the pigs rooting outside the small units as they drove past.

Farrell became so disturbed at seeing the pigs where he and his wife had once lived that he refused to travel that stretch of interstate. He always took the back roads.

Even with that maneuver, he couldn't ignore the bright, immense star that the pig farm's owner illuminated each Christmas season. Placed high on the farm's water tower, that star was visible across the desert from twenty miles in any direction.

During the early seventies, my mother worked at the army depot as a secretary to the commanding colonel. Occasionally, when he wasn't patrolling the bunkers in a Jeep, my father would check her identification at the gate before allowing her to pass. I considered those encounters curious—that two people, once married, would pass by the same gate in the godforsaken middle of the desert, so close to all those weapons of mass destruction.

That night in the Red Apple, I asked my father, "Does the pig smell bother you, working so close?"

"I can't stand it." Raylene twisted her napkin. "I hate pigs. They stink even worse in the summer. I hold my breath every time I drive by."

My father sneered. "I kind of like the pigs myself. When I drive to work and see them walking around, I know that no stupid bastard has had an accident with the chemicals or bombs. If I ever see those pigs lying on their backs with their trotters pointed to heaven, I'll know they've been gassed. Then I'll whip the rig around and drive far away as quick as I can."

"I hope you're planning on stopping by for me," she said.

"I just might, now that you mentioned it."

"He's got no sense of smell so those pigs don't bother him. If he could smell halfway decent, he couldn't work with that awful coyote bait."

"It's a living," he said. "And you don't mind spending the money."

"You got four kids, Rudell! I stretch every dollar as far as I can. I'm getting up before dawn and driving a school bus."

"All right, Raylene, all right." He held up his hands, palms toward her. "Remember, I'm working hard, too. Security guard and trapping and fence building. We're both busy."

She shook her head and looked at me. "Sometimes I worry

about him out there with all those chemicals and bombs. But I think it's safe, don't you? On the Fourth of July, the army put on a picnic for all the workers and their families. They let us get on a little train that ran out through the bunkers. They even let kids ride."

Raylene seemed to want a response from me, so I said, "It sounds plenty safe to me. Otherwise, they wouldn't let kids near it."

I wouldn't tell her Farrell's story. A lie didn't hurt.

The waitress brought our food, carrying three plates at once.

She set the T-bone in front of Raylene. The steak had a little wooden stick that said RARE. "Honey, that might bawl when you cut it," the waitress told Raylene. "If it's not just exactly the way you want it, I'll take it back to the cook."

"And this goes to the gentleman." She set the baked stuffed heart in front of my father. It resembled the diagrams of hearts in the biology text. Valves and chambers filled with stuffing.

My own heart became troubled anytime I thought of my father. Did his bother him? Seeing the heart on the plate struck me as sad and ironic.

"And this is for the young gentleman."

When she set the chicken-fried steak in front of me, I realized I didn't want milk gravy all over the meat, but I'd forgotten to tell her.

Raylene cut her steak and blood oozed onto her plate. She took a bite and said, "Plenty rare. Just how I like it."

My father's lean, strong hands cut the heart into small sections and he began to eat. After swallowing the first bite, he shook more salt onto the meat and stuffing. He pointed his fork at me. "They feed you good at that fancy school?"

I nodded. "We've got a good cook in the fraternity."

"Who's paying for it?" Rudell set down his knife and fork.

It's none of your damn business, I thought. "I got a scholarship and I've been working summers in Oscar's store."

"Oscar must be doing okay. He's a good fisherman. A fair hunter."

"He's a good hunter, too." I said. "And he's building up the guide business." I didn't want anyone to shortchange Oscar, especially Rudell.

"What do they give you a scholarship for? How does that work?" Raylene seemed genuinely interested.

"For good grades," I said. "I worked hard in high school."

A sly look came over Rudell's face. "If you're getting all this money, how come you're still washing dishes?"

"The scholarship pays my tuition, but not all my room and board." After I said it, I realized he probably didn't know those terms.

"You can get a job in Monument or Irrigon without a bunch of fancy learning," he said. "If you want to work at the depot, you got to go in the army or some other branch first."

Raylene looked at my father. "Maybe he wants to live in the city. Pendleton's real nice. Walla Walla probably is okay, too. If we lived here, you'd be near the Veteran's hospital."

"Now go and think. What would I do in a city?"

"For starters, you could be a car salesman. Then we could afford us a brand-new car."

"Nothing's wrong with that Olds," he said. "It's a '51 and it's only got seventy-two thousand miles on it. It'll go a hundred without an overhaul."

"I know there's nothing wrong with it. I'm just saying a new car would be nice."

Figuring maybe they were through asking me questions, I started to eat again. The chicken-fried steak was too cool and the gravy had started to congeal.

Raylene seemed to look beyond me. "Your father showed up in that Oldsmobile and drove through Hardman like he owned it. He looked awful handsome in his army uniform, and he was wearing some kind of fancy city hat. He was concerned about his hair going, and that covered it up some."

Rudell rubbed his hand across his receding hairline. "That Olds only had five thousand miles on it. Those people bought it brand-new in New York City and drove out to Monument to take over Mom's place. They figured they needed a truck then, so they offered me a sweet deal."

I didn't know who he was talking about, but it seemed odd that anyone from New York would wind up at Monument.

"I was only fifteen. I been barefoot and babied up ever since."

"Not barefoot," Rudell said. "She came with five pairs of shoes."

"You know my shoes hardly fit anymore," she told him. "My feet are all swelled up from your four kids."

He looked at me. "You got a dog at your door and a woman at your door. What's the difference?"

"I don't know."

"When you let the dog in, it stops whining."

"Very funny, Rudell," she said. "Very funny."

When the waitress came to pick up the plates, my father's was slicked clean. Raylene asked the waitress to put her leftover steak in a box. The waitress scowled at my leftovers. "Not hungry tonight?"

"We got to talking."

"For dessert tonight, we have pie, chocolate mint cake, and cherry cobbler. Pie's up there." With her chin, she pointed to the white board above the cooler.

"Up for dessert, Professor? Chocolate mint cake? You probably don't want mint after playing 'Chicken' with that chopper."

Even the smell of mint made me nauseous. "I'll take apple, please. But just at room temperature. And no ice cream."

"The steak filled me up," Raylene said.

"Wenatchee has the best apples in the world. Your uncle Hoot, uncle Bob, and I went to pick apples there one fall. Bob was just a kid and had trouble keeping up. The field boss wanted to sack him, but Hoot and I picked so good, they couldn't afford to lose us."

"Now you got to work with Mexicans, if you want to pick," Raylene said. "Mexicans are getting all the jobs, if you ask me."

We had almost finished dessert when Rudell said, "I'm going to run elk camp up on Sunflower Flat again. You should come up. I guarantee meat but not horns. Sometimes a cow steps in the way just as I'm squeezing off a shot. So do you want to come up?"

"I'm pretty busy at school." The term before, I only had a 2.0 average. And there was the promise to my mother.

"You've been up to Oscar's camp?"

"You bet."

"But I reckon you got skunked."

"We didn't get any elk." Actually, we hadn't even seen an elk.

"I always kill elk," he said. "Oscar doesn't work at it hard enough."

I flared. "Well, when he gets them, at least they're legal."

Sensing the tension, Raylene started looking in her purse. "It's awful cold at elk camp. I was thinking of making you a sweater." She pulled out a yellow tape measure, the kind they use in clothing stores. "Stand up right here. I got to take your measurements."

I thought she was kidding.

"Go on. Stand up."

"Raylene makes beautiful sweaters," Rudell said. "That's something she can do."

I stood and stepped out of the booth, so I was facing the window. After borrowing a pen from the waitress, Raylene began measuring my waist, shoulders, chest. I got a little tingly from her light fingers running over me.

"He has your build," she told my father. "Maybe ten pounds lighter."

"He needs to eat some elk meat and build fence. That might fix his droopy shoulder, too."

I was self-conscious about the shoulder, a result of the accident. I didn't buy any shirts with horizontal stripes.

Outside, movement caught my attention. Bill Kelso stepped onto the sidewalk from the street and did a mock double take. Neither Raylene nor Rudell could see him start to imitate her movements with the measuring tape. How the hell did he figure out where we were? I wondered.

Seeing Kelso caused me to drop my arms.

"Stay still. I got to get your arms right. Sleeve length is one of the most important parts. Now spread your arms wide."

She wore heavy perfume, and her hair tickled my nose.

Kelso put his hands close to his crotch and pretended to measure a penis. He frowned, then held up four fingers. "You got four inches," he mouthed, and shook his head. He acted out measuring his own, then held up eight fingers and grinned.

"There, that should do it." She wrote down the last figure and turned toward the window. "Did you see something out there?"

Kelso strolled down the sidewalk, an innocent passerby.

"I thought maybe that guy was in one of my classes."

When the check came, Rudell let it lie as if time didn't matter. "Elk season is my favorite time of the year," he said. "It's crisp and cold. When the snow falls, you can track them. Nothing tastes as good as fresh elk liver fried with Walla Walla sweet onions. You better come up."

"I've got to study," I said. Even so, elk camp sounded tempting. Late fall with its golden days and chilly nights was my favorite time of the year, too. If I went to elk camp, I'd get to know my father better, whatever there was to know.

"Well, take some time and come up. I'll show you the ropes." After studying the bill a moment, my father left a twenty and a ten on the table.

Raylene frowned. "That's a pretty big tip."

"Them waitresses work hard. You should know that. Besides, I might pass this way again."

Before leaving, he bought a five-pack of Roi-Tan cigars. Outside, he lit one with an Ohio Blue Tip he scratched with his thumbnail. He offered me a cigar. "You smoking cigars these days, Prof, or just a pipe?"

"No thanks." I didn't want to smoke, but I liked the smell. It reminded me of my grandfather and his pipe.

"You'd like elk camp. A little smoking, a little drinking. Mostly lying. I guarantee meat on the table."

Part of me wanted to go, if for no other reason than to show the old man I could outwalk and maybe outpack him. I knew he was damn tough, but I figured standing around as a security guard must have slowed him some, and the smoking would cut his wind. Besides, he was forty-seven.

"We better get it down the road," Rudell said.

"Think I'll walk back and clear my head. Anyway, I've got to stop at the library."

"Careful, or they'll wind up calling you 'Four Eyes,'" my father said.

Raylene hugged me close, and I could feel her soft chest against mine. "Craig, I'm just so happy you're not crippled up bad or anything. That mint chopper gave us such a worry. Ormand's accident, too." She let go. "You look fine now, just fine. Doesn't he, Rudell?"

"Except that big nose makes him look like Hoot. Spittin' image at that age." He grinned and I could see his fine white teeth. "If I was Craig, I'd sue the doctor for letting me recover so ugly."

I laughed and Rudell put the cigar in his mouth. He stuck out his hand and I shook it. He held on a little longer than he needed.

"Hope things turn out all right with Ormand," I said—more to her than to him.

"Would you just keep him in your prayers?" she asked.

"Sure."

As they drove away, my father half-waved. Raylene turned around and waved hard. I raised my arm, then lowered it. I couldn't figure if it was a good-bye or a greeting, but I felt it was something incomplete, like the hand itself.

The image of Raylene pressed close against him in the car remained etched in my mind. Newton had married Anna when he was forty and she was fifteen; then they had children rapid-fire— just like my father and Raylene. In a curious way, I was jealous of Rudell. I hadn't slept with a woman yet and didn't know that emotion or sensation. I wondered what mysterious power my father possessed to make a beautiful fifteen-year-old girl fall in love with him.

Much later, after my own life had taken severe punches, I would realize that often people make choices not out of desire but out of desperation. However, that night at the Red Apple, I was far too young to understand. I believed in opportunity, motivation, and education. And like most young people, I never expected to compromise or sacrifice.

■ ■ ■

Kelso barged into my room just past midnight. "So give me the lowdown. All the juicy details."

"I'm studying. I've got a big exam at eight."

"Okay. Just tell me how old your stepmother is."

I glanced up from the book. "How old do you think she is?"

"Young enough to be your sister. Young enough for incest. Boy, she was standing close to you. Did she measure your doofus hard or soft?"

"Get your mind out of the gutter."

"Come on. You can't tell me you weren't thinking about it. I'm guessing she's twenty-five."

"It's none of your business."

Kelso debated for the college team, and now he raised a finger as if making a debate point. "First of all, you're our brother. That makes her our mother, too. We're all family."

Someone chuckled from the hallway.

"Who's out there?"

Two other Delts moved to the doorway. Dennis and Tobin. "We've got a bet," Tobin said. "I say she's twenty-seven. I like my women older and bolder. She can't be twenty-five. Look how old your father is."

"I've got to study. I don't have time for your bullshit."

Kelso held up another finger. "Point two. I washed dishes for you in exchange for the juicy lowdown. Query? How old is Craig's stepmother/sister? A simple answer will suffice. A number."

I stood and tried closing the door but Kelso held his ground. "Just speak the truth. The truth will set you free and we'll leave you alone."

"Amen." Dennis stood with folded arms. "I'm guessing twenty-eight. Twenty-eight and still looking great."

"Let me close the door and I'll tell you. Just get the fuck out."

"No deal, Lucille." Kelso smirked. "Is she older than a senior?"

"Of course she is."

"But not by much. Say 'twenty-five' and I win. Then we'll leave you alone."

"She's twenty-seven." She could have been twenty-eight, depending on her birthday. "Now let me study."

"Twenty-seven and I'm in heaven," Tobin said. "I'm going out to the Green Lantern and drink up your money," he told Kelso.

"I'm coming, too," Dennis said.

After reluctantly paying Tobin five dollars, Kelso still didn't leave. "So how old's your father?"

"That's for me to know and you to find out."

"That's exactly what I'm trying to do. I said 'all the juicy details.'"

I figured he wouldn't leave until I told him. "Forty-seven."

He whistled. "That's damn near dead. Twenty years older. Are you going to tell Libby?"

"Tell her what?"

"Think of it. You've got your father's genes, his inclinations, his habits. The girl you're destined to marry is still in a nursery somewhere." He grinned wickedly. "She can't even speak yet. Your future wife is still peeing her diaper, eating pablum, sucking her thumb. And Libby will be an old maid compared with her. You need to tell Libby right now you can't marry her. It's the only decent thing to do."

I tried pushing the door closed again. "Get the fuck out!"

Kelso stood his ground. "When you marry your future bride, your innocent sweetheart, Libby will be past forty. By the time your own children graduate from college, she'll be hard of hearing, blind, perhaps even demented."

"You're demented," I said. "I'm not anything like my father. Nothing at all."

"You look exactly like him," Kelso said. "It's not your fault, any of it, including this uncontrollable desire for young women. And who can blame you? Libby will be losing her teeth and you'll have this sweet and tender young thing."

"My father and I are totally different."

He shook his head. "Remember freshman English. We all read *Oedipus*."

"More bullshit."

"The apple doesn't fall far from the tree. Call it destiny, fate. You can't escape it. That's the beauty. Nothing you try to do matters."

Finally he left and I closed and locked the door.

I considered my father and Raylene, my grandparents on the Lesley side. No, I didn't come from typical Whitman stock.

■ ■ ■

When a bulky package with an Irrigon return address arrived in campus mail the second week in December, I was surprised. I thought Raylene had been making an empty promise, but she had followed through. Back in the dorm room, I unwrapped the sweater—a rich ivory color. Two large male mallards winged across the chest. On the back, a brown female nestled in bright green cattails. When I put it on, the sweater smelled of rich wool and the scent Raylene had worn at the Red Apple. No one at college had a sweater like it. In fact, I had never seen anyone under fifty wear such a sweater. Sometimes, I put it on and strolled campus for a gag. People asked when I was transferring to Fairbanks.

17

RUDELL AND RAYLENE

Rudell followed his father's footsteps in many ways. He spent much of his time prospecting for gold and especially searching for the legendary lost Sledgehammer mine. Like Newton, he had a taste for young women. He told Raylene, who was fifteen when they met in Hardman, that he had a summer place and a winter place. With the two places and a '51 Olds, she must have thought, *Rich rancher*. I'm sure her parents considered him a catch.

The summer place, where they lived when they first married, proved to be a one-room shack set back a hundred yards from the John Day River, about two miles outside Monument. It had no running water and no electricity. What Rudell called the "winter place" was actually his elk-hunting cabin on Sunflower Flat. This was cooler, exposed to the breezes, but it was equally "rustic."

Years later, Ormand showed me the summer place, or what was left of it. The shack was one room, twenty feet by twelve. The wood had never seen paint and the tar-paper roof had collapsed.

Large cracks between the sideboards allowed the sunlight to stream in, illuminating a carpet of broken glass and Annie Green Springs bottles.

"Some hippie winos lived here about ten years ago," Ormand said. "They left it such a mess, no one's been near it since."

Except the rats, I thought. The reek of rat urine was undeniable.

Seeing there were no pipes for plumbing, I asked, "So you carried your water from the river?"

Ormand nodded. "There was an outhouse. I think it was over there." He pointed to a tumble of boards fifty feet from the house. "We had to carry a hoe and bang the ground in front of us to scare the snakes off."

Cheat grass, tumbleweed, and thistles grew in what might have been a yard, but there had never been one.

"Dad killed a couple big snakes not too far from this place and he dynamited a whole den of them up in the rim rock." Ormand indicated the basalt ridges on the hills that rose behind the shack. "He was crazy about dynamite. Used it every chance he got. Using dynamite was one thing he learned in the service."

He missed a great opportunity by not blowing up the summer house, I thought. My mother, Ronna, and I had lived in some shabby rental homes. "You always have to live in crummy places at first," my mother said. "Then after you've been in town awhile, you figure out where the better places are." She never had time to locate a good place before we moved. As a result, we always moved a second time, when she found someplace better.

But despite the problems with mice, heating and plumbing troubles, infestations of yellow jackets, there was no comparison with my father's homes, where Ormand spent his youngest years. My mother sewed curtains and hung thick towels in the bathroom for a small taste of luxury. With every move, she took her yellow love seat, the chest-on-chest, and the prize drum table, which always stood in the front room so company could see it when they walked in. Perhaps Rudell's "summer place" had once been better than a Third World shanty, but not by much.

· · ·

The winter place, a little elk camp on Sunflower Flat, was his favorite, a place to escape, tell stories, drink whiskey, and bring hunters. Before there were guides, my father was a hunting guide for deer and elk. He brought hunters to the camp, and even though it was run-down, they sought him out for his skill, his instincts, and his marksmanship.

He was a crack shot while hunting, fighting in the army, competing with personnel at the Umatilla Army Depot. He didn't have a guide's license or a Web site, or a helicopter to herd the elk toward the hunters the way some of the big guide outfits do today. And he didn't charge five thousand dollars for a hunt.

He asked a minimum fee for each gun—fifty dollars at first, later seventy-five. He guaranteed meat, but not horns.

"I got two hat racks," he said. "That's all the antlers I need. Besides, cows and spikes taste the best."

One of his earliest clients was a man named Marion Stokes, one of the founders and principal architects for Safeway stores. Each November, Marion and his wife, Clara, came out to Sunflower Flat, staying in the old cabin my father had bought and used as a hunting base.

One year, Marion and Clara brought another couple with them, the Parkers. Before light broke on opening day, my father positioned them in Wildcat Canyon, then backtracked to the Hell Hole, a precipitous canyon that broke off the flat half a mile behind his camp. Wildcat Canyon merged with the Hell Hole, and Rudell planned to drive any elk in the hole toward Marion's party.

The night before, he had slept in an elk hide to mask his human scent. The day would be a good one, he predicted.

After waiting in the dark canyon for an hour, Marion grew restless. He wanted to be moving but Rudell had told them all to stay put.

As light broke, Marion heard a shot, followed by four others spaced a few seconds apart. He studied the trees and clearing below his stand, believing Rudell was driving the elk toward him.

"I thought maybe your dad got one down," Marion said. "Elk are hard to stop, so I figured he kept shooting until he was sure."

But the elk herd took some other route and Marion never got a glimpse.

Marion continued. "About twenty minutes later, Rudell came hiking back around the hillside. Steam was rising off his head, he'd been moving so fast. He waved and I headed toward him, figuring he was trailing the herd.

"'Where'd they go?' I asked him.

"When he stopped panting, Rudell said, 'Got your tags?'

"'Of course,' I said. 'We've all got tags.'

"'Get 'em out. Get your knives out, too!'

"When we hiked around the hill, back into the Hell Hole, we saw he had a bull down, a nice one. He told me to tag it, but I thought I'd let Clara tag it, so I could keep hunting.

"'I didn't shoot it,' she said, and your father grinned.

"'I shot it for you. They all eat the same.'

"Then behind a couple trees, we noticed he had a spike down, too, and Parker's wife tagged that one.

"'Damn good shooting, Rudell,' I told him. Two elk with five shots was remarkable.

"He just kept grinning. 'I put the sneak on them and really got into the herd. They never smelled me.'

"Downslope were two more cows and another spike. We were amazed. Nobody could believe it. Then Parker got mad and claimed Rudell must have shot some the day before, but all of them were fresh. We spent the whole morning skinning elk and sawing them into quarters.

"Rudell hiked back to get that old horse he used to pack elk up the canyon. Parker stayed mad as hell. He hadn't fired off a shot or even glimpsed a live elk."

The horse Hammer packed three elk out of the canyon that afternoon. By then, he was stumbling. They left Parker to stand guard over the other two elk so the coyotes or lynx cats wouldn't get them. My father brought him a bottle of whiskey, a frying pan, some bacon for grease, and Walla Walla sweet onions. That night, all of them got drunk and stuffed themselves on liver and onions.

Parker never got over being mad, so he and his wife left the next afternoon with their two elk. Clara offered him the bull's horns, but he refused.

"I never heard of anyone killing five elk with five shots," Marion said. "It was wonderful shooting, but it made the hunting season awful damn short."

"I never did see Parker again," Rudell told me. "I guess he told half the people at Safeway what a piss-poor guide I was. I plumb shot myself out of some jobs. But Marion still came back every year."

After a time of discontentment, Rudell moved his family to a shabby house in Irrigon, Oregon, and he got a job working as a security guard at the Umatilla Army Depot. Rudell patrolled the vast complex to make certain no one trespassed and the stored weapons remained secured. Whenever possible, he went hunting and prospecting.

Old-timers from those days remembered Rudell as a "good old boy" who liked to play cards and drink beer. Some remembered his prowess as a hunter. "He just loved to get away in the wilderness and hunt," one said. "And he loved prospecting for gold."

Raylene had no such respite. By Ormand's account, Rudell doted on her and tried to buy her what she wanted, given his limited means. When he was home, he cooked, yet that didn't stop him from taking time off when he felt like it, leaving Raylene behind to deal with the heat, and the kids, and the snakes. Of course, she was still a kid herself. In six years, she and Rudell had four children and she suffered two miscarriages. To help make ends meet, she took a part-time job driving a school bus.

She needed better living conditions and talked of a trailer with running water. They shopped for trailers and Raylene admired the new double-wides with shiny appliances, fireplaces, and ample space for six people.

"You should have seen her face fall when Dad showed up with that used Spartanette." Ormand shook his head at the memory.

"It was forty feet long and eight feet wide, kind of like living in a submarine."

Raylene wanted a fancier car at least, so Rudell went to Portland and bought a 1958 Cadillac Seville from one of the shyster lots on Eighty-second Avenue. The car threw a rod before they'd had it a month. Then the electric oil pump went out and no one knew how to fix it. It never ran again, but my father hung on to the Cadillac, even towed it to Monument after Raylene had left him, where it sat until he decided to dump it over a cliff and into the river.

They were getting by in Irrigon, but my father tried a business venture that proved disastrous. His older brother Hoot wanted Rudell to partner with him in the logging business. Hoot had two trucks but was going broke. The rest of Rudell's brothers and sisters argued against going into logging because my father didn't really know anything about it. In addition, the competition was fierce for logging contracts. The big outfits had advantages the small gypo loggers lacked.

In spite of his relatives' warnings, my father joined Hoot and bought one of his logging trucks. He moved the family to Hardman and rented a house from Hoot and his wife, Marie. Considering that he also purchased groceries from Hoot's small store, he fell hard into debt.

Rudell wasn't a logger. But he liked the freedom and being outdoors. When the trucks or equipment needed repairing, he was slow to get to it. Frequently, he hunted or took naps instead of working. Another logging outfit sabotaged their trucks and spiked their trees. Worst of all, the brothers couldn't get contracts for enough trees to keep both trucks running.

In one of those unfathomable family disputes, Hoot sued Rudell. In the settlement, Hoot got my father's beloved "winter place," the little elk camp on Sunflower Flat. Broke and discouraged, without a base for his guiding, Rudell moved his family back to Irrigon and began working at the Umatilla Army Depot once again. He settled for the sort of regular job he disliked but which my mother had aspired to.

■ ■ ■

After this move, another characteristic of Newton's showed in Rudell—a mean streak.

My aunt Sally explained that when Newton came home from prospecting, he punished the kids, especially the boys, if they didn't perform their chores around the ranch. He singled out Rudell more than the others for his fits of temper. My father moved slowly and talked even slower his entire life. At times, he almost seemed "slow," in the sense of simpleminded, but in fact, he was one of the brightest students Monument ever had, by all accounts.

However, he lagged at getting around to his chores, and Newton beat him repeatedly. Sally told me, "Newton started kicking Rudell while he was still on the porch trying to get his boots on, and he'd kick him and kick him all over that porch, then onto the ground. He kicked your father like a dog."

When Newton died, Rudell was fourteen. I doubt he cried much at the funeral.

Back in Irrigon, after the debacle with Hoot, he began taking things out on Ormand.

In that regard, he complemented Raylene. Perhaps she had been mean from the beginning or perhaps hardship drove her to it. In any case, she went after all the children, but Ormand more than the others.

"I think I reminded her of Dad," Ormand said. "I talk slow and I move so slow, I can't get out of my own way."

■ ■ ■

Eventually, I received a letter from Aunt Sally with bad news about Rudell. Raylene had taken the four kids and run south to California, leaving him "high and dry," as my aunt put it. Sally never mentioned the long-haul truck driver, Raylene's lover, who was closer to her age. Ormand filled me in years later. He had returned from junior high school to find the furniture, clothes, dishware, his siblings, and Raylene herself all waiting in an eighteen-wheeler with a sleeping cab. They pointed the Bekins truck toward the Interstate and left Irrigon in the side-view mirrors.

When Rudell came home from the Army Depot, he found everything cleaned out except for his clothes, guns, and a pair of chopsticks from the Chinese restaurant in Hermiston. "He was blindsided," Ormand said. "Sucker punched."

The way I saw it, Rudell had been clobbered in a similar manner to the way he leveled my mother those many years before. But she had gathered some stiff-necked reserve and bounced up like a punched Palooka doll. Not Rudell. "He stayed down for the count," Ormand said. Somehow, I figured there was justice in the blow.

Upon discovering his wife and children missing, my father's first impulse was to go after them and kill her boyfriend, Chad. He even thought of killing her, if he couldn't persuade Raylene to come back on her own. The problem was, he didn't know which direction they took after leaving Irrigon.

He guessed east toward Boise because she had some shirttail relatives near there, and he figured she would need help with the children. Along the way, he stopped at truck stops, asking if anyone had seen the rig. By the time he got to Ontario, he realized he had followed a cold trail.

They were headed to California and, knowing that Rudell might not be far behind, "We hauled ass!" as Ormand put it. West to Biggs Junction, then south through Madras, Bend, Klamath Falls, then bearing west to Weed and down I-5. They stopped once for gas but didn't take the time to eat. The kids grew hungry. "I can't tell you how hungry we were by the time we got to California. Mom and Chad wouldn't let us out of the truck for fear we might be recognized and somebody would tell Dad. I ate the most, so I guess I got the hungriest.

"Chad wasn't all that much for kids and probably figured by then he'd bit off something real hard to chew. When we kept complaining about how hungry we were, he finally pulled over and ran into a place called The Olive Pit and bought two jars of green olives, one with pimiento and one with just the pits.

"He tossed them into the back of the rig. 'Now stop complaining and start eating, you little brats.'

"I still can't stand green olives or pimientos. Even today, I won't eat one. Now a black olive I can take, but not a green one. Not for all the tea in China."

I know exactly how Ormand feels, because I can't stand pickled salmon. When I went to Ketchikan to earn money longshoring for graduate school, I rented a place that had a five-pound jar of pickled salmon left behind.

Things cost more in Ketchikan than I had anticipated, and soon I was out of money, waiting for my first check from the longshoremen and reduced to eating leftover pickled salmon. Even the thought of it today makes my eyes cross.

In the summer of 2004, I passed through Corning, California, which heralds itself as "the olive capital of the world." Unable to resist, I stopped at the tourist trap called The Olive Pit and bought Ormand a one-pound jar of green olives stuffed with pimientos. Assuming he never opens it, he'll always have something to eat.

■ ■ ■

After fleeing to California, Raylene and Chad moved constantly, because they feared Rudell was on their trail. And for six months, he followed them like a hound. At first, they landed in San Jose, figuring the city was so big he couldn't find them. Chad took a job as a welder, but only lasted a couple months.

Next came Los Gatos. That might have worked but Ormand had a freak accident. While eating his lunch and reading a book, he was crushed in the cafeteria/gymnasium's automatic bleachers after a careless janitor turned the key that retracted the bleachers. Ormand spent nineteen days in the hospital; then they had to move the moment he was released. Raylene and Chad feared the publicity resulting from the accident would tip off Rudell as to their whereabouts. However, Rudell was still checking school rosters in San Jose.

After Los Gatos, they moved to Hayward, where Raylene found work as a waitress. Finally, Chad left.

"Mom had a lot of boyfriends and most of them whipped us," Ormand said. "She was still afraid of Dad and kept moving. Sometimes Dad would go back to Oregon and ask the postmaster in Hardman, where her parents lived, if they had any out-of-state mail. When he got a lead, he'd come looking again."

But each time he came after them, Raylene had moved again, sometimes dragging along a boyfriend, sometimes going it alone. She took jobs waitressing, bartending, cleaning motels. In El Monte, she worked for Fairchild, assembling semiconductors.

"That was the best job because she got benefits," Ormand said.

All the moving played havoc with his learning. "I went to ten high schools in three years. I can't even remember all the towns. One time, we checked into a school the day before Christmas vacation and checked out the day after it was over. I never even got a locker assignment."

Because both his mother and her boyfriends beat him, Ormand finally ran off and returned to Monument, where he attended high school and helped Rudell build fence.

"I missed a lot of school building fence with Dad, but that wasn't what kept me from graduating. The trouble was, those California credits just never caught up with me. Maybe they couldn't find Monument.

"I didn't figure schooling mattered that much anyway. The day I turned eighteen, I went into Pendleton and joined the marines."

18

ESTACADA

"Let sleeping dogs lie" is the adage that best describes my attitude toward the old man through the next ten years. During that time since our meal at the Red Apple, I stayed busy with college and teaching jobs in Wisconsin and Michigan. Then I came back to Oregon, fell in love, and got married.

My wife Payette's beauty lit up any room. People stopped their conversations to ask about her work, interests, and Indian heritage. Smart and ambitious, she took classes at the local community college, worked downtown in an Indian art gallery, and took care of her daughter, Tiffany. Before we married, she was a single parent, much like my own mother.

We settled into a farmhouse out near Estacada, where Tiffany had room to play. I was back in rainy, green Western Oregon. But being close to Portland and having Payette more than made up for the climate. On our rented place, seven lilac bushes bloomed in the spring and trilliums sprang up in the pine woods. We enjoyed long evenings sitting at the kitchen nook watching the twilight fall. Payette cooked pot roasts with lots of carrots, her favorite vegetable, and embellished our meals with wild rice her Ojibwa relatives sent from Wisconsin. In the winter, we played in the fields of bright snowfall, and during summer, we sunbathed and made love beside an old weathered barn on the back of the place. Deer, raccoon, and coyotes were our neighbors, and life seemed idyllic.

In 1973, a second child entered our lives, changing our relationship more than we ever could have imagined. This child was Wade White Fish, Payette's illegitimate cousin from a reservation in the Midwest. At the time, he was five.

I was visiting Payette's parents one evening, when I heard a high, haunting whining from the back bedroom. Payette's father had talked about getting a hunting dog, and I thought he'd taken in a puppy, so I went to see. When I turned on the light, I was amazed to discover a small, thin boy whining in the back room. He lay on the bed, half-covered with a worn Pendleton blanket, and seemed not to notice when I entered.

"Are you afraid of the dark?" I asked.

His whining changed pitch. "I can leave the light on."

The boy's obsidian black eyes had a vacant, far-off look, and he didn't acknowledge when I spoke to him. After watching him whine and drool for a few minutes, I decided he was severely retarded and quietly left the room so as not to disturb him. I left the light on.

Payette and I learned from her parents that by age five, Wade had been in nineteen different foster homes and several state institutions. His natural mother drank. This was ferocious drinking—day after relentless day of alcohol abuse. No fruits or vegetables could be purchased on the reservation. A fresh apple, orange, or head of lettuce required a fifty-six-mile round-trip to a large grocery store. No vitamins, no folic acid, no prenatal visits to the Indian Health Service doctor.

Three weeks after our visit, when Payette's parents decided handling Wade was too much for them, I tried talking with her about the boy. "It's sad thinking of Wade going back to foster parents."

"Stop it right now. You're not going to make me feel guilty. He's not my kid."

"Maybe we could have our own child sometime. What about that?"

"No way, José. You should have seen me the first time I got pregnant. A darned watermelon with legs. I don't need that again. Anyway, you might go chasing around like my ex did."

"I wouldn't."

"All men are the same. The little head does the thinking for the big head. Besides, I'm going to be a grandmother way too young already."

I hadn't expected this. To me, marriage meant having children, and I assumed that since she already had a child, she would want to have another with me. Sometimes, I turned melancholy when I thought about not having children of our own. During those times, our lovemaking seemed mechanical, not passionate or purposeful. But she was clear on the child subject. Once she had said, "I don't plan to make motherhood my whole life. Got too darned much living to do."

Her stubbornness always puzzled me. My own mother had been one to sacrifice, compromise, make do. Now I thought that taking on Wade would be good for our marriage. I had always wanted children, perhaps in part to prove that I could be a good father—responsible in a way my own father and stepfather were not. And I thought a child, even a damaged child like Wade, could help to bridge the drift I was starting to feel with Payette.

"Listen," I said. "Tiffany might like a brother or sister. I'm convinced we could help Wade."

"I'm not a charity."

"Just think about it, would you?"

Early one morning, Payette got out of bed and went into the kitchen. I followed and saw her pouring a small glass of amaretto. She had been crying.

I poured a glass, too, and joined her at the kitchen nook. "What's up?"

"When I married you, I knew you'd never beat me."

I was puzzled by her remark. "No, I wouldn't."

"I was worried that if I married an Indian, he'd beat me."

"I'm glad you married me," I said, taking her hand.

"I'm not a good person. I try, but I'm not." She sipped her amaretto.

"You're a good person. None of us is perfect."

"I know you want your own children, Craig. But I just can't." She squeezed my hand. "I planned on traveling light, getting out of Oregon, but then Tiffany came along. After Henry split, I was really stuck, until I met you. I know what I want, but I feel so guilty, I can't stand it." She sighed. "It was bad enough before, but now I'm thinking about Wade, too. He's so scrawny and pitiful."

"We could try." I drank some amaretto.

"I don't see how. I've got classes, my job, Tiffany, and you, of course. I want some kind of life."

"Look at the upside. With Wade, you wouldn't have to get pregnant."

She chuckled. "Stop making me laugh. I don't understand why things can't be simple. I didn't bring Wade into the world. It was my darned uncle, catting around with that bitch from Fort Berthold."

"My mother can help us out some when she's not working. She always wanted to have more children." The nook was beginning to smell like amaretto.

"She wants us to have our own children. I know exactly what she wants. I've never seen such a transparent woman."

"Wade's not all that bad. He's gotten better at your folks. Maybe they're just too old to watch him. Here, he's got us and he can learn from Tiffany. He'll keep improving."

She removed her hand and looked directly at me. "Just because he's my relative doesn't mean I'm going to carry the full burden. It's got to be fifty-fifty. Do you promise?"

"Cross my heart." I splashed more amaretto in each glass and we toasted.

. . .

During the early seventies, the prevailing wisdom among educators and health-care providers held that love, a stable environment, good nutrition, and special-education classes could solve early childhood development problems and prepare the students for the "mainstream." This was a nice idea and we bought it wholeheartedly. However, in Wade's case, no one could accurately measure the irreparable damage of a mother's steady drinking.

"Probably autistic," one of the doctors declared after evaluating Wade at Shriner's Children's Hospital. Still, he suggested that the boy might improve dramatically, given the right conditions. He held out a spark of hope that matched the tiny spark of light behind Wade's dark and brooding eyes. A sign at the hospital ignited my imagination: SAVE A CHILD AND YOU SAVE A UNIVERSE.

Maybe Payette didn't want any children of our own, but we could save this boy, I figured. Working with him—her relative—would increase our love. And it would provide me with the opportunity to be a loving, caring father, striking a sharp contrast with my own father. All he hadn't done for me, I would do for Wade and Tiffany.

Wade improved dramatically for the first six months we had him. Four weeks of antibiotics cleared his sinus infection, and his nose stopped running green snot. He began to speak—only a few words at first, and those were garbled because of hearing difficulties and an incomplete palate.

Due to my teaching schedule and Payette's studies and work schedule, we placed Wade in a day-care program run by the Campfire Girls. Several of the day-care providers found Wade sad but charming, and they were sympathetic to his plight.

As the months progressed, he began to socialize with the other children. Those in wheelchairs were his favorites. After he put on a little weight and grew stronger, the supervisors allowed him to help push the wheelchairs and feed two children with cerebral palsy.

Campfire Girls had two dogs that captured Wade's imagination. On the drive home from day care, Wade would stick his head out the pickup window and howl. But sometimes at the center, he'd drop to the floor, growl ferociously, and try to bite the other children's legs. When this happened, we'd get a call and a note about his "inappropriate" behavior.

Psychologists labeled him "retarded," "learning disabled," "emotionally handicapped," "trainable mentally retarded," but he didn't fit comfortably into any category. Eight years later, I would finally learn the diagnosis was Fetal Alcohol Syndrome, but the label didn't matter as much as his unpredictable behavior. The question always remained: What do I do with this challenging boy?

Having a problem child like Wade divided our friends into two camps. Here he's welcome; there he's not. Some tolerated him, but others didn't. The divisions were sharper than I would have imagined, and, curiously, seemed to have little to do with whether or not the friends had children of their own. Some members of the first camp found projects to keep him occupied—digging a trench, stacking wood, shoveling bark dust. He thrived on supervised physical activity. These folks cut him slack. The Stevensons and their two boys overlooked his faults, even when he left their gate open so the llamas got into the alfalfa. That evening, he helped the boys do their chores and saddle the llamas for a jerky ride around the ranch.

He was hell-bent on leaving gates open. When he let Red York's cattle out, the grouchy old bachelor just brought out two cow whips and said, "Wade, you better help me drive them home." Shep, the cow dog, snapped at their heels while Wade shuffled behind, mimicking Red. "Go, Bossie. Hurry along, Clarabelle."

Wade also engaged in infuriating behavior such as smearing his feces on a wall or flooding a bathroom. On another occasion, when we visited friends with young girls, Wade followed the youngest child—a three-year-old—into the bathroom to watch her pee. After she pulled down her panties and sat on the toilet, he peed in the bathtub. Our friends were outraged that the two were in the bathroom together and that he had exposed himself. They told me I was welcome to visit at any time, but Wade was banished.

In retrospect, I suppose I lost half my friends. Still, I accepted that loss because I was so pleased at the progress Wade was making. For good behavior one week, the kindergarten teachers awarded Wade a special fireman's hat featuring flashing lights and whistles. He wore this proudly, and during recess, ran helter-skelter on the playground screaming "Fire" at the top of his lungs. Most of the other children were so lost in their worlds they seemed not to notice.

At home, one maddening habit Wade displayed was tearing apart anything mechanical. This included alarm clocks, an expensive pocket watch Payette had given me for Christmas, a toaster oven, and a portable radio. In the process, he lost parts or damaged them so the appliances were beyond repair. For these infractions, he was sent to this room and denied television, but those measures had little effect.

Tiffany, an only child for her first seven years, resented Wade's presence in the house and tattled on him at every opportunity. Much later, we learned that sometimes she created messes or wrecked things to get Wade in trouble. He was inarticulate and unable to defend himself. He was dark with a twisted lip and a furrowed brow. He drooled. Even when he claimed innocence, he appeared guilty. By contrast, she was a bright, clever, outgoing child—more than capable of fooling her parents. For obvious reasons, she remained her mother's favorite, and Payette constantly fussed over her clothes, hair, makeup, anything dress-up.

If losing friends was unsettling, losing relatives was worse. I never expected their intolerance. More than anything, I felt my uncle Oscar would stand behind Wade. Oscar had a severely retarded daughter he'd had to put in the state home at Fairview when she turned seven. If anyone could understand the challenges of raising a damaged child, I figured he could. But Oscar had no tolerance for Wade and seemed to resent his every action. Later, I realized that his resentment came from the fact that Wade resembled his daughter in many ways and reminded him of her.

Perhaps Wade sensed Oscar's tension and it triggered negative responses. At my uncle's house he destroyed a coffee table with a small hammer. Outside, he took off his belt and whipped Oscar's black Lab, Ace, a large, genial dog tolerant of children. When Ace retreated to his doghouse, Wade poked and poked the dog with a rake handle until Oscar stormed outside and cuffed him to the ground.

■ ■ ■

Although Wade's behavior could be maddening, sometimes he made a good companion. Outdoors, he was usually active and cheerful. He ran through the woods and fields, bringing home shiny stones, bird bones, feathers.

One November, Payette took Tiffany to visit relatives in Wisconsin. After work, I'd let Wade watch *Sesame Street,* and I'd hike the half mile to farmer Red York's stock pond, which had earthen dikes, cattail edges, and willows on the east end. Toward dusk, during the winter months, small groups of ducks flew in from the Clackamas River. Sometimes, I'd spot a couple of teal or mallards and shoot them for dinner.

Wade was fascinated by the duck feathers I gave him and would keep some of them in his dresser drawer. He also wanted to hear the ducks' names, but even though I'd repeat the names for him many times, he couldn't remember. I told him about saltwater coots, just because I thought that name might stick. There were no coots near Estacada, but the name became one of his favorite words, and as he tried to fall asleep, he'd repeat, "coot, coot, coot, coot."

One day Wade couldn't watch TV because he'd broken off the antenna. I agreed to let him come along to the pond, even though my general policy was to keep him far away from the shotgun. I stored it in the attic between hunts, locked securely. And I kept the shotgun shells locked away in a basement trunk. Each time I left the house, I counted shells, so none would be left unsecured.

My shotgun was a well-used Remington pump twenty gauge Wingmaster that I'd purchased on time from my uncle Oscar's sporting-goods store in Madras. He was just starting up the business then and couldn't afford to carry items on credit, so I'd borrowed eighty-nine dollars from Beneficial Finance and paid it back at a little over ten dollars a month for a year. I earned the payments working in my uncle's store. Because I was only fourteen at the time of the purchase, my mother had to cosign the loan. She didn't own a house, but she put up her used Pontiac as collateral. The loan papers read: "Doesn't own home. Has old Pontiac—runs good. New rubber on front." My mother had purchased two tires that autumn from Les Schwab's tire dealer. In those days, he was just starting out in Prineville, Oregon, and my mother liked him because he changed flat tires free for women drivers.

Wade and I arrived at the pond by early dusk, and even though I cautioned him about the importance of being quiet, he rustled in the dry leaves under the willows. I crouched in the cattails at the east bank. Red York's tractor thrummed a couple fields away, and the cold evening wind carried the scent of silage.

"Tracto," Wade said. His incomplete palate kept him from pronouncing r's.

"It's farmer York," I said. "Now you've got to be quiet."

"Yo'k," he said. The wind grew chillier and he shivered. His teeth chattered.

"Shhh," I said, squeezing his shoulder and pulling him closer. A small group of ducks appeared high above the pond. Their quickness indicated teal. They circled the pond, still far beyond range.

"Close your eyes," I whispered. "Keep them closed." I was afraid if Wade saw the circling teal, he'd cry out with excitement.

Wade squeezed his eyes shut.

"Good boy."

In the distance, Red York shut off his tractor and it dieseled loudly. I heard him call his dog Shep.

The ducks folded their wings and started to drop toward the pond. Their wings whistled.

My thumb touched the shotgun's safety button. I kept my face down.

Suddenly, Wade's eyes opened wide as the whistling grew louder. Spying the ducks dropping, he said, "Coots." Then he leapt to his feet, calling excitedly. "Coots, Dad, coots. All ove' the place!"

The ducks flared, veering to the north, back toward the river. Slipping off the safety, I stood, throwing the shotgun to my shoulder and gauging the distance. A long shot at best.

"Don't shoot, Dad! Don't shoot!"

Startled by his voice, I froze for a moment, then clicked the safety on.

He tugged at my coat sleeve. "Don't shoot p'etty coots."

His face pinched in worry and earnestness. I thought he was going to cry.

"It's all right. I'm not going to shoot." I shook my head, conjuring the ducks' dark silhouettes as they winged away—dots in the night sky. "It's too far anyway."

"Coots p'etty. So beautiful." He half-smiled.

I ejected three number-six shells from the shotgun, then dry-pumped twice to make certain the chamber was clear. I tucked the waxy shells into my pocket and rested the gun on my shoulder.

"Let's go home and rustle up some supper."

We headed back to the house, the porch light drawing us from the pond like a beacon.

That night, I fixed macaroni and cheese Hamburger Helper and sliced tomatoes. Wade had orange juice and I drank coffee, knowing that I would be up late grading papers. I missed Payette and Tiffany. This is like a single parent's supper, I thought. One dirty frying pan, some plates and utensils. I made certain he took another vitamin, then helped him with his bath and tucked him into bed. I read *Curious George* and *Little Toot*, a book about a courageous tugboat.

Later that evening, as I sat at the kitchen table grading papers, snowflakes began to snick against the window. A melancholy emptiness overtook me as I thought of Payette. The year before, the three of us had gone out into the field during the first snowstorm and made snow angels. Tiffany had giggled with delight. Payette's raven black hair framed her face and a few damp strands clung to her forehead. She was wearing my old red-and-black Filson jacket because she didn't want to get her new goose-down parka dirty. She had a maroon stocking cap pulled down to her ears, but her face was exposed, and I kissed her cold nose and lips.

Now, I wondered if it was snowing in Wisconsin. She hadn't called. I couldn't call her because it was past midnight in Stone Lake. Did she miss us? Did she miss me?

Wade's voice came from the bedroom, high and haunting. "Coot, coot, coot, coot," he repeated into the dark and restless night.

■ ■ ■

When dealing round-the-clock with a difficult child like Wade, parents frequently stress the "challenge" and "reward" of working with special needs kids. They don't talk much about *revenge*, but I occasionally used Wade to get back at people who deserved a comeuppance. This became easier to do as both his behavior and speech improved. He would act normal for a couple minutes, but then he'd take off on a tear, startling everyone in the process.

One day, I spotted a great used pickup at the Oregon City gas station where I traded. It was a fire-engine red four-wheel-drive Ford—perfect for fishing and hunting. Buoyed with enthusiasm at owning an almost-new truck, I drove to my bank, leaving Wade in the old Chevy while I went in to talk to the loan officer. The officer's hair was razor-cut and he wore one of those yellow "power ties" that were popular then. While he wasn't the teacher type, I figured the deal could be struck in a few moments—"Instant Approval," as the TV jingle offered. However, in his polite but firm (and just a little smug) way, he denied my application.

He cited the reason: The community college had no tax base, no firm financial standing. Each year we had to seek the approval of county voters for the following year's operating budget. Often, those levies had failed during our first attempts, and it was possible the college might close down completely.

Crestfallen, I left the bank, scarcely believing I had been so soundly rejected. Wade remained in the car, pretending to drive. The windshield wipers screeched back and forth against the dry glass. I shut them off. "It's not raining, Wade."

He squinted at the blue sky. "It might rain."

"What makes you think that?"

His lower lip hung out. "I'm thirsty. Can I have a pop?"

I shook my head; then I had an idea. "Just go in the bank there where Dad was and get a drink of water."

Of course, the bank held no drinking fountains, but Wade marched through the wide glass doors, eager to find one. I stayed outside, counting five minutes on my watch. When time was up, I stepped inside.

Chaos.

Wade was running quickly from one section of the bank to another, and two tellers had abandoned their posts and were trying to catch him without looking as if they were in active pursuit. Yellow Tie was after him, too, but slowed by his wing tips.

These were the days when people smoked, and the bank contained two tall cylindrical ashtrays filled with sand. Wade had tipped both of them over. Sand, cigarette butts, gum, and wrappers trailed along his footpath. Two of the chained pens had been ripped out and lay on the floor, along with a flutter of pink withdrawal slips.

Pretending naïveté, I asked, "Say, has anyone seen an Indian boy in here? Six years old? But he looks smaller."

The tellers and Yellow Tie paused in their pursuit.

"Hey, Dad," Wade said, recognizing my voice. "I can't find a darned old drinking fountain anywhere. I don't think they got one."

"Well, let's get a pop across the street then," I said, and he scampered out ahead of me. As I approached the doors, I took care not to step on any gum.

Outside, the sun felt warm and the sky resembled a robin's egg. Later, I would get a loan at the Portland Teacher's Credit Union.

■ ■ ■

The September after he turned seven, Wade entered grade school.
The school tried mainstreaming him, the vogue theory at the
time, but failed utterly. Wade constantly leaped from his desk,
raced around the room, slammed cupboard doors, turned water
faucets off and on. Putting him in his own space with paint or
Play-Doh proved useless. He poured out the paint or threw Play-
Doh at the other students while cackling and giggling like a Bed-
lam inmate.

Our lives were interrupted by a threnody of complaints from
counselors, teachers, administrators. Somehow, their attitude was
to blame us for his behavior. Punishment fell on us during those
periods he was suspended.

"This is way harder than I thought," Payette said. "I can't miss
any more work. Sometimes I think having him is unfair to Tiffany.
He takes up so much time."

"I'll call in sick," I said, even though I'd run out of sick days.
"It's only a three-day suspension."

"Three days seems like three years." She shook her head.
"Things will never be normal for us, will they? I feel trapped. He's
like an anvil chained to my neck."

Ritalin, Dr. Feingold's sugar-free diet, behavior modification—
all proved useless, perhaps worse than useless because they held
out false hope. Finally, we found a special-education class where
Wade's behavior improved, primarily due to dedicated teachers
and lower expectations. Once again, Wade was allowed to help
wheelchair-bound students. Perhaps twice a week he'd come
home proudly with a good behavior badge or note: "Wade showed
improvement this afternoon."

Two years into the classroom, the teachers promised breakthroughs. "He's almost ready to read and tell time," they insisted.
At home, I read him story after story until my eyes drooped. I
made sure he continued to watch *Sesame Street*. I crossed my fingers until they ached. But no breakthroughs occurred in spite of
hard work and good intentions.

My father's parents, Newton and Anna Lesley, with seven of their children shortly after arriving at the homestead in Monument, Oregon. Anna's brother Elroy is in the back row, far right. (1911)

My father, Rudell Newton Lesley, in his army uniform. (1944)

Newlyweds Rudell and my mother, Hazel Jane, in Hattiesburg, Mississippi. (1945)

My mother, father, and I in The Dalles, Oregon. (1945)

My mother's parents, Oscar and Flora Lange, in The Dalles.

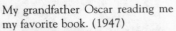
My grandfather Oscar reading me my favorite book. (1947)

I had a pair of cap pistols when I was four.

Grandma Lesley visiting me in The Dalles. (1949)

Christmas bounty at my grandparents' place. (1950)

My stepfather, Vern Hecker, and I on my first day of school. (1951)

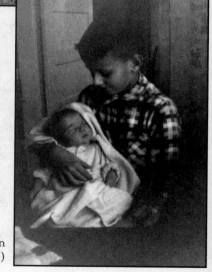

Hatless and Horseless at the Pendleton Round-Up. (1951)

Holding my baby sister, Ronna, in Baker City, Oregon. (1956)

With my pal Danny Freeman. (1957)

On the road. (1957)

My mother, Ronna, and I outside
Baker City. (1956)

Ronna on her second birthday
with my mother's signature lamb
cake in Madras, Oregon. (1958)

Mom working at the Warm Springs Indian Reservation. (1958)

My uncle Oscar Lange and my foster son, Wade White Fish, at Oscar's Sporting Goods in Madras. (1974)

My grandfather Newton and uncle Martin Lesley (my namesake) the year before Martin was killed.

Standing outside Uncle Hoot and Aunt Marie Lesley's Hardman store. (1981)

My wife, Katheryn Stavrakis, holding our daughter Elena, and Wade in Portland, Oregon. (1982)

With Raymond Carver in Port Angeles. (1982)

Wade by the woodpile. (1984)

Rudell, Elena, and I. Elena was born on his birthday, March 18. (1983)

Mom doting on her grand-
daughters. (1986)

Rudell's place in Monument,
Oregon. (1989)

Elena, Kira, and I with my friend Robert
Stubblefield in Monument. (1989)

My aunts Sally Smith and
Lela Sloan.

Above Cupper Creek where Rudell saw Bigfoot in 1980.

Kira holds a campaign sign for Elena, who became president of Irvington Grade School in Portland. (1993)

Ormand, Craig, and Huston Lesley the day after Rudell's funeral in Monument. (2001)

Ormand leaning against a fence jack he and Rudell made with red-hearted juniper thirty years earlier. (2004)

Kathy and Elena at Elena's Brown University graduation. (2004)

• • •

The longer he lived with us, the more Payette resented him. By this time, she was working for the Indian Education Program at the Northwest Regional Educational Lab, and she threw herself more and more into conferences and travel, spending fewer nights and weekends at home. When she was home, she concentrated on Tiffany. I sensed Payette's distance and tried to appease her anger. Because Wade was her relative, I assumed that underneath her dark moods, she was pleased at his progress, but I was wrong.

Payette and I disagreed about the boy. While I concentrated on the strides he was making, she emphasized the difficulties. After she returned from a three-day conference on Indian education for kindergartners, she stayed especially moody, ignoring Wade in spite of his strategies to gain attention.

"You haven't had one good word to say since you got home from the conference," I said.

"What's to say? I can't deal with him. I'm not a saint. If you think you are, go right ahead."

Eventually, she turned over the doctor's appointments, school conferences, and disturbing calls from the teachers entirely to me.

When she bathed, Payette started locking the bathroom door because she didn't want him coming in and watching her. Our lovemaking became infrequent because she was convinced he lay awake at night listening. His sleep was always restless, whether or not he took Ritalin, and sometimes he did awaken and wander the house.

■ ■ ■

Clearly, Wade and I were moving in one direction while Payette veered in another. For over four years, she and I had held together a frantic schedule of community college teaching (five classes three times a year, plus summer school for extra pay), her classes and jobs, day care for both children, endless rounds of appointments with doctors, psychologists, counselors, and teachers. Now our relationship was unraveling, but I didn't know what to do.

Payette applied to a special program Harvard University offered qualified Indian students. If she were accepted into the program, she would receive a master's in education after a year's study. At this time, she held a secretarial science degree from Clackamas Community College and two terms of additional classes, but no associate of arts degree. Harvard would allow some credits for "prior learning experience," including time spent working on Indian Education programs at the Northwest Regional Education Lab.

I first saw Harvard's program as a wonderful opportunity for her. Almost two hundred students attended it, although many turned out not to be enrolled tribal members, but Indian "wannabees." According to Payette, Harvard had not bothered to verify the backgrounds of many students. Jamaicans, African-Americans, and Anglos all passed until some standards for verification were eventually established, with Payette serving on the committee. No matter their stripe, the students were not taught by the usual Harvard professors but rather by adjuncts brought in from Rocky Mountain College in Billings, North Dakota State, and other institutions.

After completing her master's degree in nine months, Payette found it difficult to get high-powered employment off the reservations or apart from the political internships available in Washington, D.C. Personnel officers were skeptical about her lack of a B.A. "Everybody wants to know your darned pedigree," she complained.

■ ■ ■

Moving to Cambridge had meant separation from me, Wade, and Tiffany, a separation I realized Payette wanted. We agreed that I would watch the children so she could concentrate on her studies.

On the journey east, we had stopped in Billings to visit her sister Eve and watch our brother-in-law Jerry play in a softball tournament. Eve, who had two children of her own, agreed to care for our kids so we could have a little time together. During Jerry's game against Helena, Payette and I decided to take a walk to the basalt rimrock above Billings. We carried Cokes and hamburgers smothered with fried onions so we could have a little picnic.

To the west, the setting sun cast a deep maroon glow. The wind picked up, carrying the scents of juniper and sweetgrass. Below, we could hear the thunk of metal bats and the cheers of the crowd.

Payette finished her hamburger and crumpled the napkin, letting the wind carry it fluttering along the rimrock. "I love fried onions," she said.

"Hey, Indians aren't supposed to litter."

She sipped her Coke, then set it on a rock. "I don't want to be married anymore."

I had a mouthful of hamburger but couldn't remember to swallow.

"I've never loved you," she said, eyes lowered, as if watching the action on the field. "I thought I could learn to love you because you're a good man, but it doesn't work that way."

I finally swallowed, but was unable to make my mouth say, "You never loved me?" The crowd cheered and two men ran around the bases, but I couldn't comprehend any of it. "You don't mean it—about not being married."

"Yes, I do."

"What about the kids? They both need us."

"Wade just makes everything worse."

"You can't do this."

"You can't stop me."

She did mean it. The divorce would take a while, as divorces do, although we made a couple of gestures about getting back together. Both Tiffany and Wade lived with me a semester, but they fought constantly, so, eventually, I sent Tiffany to stay with her grandparents.

Wade stayed with me because no one else wanted him and I did. I vowed to raise him right and show up all of those who had abandoned us—especially Payette, but my father, Rudell, too. He had run off on me first, and then Payette pulled the same stunt. I was determined not to quit on Wade. I was too stubborn and defi-

ant and naïve to back out. Children's Services wouldn't get him,
and I wouldn't send him back to the reservation.

I was smart, hardworking, well liked. Wade had progressed
miles since the doctors had diagnosed him first with autism and
severe retardation. His speech had improved, too. Surely, I can
bring him along, I thought. Lots of people were single parents. I
knew I could do it.

19

HIT MAN

Ormand didn't get the calling to be a minister until after the devil tempted him to be a hit man. The hit man summons came during the time Ormand spent as a marine stationed in Cherry Point, North Carolina. In some ways, he made a perfect marine. Ormand was tough from building fence and he knew about killing after running traplines and shooting game for table meat. Like my father, he was a crack shot. The marines taught him how to kill men.

"All the movies in those days glorified hit men," Ormand said. "They drove fast cars, slept with beautiful women, and had lots of money. Being a hit man became my fantasy. Anyway, I was pretty impressionable back then. And I had a nasty mean streak."

For Ormand, the hit man fantasy became a reality.

Fort Bragg sat practically next door to the marine base. With so many military personnel in the area, numerous clubs offered entertainment devoted to the baser instincts—stripping, prostitution, gambling, and drugs. Money flowed freely from the young men's pockets, and the competition for that money was ferocious.

"Clubs stole beautiful bartenders or great dancers from one an-other," Ormand said. "Some women just had an attitude or body that attracted men like honey, and the word got around. All of a sudden, your place became top dog."

Many club owners and managers came with shady back-grounds: pimping, loan sharking, extortion, income tax evasion, manslaughter. They hired marines, including Ormand, to serve as bodyguards and bouncers, run errands, steal girls from other clubs. Frequently, the managers offered to double the girls' present salaries, at least to tempt them away. Later, they'd sign the dancers to restrictive contracts and hang on to them with threats.

Even though Kingston County, North Carolina, regarded itself as Bible Belt, the good citizens turned a blind eye to these illicit activities. Some profited directly from the clubs through rents or liquor distributorships. Others believed that they could protect their own daughters if the young men had outlets for their base desires elsewhere. The whole county benefited from revenue and business taxes.

Tony Ricardo ran a cluster of clubs and had a serious six-figure income. When Tubby Powell, another club owner, muscled in on Tony's territory, he decided to strike back hard.

Tony hired Ormand to kill Tubby and offered my brother two possibilities. He could use a sawed-off twelve-gauge shotgun, be-cause the police couldn't run ballistics tests on pellets (but Or-mand was instructed to pick up the tell-tale wadding from the shells). Or he could stick a pistol in Tubby's ear, pull the trigger, then drop the pistol.

"I was a good shot with a pistol," Ormand said. "Whenever I built fence I carried a twenty-two pistol. I'd shoot chukars, quail, grouse. Usually I could hit them in the head. Tubby was no prob-lem at all."

Tony gave Ormand $2,500 in advance, with another $2,500 guaranteed after the job was completed. He also gave him an un-registered .32-caliber Smith & Wesson automatic.

Ormand put on plain clothes with loose trousers so he could pack the .32 in his front pocket unnoticed, then drove out to the

High-Spot. In order to appease the bluenoses, few of the clubs had bright neon signs, and the High-Spot's sign was very discreet. Still, every serviceman knew its location.

My brother parked the rental car (procured with a false ID) and went inside to look for Tubby, who usually occupied his own table near the dance floor. Although Tubby wasn't there, Ormand ordered a drink and sat at the bar. He didn't want to get involved with the dancer, a pale brunette with large breasts.

"She was definitely second-string," Ormand said. "Not much of a dancer. I felt kind of sorry for her because the crowd was sparse in the afternoon. The really good-looking women danced at night to draw in the servicemen."

When Tubby didn't show after an hour, Ormand went back outside to wait in the car. The club was located beside a lake, so he decided to walk over and observe the wild ducks. The red-winged blackbirds rustling in the cattails reminded him of home.

"Suddenly, I heard this voice, like the voice of God. It said, 'Ormand, you're not a hit man! You're just a dumb hick from Monument! What are you doing here?'

"Right then, I realized I couldn't do it. When I took the gun out of my pants, it illuminated, and I threw it into those cattails. For all I know, it's still buried in the mud."

He needed to return the money to Tony and tell him the hit was off, but he was afraid Tony might have him killed for failing. The code demanded that an assigned hit had to be completed, especially if the hitter had taken the front money.

"I think Tony's wife helped me out some," Ormand said. "She liked the young marines that always hung out in the clubs. She was beautiful and slept with them when her husband wasn't around. Even though she was past forty, that woman was a knockout."

For whatever reason, Tony took back the money and remained on good terms with Ormand. So did Mrs. Ricardo. When Tony was doing jail time, she and Ormand had a fling.

Adultery is bad, but nothing like murder.

"I knew the Lord wasn't in what I did with Tony's wife, but He sure stood beside me out by those cattails."

■ ■ ■

In 1976, back in Monument, Ormand sold a coyote pelt for fifty dollars and bought a pair of Acme boots and a bottle of whiskey at Boyer's Cash Market. He spent the afternoon walking around town showing off the boots.

Later that evening, he started drinking and discussing his philosophy of life with Jim Hebo, a bitter, one-legged Vietnam veteran who had served as a medic. From time to time, Jim's girlfriend, Jody, added her comments.

Disagreeing on a number of issues, both men were drunk by 10:00 P.M. At that time, Jim demanded that Ormand leave the trailer he shared with Jody.

Ormand agreed to leave but said he needed to piss first and headed for the bathroom. Jim seized a .44 Magnum and shot Ormand in the neck.

As Ormand bled profusely on the bathroom floor, Jody screamed at Jim, ordering him to help Ormand before he bled to death. She warned him that if Ormand died, he'd be charged with murder. Sobering a little and using his skills as a medic, Jim kept Ormand alive until the ambulance arrived and rushed him to the hospital in John Day, where he received five units of blood. "If he wasn't such a big man, he would have bled to death," the doctor said.

When the police interviewed Ormand at the hospital, he claimed the event was an accident and that he didn't plan to press charges.

"I sort of considered it an accident between drunks," he told me later.

Although skeptical, the police decided to let it go.

The bullet damaged the cluster of nerves at the base of Ormand's neck, resulting in damage to his right side. He can't raise his right arm above his head or hold it straight out in front of him. He has to twist sideways for the simple task of shaking hands.

When Ormand tried collecting disability after the shooting, he learned that Jim and Jody had filed a breaking and entering report against him. Each had made a statement that eventually kept Ormand from collecting disability, because the authorities concluded "the disability occurred during the commitment of a felony."

Forced to give up fence building, Ormand remarked, "Getting shot was a bad career move."

■ ■ ■

While he was recovering, Ormand had a vision that changed his life. "I had a slow recovery," he said. "I couldn't use my right arm and I was pretty helpless, so I moved in with Lester and Bunny Oates down in what they call 'Mill Town.' All those houses have the same floor plan, just like where I got shot.

"After staying there about a month, one night I got up to go to the bathroom, but when I opened the door, the bathroom was gone. I saw this staircase leading up into darkness."

"You probably wandered into the hall by mistake." I knew Ormand would have been taking Vicodin or Percocet.

"No, it was the bathroom door. I recognized the frog decal Bunny stuck up. I closed the door and stumbled back to bed. 'Wake up, Ormand, you're dreaming,' I said. So I got up again and went into the bathroom. Nothing but that staircase!"

"Sometimes you dream the same things over and over again."

"But I was wide-awake by then," Ormand insisted. "The third time I saw that staircase, I decided to climb. It seemed to take a long time. I passed through the fog, and at the top of the steps, I saw a shining pulpit and a dark figure wearing a sou'wester.

"His arm pointed directly at me and he cried out, 'There is a good man!'

"His words struck me. I knelt and gave myself over to the Lord. Gave over my anger. When I stood, I was in the bathroom. I looked in the mirror and my hair was electrified—all of it standing straight up. Since my hair is curly, I knew a transformation had taken place.

"Then someone was pounding on the bathroom door. When I opened it, Bunny's face went white.

"'Ormand, what happened to your hair? I heard somebody yelling and got up to see if you were all right. You look like you've seen a ghost!'

"'Bunny, it's okay. Calm down.'

"Lester was up by then, wanting to know what happened. Bunny made coffee, and when she handed me my cup, I reached out and took it with my right hand. It only worked halfway, but that just reminds me I still have a ways to go."

Growing up, I had heard similar stories from my relatives, and I believe that it took a miracle to save me after the mint chopper accident. Still, the universe never reveals itself to me as directly as Ormand described.

"Why was the minister wearing the sou'wester?" I asked.

"That was the Holy Ghost telling me I'm going to have a lot of storms in my life."

After the vision with the figure wearing the sou'wester, Ormand began studying the Bible more closely and eventually became an apprentice preacher. Although he hadn't had formal training, as with many rural preachers, he'd been moved by the Spirit. Now, he offers daily witness, prayer, and spiritual uplifting to friends, neighbors, and newcomers. On occasion, if the regular minister is called away, Ormand will preach or conduct a service. He led our father's memorial because the scheduled preacher left to visit his sick wife in the Bend hospital.

Part of Ormand's testimony results in beautiful walking sticks carved from mountain mahogany. Each piece bears a key Bible passage. He offers the sticks as gifts, and Boyer's carries a few for a modest price.

Having recently joined the city council, Ormand preaches a little about civic activities and ethics. His answering machine message says, "This is Ormand. If I'm not here, I'm out trying to help somebody, or I'm trying to help myself."

20

OREGON CITY

After the divorce, I attended graduate school for two more years, earning an M.F.A. at the University of Massachusetts. When I returned to Oregon, after-school day care remained a constant problem. Hyperactive and inattentive at eleven, Wade was also too old for most programs. Few caregivers had the patience or flexibility to accommodate him, especially if they were accustomed to dealing with middle-class "normal" children. A respite program was available through the county, but this was more harmful than helpful. These children—constant firestarters and masturbators—were worse than Wade, and he picked up bad habits. One boy wore a football helmet device so he wouldn't hurt himself when he smashed his head into the wall and shouted, "I'm okay! Are you okay?"

At home, helmetless, Wade smashed his head into walls until he threw up.

The trick was to seek out eccentrics who liked children. One of these was a painter whose only subject was his nude wife. Another was a woman who fed every pigeon in Oregon City and had

Wade accompany her on excursions under bridges, along the railroad tracks, below the free municipal elevator. The arrangements with eccentrics usually lasted only a couple of months before they ran out of patience and headed off to other projects.

I found some care through church references. Burkee, a hardfaced woman, ran a Lutheran child-care program on Sundays and provided in-home care for two men on state disability. One seldom came out of his room, and I never heard him speak. The second, Otto, talked constantly, primarily about his Spokane motorcycle club, the Desert Demons. He was wiry with the abject appearance that some people on disability wear. He and Burkee chain-smoked. His oversized jeans hung low on his hips, and he rolled up the bottoms to reveal black scuffed motorcycle boots. He had a flat-head Harley stripped in the dining room, but I never saw it up and running. The motorcycle was a constant fascination for Wade, as was Sarge, a male German shepherd that whined incessantly, like Otto did over his aches and injuries from bike accidents.

"When I wake up, I'm always thankful something hurts," Otto claimed. "If I ever feel decent, I know I died in the night."

Burkee and Otto epitomized backsliders, but I didn't care as long as they watched Wade.

Wednesdays, I taught a night creative-writing class at the community college. It finished at ten, but frequently I talked with students after class, so I picked Wade up around eleven. He would be glued to the TV set watching wrestling shows or demolition derbies while Burkee and Otto split a case. Although I'd be exhausted, I'd join them for a beer and watch the mayhem. During commercial breaks, Otto retold stories of his Spokane motorcycle gang.

As I drove up one night, I saw the front room picture window had been broken and boarded up with two sheets of scrap plywood. I hope Wade didn't do that, I thought. Looking closer, I saw boot prints in the mud under the windowsill. Chances were one of Otto's friends had kicked out the window. Long shards of glass remained visible in the illumination of the naked porch light. Someone had done a poor job of sweeping.

When I shoved open the door, the cigarette smoke and tension were thick enough to cut. Sarge had a large white bandage on his right thigh and a plastic collar around his neck, keeping him from licking at the wound. Under the smoke, the place smelled of mildew, cooking grease, and stale beer.

"Jesus Christ! It's about time you showed up!" Otto said.

"Give him a beer," Burkee said. "He's gonna need a drink."

"I only got three left," Otto grumbled, but handed one to me anyway.

"Thanks," I said, trying to ease the tension. "Did old Sarge get hit by a car?"

"We got the bejesus scared out of us today," Otto said. "We're still plenty shook."

"I can barely light a cigarette," Burkee said, but she managed. After taking a long drag, she held out both hands so I could see them trembling.

On the sofa across the room, Wade sat silent, his head drooping to his chest.

"What's going on?" I asked.

"I still can't believe it," Burkee said.

"Wade stabbed Sarge. Just like a dirty Mex." Otto crushed his beer can.

I was stunned. "Stabbed?"

Otto stood, a little unsteady. "Come and look at this." He limped toward their bedroom and pointed under the bed. "Blood all over the place."

I saw a dark reddish stain the size of a dinner plate. Then I noticed drop-sized stains across the floor.

"Sarge crawled under the bed to hide from the little shit. After that, the dog jumped out the window."

I was incredulous. Sarge and Wade were pals. "Are you sure Wade stabbed him?"

"Do you think we'd make it up?" Burkee had followed us in. "Do you think we broke our own goddamn window?" As she drew on her cigarette, the deep circles under her eyes seemed to darken. "He stabbed Sarge with my best kitchen knife."

I didn't say anything.

"We come home to blood everywhere," she said. "The boy was missing, the dog gone. I swear to God, we thought the worst. I didn't know what to tell you, what kind of story . . ."

"She got all dizzy from her blood pressure," Otto said. "I thought I'd lose her, too."

"I'm sorry," I said, not really caring about Burkee. Wade was my main concern. "So what happened exactly?"

Otto shrugged. "The police got some wild story about a monster. That boy's crazy. Completely loony."

"You called the police about a dog?"

Burkee flared. "What do you expect? Your boy was gone." She turned to Otto and leaned against him. "You remember that awful time my boy went missing? The coroner had him as a John Doe for six months after the hit-and-run. All that time, I thought he was in California."

"Don't drag that up again," Otto said. "Don't go beating on yourself." He put his arm around her shoulder. "Wade ran off and left the door wide open. We could have been robbed."

Burkee wiped her nose on her sweatshirt. "I don't want any more days like this one."

Otto held her tighter. "It's all right now."

"My boy's dead. That's his dog—all I got left. I'm heartbroke."

She needed comforting, but that was Otto's job. I had to find out more about Wade. "Can you think of any reason he'd stab Sarge?"

Burkee held out her hand as if to steady herself. "I got to lie down a minute."

"You go ask him," Otto told me. "You try to get a straight answer from that kid."

I thought she was going to bed, but they both followed me back into the front room. Otto sat in the La-Z-Boy and Burkee lay down wearily on the couch.

"I'm wrung out like a dishrag," she said.

I turned to Wade. "Why did you stab Sarge? You're his friend."

Wade's shoulders slumped. Saliva bubbled from his lower lip. He drooled.

I gripped his shoulders, trying to force him to look at me. "Wade?"

I was half-convinced this was a nightmare. Maybe I'd stopped the pickup somewhere and fallen asleep. I gripped tighter. "Just tell me. You're not going to get into any more trouble."

He wouldn't look up, but his face twisted and I loosened my grip.

"You won't get anything out of him. Cat's got his tongue." Otto leaned forward in his La-Z-Boy and rubbed his temples. "I'm getting a headache from all this trouble."

"Where's the knife?" I asked him. In some crazy way, I imagined it might tell me something, point to a culprit other than Wade.

"The police took it," Burkee said. She nodded as if for emphasis. "Now we got the police mixed up in our business."

"They'll keep an eye on us, all right," Otto said. "My buddies are going to love that." He glared at Burkee. "You should never call the cops."

She snapped at him. "Maybe you should find some new drinking buddies."

After lighting another cigarette, she turned to me. "We got home to this mess and couldn't figure it out. Like I said, we thought the worst. Anyway, the police followed the trail of blood outside and found Sarge lying under a big rhododendron a couple houses away. They called animal control and took him to an all-night vet."

"I can imagine what that's going to cost," Otto said. "The mutt ain't worth that much."

"Goddamn you!" she said to Otto. "He's my son's dog so shut your fucking mouth!"

Otto turned to Wade. "The boy came slinking back. Too curious about the police cars and flashing lights."

"I cried when I saw him. Broke down crying. That's how relieved I was."

"Damn straight." Otto struggled to his feet, pointing at Wade. "Don't you have any sense, boy? Sarge is your pal. You don't stab a pal."

When I saw Otto's anger and confusion, I had a moment of clarity. Nothing was going to be settled tonight. The main thing was to appease Burkee and Otto, then get Wade out of there before the police came back. I got Wade's jacket and put it on him. After that, I wrote Burkee and Otto a check for two hundred dollars, figuring that would cover the window replacement, the vet, and a new knife.

Sarge whined softly when he saw Wade was leaving. Dried blood still matted the fur around the dog's hip and down his leg.

"I'm sorry you got hurt, Sarge." Wade's voice sounded thin and forced. "I'll be back tomorrow and we can play."

Wade stayed quiet on the drive home. He fiddled with the seat belt, zipped and unzipped his jacket. He got ready for bed, and his pajamas were backward, but I didn't care. Once he was in bed, I tried saying a prayer. He giggled a few times, but grew still when I added Sarge to the prayer.

"God bless Sarge. Amen," he said.

"Good night, Wade."

"The bedbugs bite." He seemed to be in a better mood.

"Hey, how did Sarge get stabbed, anyway? I wasn't sure. You told the police. So tell me."

"Burkee and Otto shouldn't have left me alone," Wade said. "I was scared. Sarge was scared, too. And then I heard a monster in the basement."

A monster, I thought. The boy had flipped. I'd be lucky if the police didn't contact Children's Services and take Wade away.

"Tell me about the monster."

"It was down in the basement, behind the furnace. I could hear it breathing in and out—like this." He took a few slow, deep breaths. "And Sarge went down to see. That's when I got the knife. I snuck down, too." Wade sat rigid in the bed, eyes widened. "Then Sarge's hair stood up on his back. He growled and the monster tried to climb up the stairs. Sarge chased right behind it. He bit it and grabbed it with his mouth. Then the monster bit him and Sarge yelped and ran off."

Could there have been a rat or cat? I wondered. Did the furnace come on, making odd noises? Wade seemed convinced. "Maybe you got confused," I told him. "Maybe you thought Sarge was the monster."

Wade shook his head so violently I could hear his teeth click. "I saw a real monster and it bit him, so I stabbed it with the knife." Wade started to cry. "It tried to hurt Sarge. Sarge and I are friends."

He was sobbing by then and I understood it would be useless to try to untangle his emotions and imagination from the actual event. I smoothed the hair on his head. The boy felt feverish. "Just get some sleep tonight. We'll figure things out tomorrow. Sleep as late as you want. You don't have to go to school."

He quit sobbing. "Is it going to snow?"

I didn't know what the morning would bring. Maybe the cops would show up or Children's Services, but I doubted it. What could they do? They tried to get rid of kids like Wade and pawn them off on people like me.

In the morning I'd call the psychiatrist and explain we had an emergency. I hadn't figured out all the details yet, but it would be good to get Wade out of Portland—have a cooling-off period. How long am I going to have to go through this kind of shit? I thought. Why did I take on this responsibility?

Suddenly I remembered my father, who hadn't done a damn thing for me. Maybe I could get him to take on Wade as a kind of payback, crazy as it sounded. I started convincing myself that Wade and Rudell could team up. Wade could be outdoors and help my father build fence and trap coyotes. In a place like Monument, Wade would go to a small school and people could get to know him.

Seeing my father became important to me. I wanted a more normal life, and if I could get him to take on Wade, if only for a while, I might come up with a better plan. In my desperation, I imagined that my father might feel remorse and welcome a second chance at fatherhood by helping me out. And maybe Wade would bring my father and me closer together. Although I had never had a relationship with Rudell, something in me longed for one. I got

ready for bed, knowing sleep would be difficult. Still, the road toward Monument seemed clear.

Rain blew against the windows on the south side of the house,
rattling the panes. I kept listening for Wade to rouse, perhaps
stumble downstairs to the kitchen. My imagination conjured
nightmare scenes of Wade climbing the stairs with a knife.

Unable to rest, I got up, turned on the light, and dragged my
heavy dresser in front of the bedroom door. Then if he tried to
open it, the screech of the dresser's legs would awaken me.

My God, it's come to this, I thought. My desperation and longing are driving me to Monument.

■ ■ ■

That restless night I dreamed again of the pink raincoat and a
Japanese child who went missing back in Massachusetts while I
was a graduate student. Columbus Day, 1977, I returned from
studying to find Mrs. Kagita, rain-soaked and distraught, holding
out a child's pink raincoat.

"Yukiko gone," she said. The playground's gate swung in the
wind.

This was at the University of Massachusetts's Puffton Village,
a rabbit-warren maze of housing units set aside for married graduate students. As a single parent, I qualified for K block, units near
the back of the project. Mrs. Kagita, her husband, and their
fifteen-month-old daughter lived in the L unit, across a muddy
strip of grass from K. A shabby playground stood beyond L, and
past that, perhaps fifty feet, a culvert and small slope led to a
slough off the Connecticut River.

"Have you seen Yukiko?" Mrs. Kagita asked.

"She's probably with the other kids." In the distance, a group
of children raced through the weedy fields along the slough. I
spotted Wade wearing his orange U-Haul stocking cap. At nine,
he was the oldest, but developmentally, he was far behind the
others.

I know this much. Before I walked over to where the children were playing, I checked the slough near the culvert to make certain Yukiko wasn't down playing in the mud where the older children often went. No sign of her.

When I reached the children, no Yukiko. They didn't remember seeing her. We searched the fields and grounds for twenty minutes; then I took Wade and we went door-to-door. Mrs. Kagita was too upset to be of much help and barely spoke English, but her husband joined the search.

We had worked our way halfway through the D unit when I heard the piercing ambulance sirens. Paramedics fished the drowned girl out of the slough near the culvert. Yukiko wore a blue sweatshirt with a sunflower on the chest, dark jeans, and a single bright green rain boot. Algae flecked her clothes and hair.

I was heartsick—furious at myself for not posting someone to safeguard the culvert and slough. I figured she had wandered back in the rain-slicked dark and fallen off the culvert.

Later, at the tiny apartment, I went through the motions of fixing dinner. All I could think of was the Kagitas' grief, the death of a beautiful child.

"Yukiko was just sleeping, right?" Wade asked. "Man, those sirens were so cool. I want to be a fireman."

"Maybe someday," I said. My head throbbed.

"She's okay, right? Can I be a fireman?"

"We'll see."

Two plainclothes police officers showed up after 11:00 P.M. Wade was asleep and I had the Springfield news on, but there was no word of Yukiko's death. The officers asked detailed questions about Mrs. Kagita: Did she usually leave the child alone on the playground? For what amount of time? Was she emotionally stable? Was she happy in the U.S.?

I became offended at their questions. Surely, the Kagitas had enough grief.

Then the questioning took an ominous turn.

"Does Wade play with the little Kagita girl?"

"Not much. She's too young."

"Does he ever roughhouse with her?"

"No, they don't really play together."

"Would you say he has violent tendencies?"

I didn't answer for a moment. "No."

"We talked with a neighbor, Mr. James Morley. He said Wade knocked his son Jimmy off his bike. On another occasion, Wade tried to push Jimmy into the slough. According to Mr. Morley, your boy was very aggressive."

I felt a kick in my stomach. *That son of a bitch.* I pictured Morley's scraggly graduate-student beard, his pale blue eyes behind round spectacles, his high voice.

"Would you say Wade's aggressive very often, Mr. Lesley?"

"No. He's not aggressive."

They exchanged glances.

"Mrs. Kagita said Wade was responsible."

I was stunned by her accusation. A dead child was a horrible, unthinkable event, but to accuse another child. . . . I couldn't believe she had made such a statement.

"He was with me. We were looking for Yukiko together."

"We'd like to talk with him."

"He's taken his medicine and he's sound asleep."

"What kind of medicine?"

I didn't want to say Ritalin for hyperactivity. "It's a doctor's prescription to help him sleep. I'm not going to wake him up."

"Tomorrow morning then. Ten o'clock."

Convinced Wade had no part in Yukiko's drowning, I allowed them to take his boots and muddy clothes.

Two days later, in my presence and that of a lawyer, the officers questioned Wade out by the culvert. They tried to trick him into saying he'd been involved.

Some children, especially damaged children, appear guilty. Wade wasn't cute. Clumsy, awkward, skinny, he was a dark child from a hardscrabble reservation. Anytime Wade thought he was in trouble, his shoulders sagged and his lower lip hung out. He squinted his eyes and twisted his face.

To make matters worse, his imagination ran wild. According to the doctors, he frequently couldn't distinguish actual events from dreams or fantasies. For two days, tales of Yukiko had been circulating at school and at the housing complex. I had no idea what Wade would say, but I prayed they wouldn't trap him.

Finally, perhaps in an effort to please the police after an hour's questioning, he told them he was playing by the water when she fell off the culvert into the slough.

"Did you jump in and grab her?"

"It was scary. I couldn't see the bottom."

"Did you yell for help?"

"She made a bad sound. I saw bubbles."

"Did you run for an adult?"

"I found a stick, but she couldn't grab it. I reached out."

"So you didn't go in the water?"

"You're supposed to reach out with a stick." The lawyer finally spoke. "Every lifeguard knows that."

"She stopped moving even when I touched her with the stick. I felt bad."

"What happened next?"

"A whale came and tried to push her onto shore. But she sank. The whale didn't have arms, so it couldn't lift her."

"This water isn't very deep. A whale couldn't swim in here."

"It was a small whale."

I wanted to laugh and cry with relief. The cops had tried to trick him into a confession, but he gave them a whale story.

The lawyer conferred quietly with the police for ten minutes.

"I think that's all for today," the lawyer said. "Maybe you should take the boy somewhere like a park, play catch or go on the swings. Relax."

Off the hook.

The Kagitas didn't sue the university for having an attractive nuisance. They tried to resume their lives. The university spent

$70,000 to put up a cyclone fence so children couldn't get near the slough. The coroner ruled death by accidental drowning.

Off the hook?

The ambiguities linger. When a child, particularly a peculiar child, has been accused, shadows hover over the incident.

Was Yukiko in the water when I looked? Darkness was settling in and the slanting rain disturbed the surface. Could I have missed her?

The day after the questioning, I explored the area and found a stout stick, perhaps five feet long, jammed into the culvert's wire screen. Did the stick lend credibility to Wade's account? Or had some other child left it there?

When I showed it to Wade, he said it was a cool stick and he used it to whack for rabbits in the weeds. He played alone the rest of that fall because the other children shunned him. It saddened me to stand in the kitchen window and see him, a solitary child in the far fields.

"Is this the stick you held out to Yukiko?"

His face darkened and his mouth twisted. "Dad, that was a pretend story."

"So you weren't there when she fell?"

He squinted his eyes. "Not me."

■ ■ ■

After Yukiko's death, I tried to avoid Mr. Kagita whenever I saw him walking my way at the university. I couldn't bear to see the grief on his face or in his posture.

Even though I remained 99 percent certain that Wade hadn't had anything to do with Yukiko's death or even witnessed it, the event haunted me. I felt that I could have prevented it if I had only stayed by the culvert or positioned one of the other searchers there, thus preventing her from approaching the water.

I was also certain that Mr. Kagita wouldn't agree with me, and I always admired him for not seeking to punish my boy somehow.

The last time I spoke with Mr. Kagita, we ran into each other in the student union. It was shortly before spring break, and I was planning on going to Florida with Wade. I looked forward to driving through the South, sunning on the beach, perhaps trying my hand at surf fishing. Wade loved the ocean.

I had just mailed some postcards and turned around to see Mr. Kagita watching me. He wore a yellow button-down dress shirt, a modest blue tie, and a thin navy jacket.

Before I could speak to him, two boisterous coeds raced by. One said, "Hey, Mr. Lesley. Where are you going for spring break?" She was Leah Gallagher, one of my students, who majored in marketing. She was extremely pretty and never seemed to have a care in the world.

"Florida," I said.

"That's where *we're* going!" She laughed. "Maybe we'll see you there."

"I'll be looking for you," I said before she fell in with some other students and headed for the door.

"So young and happy," Mr. Kagita said, watching them leave.

"Yes," I said, wondering if people like Leah ever experienced sorrow.

"And how is your boy, Wade? Okay in school?"

"He's doing pretty well," I said. "He's still in special-education classes for the learning-disabled, but his tutor thinks he'll be able to read pretty soon." The tutor had talked of an imminent "breakthrough."

"I hope he will be a good student," Mr. Kagita said. "Will you take him to Florida?"

"Yes," I said. I was more than ready to get out of Amherst. It had been a hell of a year, but far worse for Mr. Kagita, I knew.

"Oranges and alligators, I think. I read about each state before I came to America."

"Oranges and alligators. You've got that right. And sunshine. I hope it's warm." I paused, then asked, "And what will you do for spring break?"

"I will go to Japan and see my wife and parents."

"That's good. It's good to see family." I didn't know whether or not I should have said "family." Of course, his family had been devastated. "Please tell Mrs. Kagita hello from me."

He had a faint smile. "I will see her this Sunday."

Then his face grew serious again. He reached out, taking the sleeve of my jacket in his small hand. "I want Wade to be a good citizen, Mr. Lesley. Please, you help him grow up to be a good citizen."

I was surprised both by the request and his earnest demeanor. Suddenly, I felt Mr. Kagita's unfathomable sorrow, and I had a wild urge to take him out drinking until we were both oblivious. "A good citizen. Yes, I want that, too, very much."

His eyes glistened. "A good citizen."

I took one of his hands in both of mine. "I promise to do all that I can. Thank you."

He nodded. "Thank you." He bowed slightly, then walked away.

"I'll do my damnedest," I whispered, knowing already the heaviness of the burden, the importance of the promise.

21

HARDMAN

When sheep ranching and gold prospecting had flourished, Hardman had been two towns—Raw Dog and Yellow Dog. No one knew for certain where those names came from, but one story had it that two prospectors fought their dogs over a land claim, and the yellow dog chewed the other one raw. Eventually, as the territory became more civilized, the residents wanted postal service, but the U.S. Postal Service wouldn't deliver mail to a town named either Raw Dog or Yellow Dog. As a result, the settlers grudgingly agreed to call the town Hardman, after Dave Hardman, the first postmaster. Still, most old-timers refused to call the town anything but Dog Town.

At a distance, Hardman, sitting on a dry and windy ridge, appeared to be a ghost town from a B Western. Up close, the impression remained, although half a dozen lights flickering in the bare windows of scattered houses and trailers suggested a few of the ghosts still hovered. Three paintless shacks had broken children's toys lying in the snow, and blackened stalks of corn by two banged-up trailers suggested the occupants once hoped for a garden.

Some places featured abandoned cars and rusty farm equipment, long past use, a few torn mattresses and sofas dragged from
half-burned houses. Stacks of spare tires hinted that some of the
old vehicles ran at one time.

As I drove through the tiny settlement, I remembered that
Raylene had grown up here. Where? All the places reeked of
poverty and isolation. None looked as if it had ever been prosper-
ous. When my father drove through in the '51 Olds, that flash of
chrome against the weather-beaten backdrop must have sparked
hope in the pretty fifteen-year-old. Her circumstances had been
desperate, and she thought of my father as a way to change them.
Now, desperation had driven me to the same territory, with my
own guarded hope. I had decided to stop in Hardman on the way to
Monument to get the lay of the land from Rudell's brother Hoot.

In Hardman, the most prosperous-looking place belonged to
my uncle Hoot and aunt Marie, who lived in back of the old Hardman general store. Although the store had been closed for five
years, the building still had faded white paint and a large orange
Union ball hanging over the leaning porch and rusted gas pump.

The front door, which opened into the store itself, was padlocked. Peering through the plastic-covered window, I could see
scattered items on the shelves: rat traps, Drāno, aluminum foil. I
figured Hoot and Marie had used up canned goods like tuna fish
and chili years before.

A narrow path through the tall woodpiles led to the kitchen
door in back of the building. No sign of Hoot, but Marie was
mashing potatoes at the kitchen stove. I knocked.

When she answered the door, Marie wore a puzzled look, as if I
were a stranger stopping for directions.

"Marie? I'm Craig, Rudell's oldest boy. From his first marriage."
As recognition lit her face, I added, "I'm on my way to see him."

"Why, of course. I see the resemblance. Grandma Lesley always showed us your birthday pictures. She came once a year, regular as rain. You must remember her cinnamon rolls."

"Made your mouth water," I said.

Marie stepped back. "Come right in. It's pneumonia weather

out there. Hoot will be so tickled. He and Charcoal, his favorite cat, went to check on the Baxter brothers down the road. LeRoy broke his knee falling on the ice."

I saw snapshots of grandchildren and a black cat on the refrigerator.

"My boy, Wade, is out in the pickup."

"Don't let him frostbite. I'm fixing elk roast. Hoot shot a spike this year."

The elk smelled good.

"Just to let you know, Wade's my foster son. I should warn you, sometimes he gets a little wild."

"Sounds just like a boy," she said. "That's why God invented belts."

"Listen," I told Wade after I returned to the pickup. "We're going to visit these people a little while."

He squinted. "Do I know them?"

I shook my head. "My aunt and uncle—Hoot and Marie. I want you to be on your best behavior."

"Hoot! Hoot! Hoot the Coot! Hoot like an owl!" He threw himself against the backseat of the pickup and kicked the dash with his black cowboy boots. He stopped. "Why don't I know them?"

"They live way out here. We never came this way before."

"It's too far. I hate riding this far. My butt hurts."

"So get out. Marie's going to feed us supper."

Wade looked around the empty town. "Do you think we'll see wolves?"

"Maybe. With wolves, you never can tell. Hoot and Marie have a cat named Charcoal."

"I don't like that name." Wade's brow furrowed. "Can I call him Charlie?"

"Why not? Maybe he'll like it." I didn't want any trouble with the cat. I didn't know what to expect. I took Wade's shoulders with both hands. "Now you treat the cat gently. No rough stuff. Do you understand?"

He nodded vigorously. "Just pet the cat." Then he asked in a loud voice, "Can I throw him sticks?"

"No, you throw sticks to dogs—not cats. Besides, I don't want any windows busted out."

Wade brightened. "Man oh man! You should have seen old Sarge jump through that window. Like Super Dog. Crash! Big smash-a-weenie!"

I gripped his shoulders tighter until he winced. "No more of that stuff. I mean it."

He didn't answer for a minute. "There was a monster. A monster was attacking Sarge and I stabbed it. The monster was trying to hurt Sarge." He closed his eyes as if remembering. "Now I know. The monster jumped out the window and Sarge chased it away so it wouldn't hurt me."

The psychiatrist had said that any event Wade imagined, or what he dreamed, would seem as real as the event that had actually happened, but I couldn't let this wild story go without a challenge.

"Think about it, Wade. You stabbed Sarge. Burkee and Otto had to take him to the animal doctor to get his thigh fixed up. Don't you remember? Sarge had to wear that funny plastic collar to keep from biting himself. You hurt him, Wade. I don't know why, but you hurt him, and nothing like that's going to happen again."

With his eyes still closed, Wade began speaking, but the voice sounded far off, almost like a bad telephone connection. "Wade didn't hurt Sarge. Sarge and Wade are friends."

My ears started ringing from the cold and Wade's odd tone.

His eyes opened wide. "I saw the monster. You weren't there, and Burkee and Otto were gone, too. Nobody was there but me, so I wish you'd shut up, Dad. Just shut up about it!"

I let go of his shoulders and slapped his cheek. A red blotch appeared. He flopped prone on the seat and began to cry.

I slammed the pickup door and stood stiff in the cold, watching the boy inside as if he were miles away. I stood until I felt the biting wind ease my hot anger.

"Craig."

I turned. The wind whipped Marie's apron and lifted her cotton housedress above her knees.

"Hoot and Charcoal just got back. Aren't you coming in?"

I forced a smile. "We're on our way. The boy's putting on his cowboy boots. He's proud of them."

"All right, then. We don't want supper to get cold." She turned back toward the kitchen.

I opened the door and grabbed one of Wade's scrawny calves above the boot. "I'm sorry. I shouldn't have done that. When you hurt Sarge, it really made me upset."

Wade didn't say anything, but he had stopped crying.

"Let's go inside. Hoot and Charcoal just came back. Let's go see Charcoal."

He scrambled out of the cab. "I just pet Charlie."

"The truth is, Rudell feels puny all the time," Hoot said.

Marie shook her head. "He's on the far side of yonder."

We were sitting at the table drinking coffee after supper. Wade had gone outside to check the woodpile. Hoot had outfitted the boy with elk-hide gloves and a red wool cap that kept falling over his eyes. "It's the smallest size I got," he had said. Charcoal padded through the snow, investigating the newcomer. After sitting on a round of wood, Wade lifted the cat onto his lap and petted it.

"Right now, Rudell looks older than I do," Hoot said. "And I got a dozen years on him. Myself, I'm running on DMSO. I get it from the horse doctor in Heppner."

"Makes sense," Marie said. "You're stubborn as a mule."

"All your dad does is sit bundled to the chin in that trailer. Keeps the woodstove blazing so hot I sweat the minute I open the door. Complains he's cold every second."

Marie looked out the window. "That boy's sure hitting it off with Charcoal. They're thick as thieves."

"He likes animals," I said, relieved they were getting along.

Hoot continued. "They had Rudell a week up to the Vet's in

Walla Walla and couldn't find a thing wrong. Run a bunch of damn tests and came up zero."

He knuckled the tabletop. "I took him down a bottle of DMSO, and we rubbed it into his knees and shoulders. He had a bad cough, so we rubbed some Vicks and DMSO on his chest. After awhile, he coughed up that poison."

"Hoot and the DMSO got him on his feet," Marie said. "Forget the doctors in Walla Walla."

"Elk camp bucked him up; too. Rudell shot this big old cow down the Hell Hole right behind the Sunflower Flat camp. I own it now, but Rudell still hunts there sometimes."

"Did he have a cow tag?" I asked, more curious than critical.

"Well, Rudell's not big on formalities." Hoot rubbed his cheeks. "Getting that cow sure cheered him up." Hoot turned toward Marie. "Speaking of cheer, where's that bottle of Dr. Tichner's? This coffee is a little weak." He stood and began searching through some bottles in a cupboard above the refrigerator until he found a plain brown bottle full of amber liquid. "Ahhh. Dr. Tichner's varmint medicine. Good for gout, lumbago, and droopy eyes." He turned to me. "Just what a young man needs. Guaranteed to make the ticks back out and the crabs abandon ship." He poured about two fingers in my coffee cup.

Marie's face tightened. "Don't you go talking like that, Huston Newton Lesley. I swear you've been out in the sticks too long. I know you and those Baxter brothers tell some risqué stories."

He ignored her. "What do you think?" Hoot asked.

I sipped the doctored coffee. I had tasted lots worse. "The ticks are showing a white flag." I had another sip. "Is Tichner a real doctor?"

"Hell, we've never had a real doctor out here. Tichner sets a few bones over in Long Creek. When a wife shoots a husband, he gets patched up over there. Saves the county a lot of grief. Tichner's got his own way of doing things, but he won't give out the varmint medication recipe. Fermented juniper berries. I know that much." He added another splash to my coffee.

"Speaking of varmints, I'm convinced they're Rudell's problem. He's been trapping wild things all these years, and one gave him mountain fever."

Marie began washing the last of the dishes. "Just to see Craig will do him a world of good."

We heard a *chunk* outside as Wade threw split pine sections on top of the woodpile. "Work's good for the boy," Hoot said. "Anyway, my bursitis won't let me stack wood these days."

"Why don't you stay the night?" Marie asked. "Start out for Monument when you're fresh. We got bunk beds."

I started thinking that Wade might be calmer in the morning. There was no predicting his night behavior. After the stimulation of a full day, he might overload and go haywire. Other times, he'd toss fitfully all night. Still others, he'd conk out. I couldn't find a pattern.

"Rudell doesn't have a phone," Hoot said. "You can call Bacon Elder and he'll take a message."

"I think I'll surprise Rudell," I said.

"He'll want to see Wade," Marie added. She hung up the dish towel embroidered with STARDUST LOUNGE. RENO, NEVADA. Looking out the window, she shook her head. "I swear. He attacks that woodpile just like our kids used to. But they were never so thin. If Wade stuck around here, I could put some meat on his bones."

Hoot shifted in his chair and squinted at Marie. "Honey, I think we're past raising children."

Marie clucked. "Time races by so fast. Well, I better go put more blankets on those beds. Sometimes when the girls come back for Christmas, the grandkids sleep on the bunks like their mothers used to." She opened a big wooden chest beside the sofa and took out some colorful wool blankets. I figured they were seconds from the mill in Pendleton.

"That sofa makes into a bed," Hoot said. "It gets kind of elbow-to-elbow in here."

"Where do the girls live?" It seemed odd that I knew nothing about my cousins.

"Jenn has a nice restaurant down near Hubbard," Marie said. "It's close to where you teach."

"I'll have to try it."

Marie went into the spare bedroom and I offered to help, but she said, "A man would just be in the way. No offense."

While she fussed with the blankets, Hoot tipped his head closer to mine. "Keep an eye out for Brandy."

I sensed a warning. "Who's Brandy?"

"Well, you might call her Rudell's 'sleepy-time gal.'"

This was a development I had never thought of. My father had left my mom, and Raylene had taken their kids and run off. Now someone named Brandy had entered the picture. Aunt Sally had never mentioned a Brandy. "Does she live with him?"

Hoot nodded. "Only when he has money. Rudell gets his government disability check the first of every month. Brandy shows up regular as the postman. She and Rudell toss a little hoo-haw for a week or ten days, but when the money's gone, she slips away. She's got another bunkie in Long Creek. He's even older than Rudell."

Marie called from the bedroom. "Hoot, sometimes you best keep your mouth closed."

He leaned back, spreading his hands. "I'm just saying my piece."

I tried picturing Brandy. Most likely, she resembled one of the desperate women I found who were willing to watch Wade. Women without skills, hard pressed for some cash.

"I'm not pretending to like her. She'll clean his bones like a vulture. That's how she is." Hoot gripped his coffee mug. "Rudell's little head is doing the thinking. She used to be a looker. Still thinks she's hot stuff."

"I get the picture."

Hoot studied the calendar hanging above the stove. It said IONE GRANGE and had a four-point buck leaping over a fallen birch. "Twentieth of the month. Most likely she'll be scratching her itch in Long Creek."

"Thanks for the warning."

"What are relatives for?"

• • •

That night after he showered, Wade went to his bunk and quickly fell asleep. Charcoal snuggled up beside him, and the boy slept soundly.

I lay awake, sweating a little from the coffee and liquor but listening to the woodstove's hiss and snowflakes ticking against the single windowpane. Cold air leaked around the window, so I threw another blanket from the chest over the cat and boy.

For a while, I studied the outside landscape, which was illuminated by the harsh farm light. A barn with a hayloft, an old blue pickup missing a tailgate, three cords of split pine. Thinking of this simple place, I stood convinced Wade might get by here without constantly finding trouble. Hard work gave him a more peaceful sleep than a pile of prescription drugs could. Tomorrow, I'd see my father and decide how he and Wade might get along. Hoot said my old man had been feeling puny. No doubt Wade could help him build fence, set traps, and do any odd jobs around the place—as long as he had a little instruction. He was wiry, but he was strong.

When I closed my eyes, thoughts of Brandy intruded, and I imagined how she might look. Rouge, mascara, a slash of lipstick, dyed red hair. I opened my eyes, trying to shake the image. Wade might have a long shot with my father. But then someone named Brandy would show up. Damn slim chance of Rudell and Wade hitting it off, even without Brandy.

22

MONUMENT

Given its isolation, you won't find Monument unless you search hard. The town lies 250 miles east of Portland, and only a secondary road leads in or out. The 140 citizens, give or take a few, live seventy miles from a barbershop, cup of espresso, or law enforcement. The last fact made it particularly attractive to my father and his cohorts.

Monument consists of modest, inexpensive homes, double- and single-wide trailers, muddy cars and trucks, dozens of mongrels and sheepdogs. In spite of the town's plain appearance, the views in any direction are breathtaking. Majestic basalt columns break the tawny mountainsides; colorful ocher and blue-green volcanic deposits shoulder out of the rugged landscapes.

In summer, yellowbells, violet birdbills, balsalm root, and lupine decorate the lush grass. Greater Canadian geese blanket the green alfalfa fields along the surging North Fork of the John Day River. Red-winged blackbirds cackle in the cattails.

At night, coyotes ring the town and isolated farmhouses, calling mournfully to one another while trying to lure away the fam-

ily dogs and cats. I can't accurately describe the millions of stars—
but let your eyes adjust to the dark for five minutes and you'll see
farther into the night than you imagined possible.

"I've got all this," my father Rudell once said at dusk while
standing a few steps from his shabby single-wide Spartanette
trailer. "And I don't have to pay for it." He flung an empty Heidelberg can toward the growing pile thirty feet in front of the
trailer. "Even the stink is free."

We stood upwind from his skunk gland and dead fish coyote
bait, essential for trapping. The stench was undeniable. But so was
the beauty.

■ ■ ■

On my first trip to Monument, the one with Wade, I had no idea
where my father lived. A mile from town, I saw a solitary woman
jogger wearing yellow tennis shoes and a bright blue sweatshirt
with a Nike swoosh—not exactly what I'd imagined finding on this
isolated stretch. After pulling the pickup to the side of the road, I
leaned out the window so she'd know I wanted her attention.

As she approached, puffs of steam came from her mouth, and
she seemed irritated at having to slow down. "What is it?"

"Can you please tell me where Rudell Lesley lives?"

Jogging in place, she shook her head. "He lives here in Monument?"

"Last I heard."

"Sorry. Ask Jerry at the store. He knows everyone."

Maybe she wasn't a longtime local, but in a town of 140 people, I took her inability to know my father's place as a bad sign.
But then, he had never been one to socialize or go to church.

At Boyer's Cash Market, Jerry Boyer knew my father well.
Rudell maintained a charge account there for his gas, beer, and
grocery items. His credit was good and he always paid near the
first of the month after he received his disability check.

In addition to providing groceries and gas, the market served
as the nearest liquor store and dry-goods store, carrying every-

thing from jeans to Acme boots. On the spur of the moment, I asked the owner what the most unusual item was he'd ever carried.

After thinking a minute, Jerry said, "Bow ties. The clip-on kind." Once he had ordered a card carrying a dozen ties, but they hadn't sold. "It was just a whim," he said.

Rudell's place lay downslope from the county power coop on a flat patch of land owned by Bacon Elder. According to Jerry's directions, you parked above the place and walked a footpath past a broken gate toward the small trailer with an attached lean-to. No dog to worry about. The coyotes had killed it three months back.

Rudell's aging trailer was silver and chartreuse. A 1958 Jeep Gladiator pickup, half-rusted away, sat out front. Beyond the Jeep, nine power mowers rose from the weeds. As Wade and I walked closer, I could pick out brands: Montgomery Ward, Sears, one John Deere.

Wade whistled. "Look at them cool mowers. Can I mow the lawn?"

"There's no grass. Nothing but weeds."

"Then why does he have all them mowers?"

"Somebody's fixing them up." Mower parts lay in upturned hubcaps and two-pound coffee cans. Nicked blades lay scattered in the grass.

"Maybe I can drive that truck."

"Stay out of it. Anyway, it's time to meet my father. You can call him Rudell."

"Is he my grandfather?"

"Only if you stretch it."

On one side of the lean-to, a blue plastic tarp covered a cord of firewood. An empty cable spool made a crude outdoor table, and rounds of firewood served as chairs. Hamm's beer cans lay in an arc about sixty feet from the trailer door. A similar arc of empty Tab cans spread out twenty feet closer. Between the two, a dog bowl lay upside down.

"I don't like this place," Wade pinched his nose. "Something stinks."

"That's just the septic tank, or maybe a cow barn someplace." I studied his face a second, wondering if he had ever lived in a sorrier-looking shack on the reservation.

The trailer door banged open and my father stepped onto the crooked porch. "Are you hungry, Professor? I got stew on." He squinted at Wade. "Bring the boy in. I don't want him messing with those mowers."

Rudell had lost some weight, so his flannel shirt seemed oversized. His hair was graying and thinning more, and his dark complexion had a sallow tinge. But he still moved with the lanky ease of someone who had worked outside most of his life. He came off the steps and shook hands with us both. "Good to see you, Professor." He clapped Wade's shoulder. "This kid's a string bean, but he's tough." He looked directly at the boy. "Hoot says you're pretty good at stacking wood."

"I'm double strong," Wade said.

My father looked fairly strong himself. He seemed to be recovering from whatever ailed him.

Inside, the trailer smelled of wet wool, a hot woodstove, and spicy stew. Rudell had placed a pan of water on the stove to increase the room's humidity. The pan's bottom was crusted with hard minerals.

"Do you live here by yourself?" Wade asked.

"Unless I get lucky." Rudell winked at me. "Sometimes company comes around."

"Why you got all them lawn mowers out there?"

"Ormand, your dad's brother, went and took a course in small-engine repair. He can fix damn near anything. Lawn mowers, weed eaters, siphon pumps, two-cylinder motors. He's a crackerjack."

I was a little jealous of the way my father was bragging up Ormand. "Those mowers are all torn apart."

"He's waiting for parts from John Day."

I hadn't counted on my half brother. Aunt Sally had told me he was living in Weed, separated from his wife and two kids. Of course, I hadn't asked about him for a couple years. "Will he be around so the boy can meet him?"

Rudell shook his head. "He went south to California. They owe him back pay at the county lockup. Anyway, I needed a break. Ever since he got religion, he's been thumping the Bible at me."

"Hey, look," Wade said. "Here's old Mom and Tiffany and me when I was little. You, too, Dad." Wade pointed to the picture on the refrigerator. It showed the family shortly after he'd arrived from the reservation. Following a church service in Estacada, we had posed in Sunday dress-up for a photographer in Oregon City's shopping mall. Payette wore a bright green spring dress, and her thick, shoulder-length raven hair shone. It stung me to see the photograph.

"I miss Mom and Tiffany," Wade said.

"I hear she went south on you," Rudell said. "Sally told me."

"Deep south."

"She was a looker." He half-smiled as he studied the picture. "You know why they call women that?"

"You tell me."

"Because they're always looking for someone better."

A joke. "Well, she's still looking then, I guess."

My father served three helpings of stew in green plastic cereal bowls. "I made this a week ago, but stew keeps."

"It's too darn spicy," Wade said.

"Eat some bread with it." Rudell ripped a fist-sized chunk from the loaf and handed it to the boy. "And don't complain about the grub." He sopped up some of the stew with his own bread. "You fellows eat hearty. We got a chore to do tomorrow morning. I planned to leave tonight, until Hoot called Bacon and he told me you was coming. What took so long anyway?"

I shrugged. His tone was critical, as if we had held him up somehow. Getting to Monument was my business and I'd do it in my own time. "We took the river road through Spray and Kimberly. Hoot said I couldn't get over Sunflower Flat with a two-wheel drive."

"Out here, you need a four-wheel drive, so we'll take my

truck." Rudell stood and took a bottle from the shelf beside the stove. "DMSO. Funny how you rub it on, then taste garlic."

He took off his flannel shirt and rubbed DMSO on his elbows. "I'd be crippled up if it weren't for this." He put some on his shoulders. "Did you see them beer cans out in front?"

"I saw them."

"That's how far I could throw until I got stoved up. After seeing the doctors in Walla Walla, I quit drinking beer like they said, so I started on whiskey and Tab. But I can't throw those Tab cans half as far. So much for getting cured."

His skin seemed a little loose, like someone who's lost weight. Even so, I could see the muscles ripple in his arms and shoulders. His chest was small but muscular, too, maybe from setting traps all those years.

When he finished doctoring his elbows, neck, and knuckles, he returned the bottle to the shelf and put on his shirt.

"You fellows better grab your sleeping bags. We'll head out for that chore in the morning."

"What chore?" I asked.

"Let's get some shut-eye. Tomorrow we'll form a posse."

I woke up just a little after two and felt the flannel sleeping bag liner against my cheek. At first I thought the coyotes had awakened me with their mournful night cries, but then I heard music playing far off. It remained indistinct, but after awhile, it grew louder. Old-time country music sounding scratchy and tinny like a cheap radio you might hear in a metal shop or school bus depot. When the song finished, I heard voices and laughter, both men's and women's. Maybe my father had country-western tapes he'd bought at a truck stop—tapes of a live performance. As the music started again, I tried recognizing the voice—Merle Haggard or Johnny Cash. No, someone older—Bob Wills or Bill Monroe maybe. Whoever was singing sounded good, but the music made me feel hollow, too, the way it sounded so long ago.

Wade slept huddled in his sleeping bag. The music hadn't disturbed him. Curious to locate the sound, I eased out of my bag and slipped on my clothes. I hadn't seen a radio in the kitchen or front room, but perhaps Rudell had one in his bedroom and was pulling in a megawatt night station from Modesto or Reno, Boise or Billings. Whatever it was, this station didn't sound local, nothing like the little one-room, edge-of-town places that give weather and read farm reports. On some clear nights, I remembered listening to San Francisco talk radio out here in lonesome Eastern Oregon, and I felt strange hearing those distant voices like next-door conversation, until they faded into yonder.

Coals glowed in the woodstove. Distracted by the music, I knocked my knee against the large round of sweet pine that served as a coffee table. Then I was in the kitchen, and the sound seemed to be coming from outside. I looked for a passing car with its radio on, but couldn't see one. In the distance, Monument's single streetlight illuminated the gas pumps at Boyer's store and two pickups in front of the Elkhorn Tavern. I peered into the closer dark. Maybe a night walker carried a radio, but I saw no movement.

Suddenly, a hand gripped my shoulder, and I dipped and whirled, heart leaping.

"Take it easy, Prof." My father's drawl. "You're acting like a city slicker—afraid of the coyotes."

His breath smelled of coffee, whiskey, and throat lozenges. When he flipped on the light, I saw he was wearing a yellow sweatshirt with the words PRAIRIE CITY DUCK SHOOT and a pair of old green pants.

"Let's have a Seven and Seven," he said, reaching for a bottle of Seagram's. "Then you'll hear the sandman instead of the coyotes. Hope you don't want ice. The freezer's on the fritz."

After he made the drinks, I took a couple swallows—sweet and strong at the same time.

"I guess your music woke me up." Now I heard a woman's voice, clear but distinct. "Isn't that Patsy Cline?"

His eyes narrowed. "Could be. I can't tell for sure."

"It's Patsy." I could make out the faint words: "Crazy for thinking that my love could hold you."

He crossed over to the trailer door and flung it open. Cold air blew in and the music grew louder still. "Outside," he said—both an affirmation and a question. "Come and listen."

I leaned out the trailer door to hear better, and a shiver ran through me—something other than cold. "Maybe someone's got a radio on. Or they have a satellite dish and are pulling in a country channel."

He handed me his red-and-black-plaid coat from off an elk-antler hook. "Go on and look. Then you tell me."

"Shoes," I said. I didn't want to step on nails or splinters, maybe Ormand's mower blades out in the unkempt lot. Slipping into the bedroom, I got my shoes and fumbled into them. Wade stirred, took a stretch, then settled.

As I stepped onto the front porch, worn bare by boots, my father said, "Listen good."

The music shifted: It seemed to be coming from my pickup. "Shit," I muttered, fearing Wade had snuck out and turned on the radio. That would be just like him. "If I have a dead battery . . ." At least there were jumper cables behind the seat.

However, as I approached the truck, the music shifted again, sounding farther away, up toward town. I walked two blocks in the cold night air, trying to locate the source. A couple of thin dogs slunk past. My breath came in silver puffs.

No music, but something scratching, like the lead to a tape or the sound a needle makes before the song. When the music started again, it seemed to be coming from the back of the trailer.

"What do you hear out there?" my father called. He stood, a black silhouette filling the trailer door.

"This is some bullshit trick," I said. "You've got me chasing a goddamn snipe." I strode to the trailer's door. "What's turned on in there? A tape player?" I stopped to listen.

"Not me." He took a slug. "I don't hear so good."

Radio voices now came from the back side of the trailer. Again, the laughter. I stepped onto the porch.

He shifted his frame so I could shove past him. I opened his bedroom door, but nothing was playing inside. "Nice joke."

He lifted both arms as if surrendering. "I swear it ain't me, Prof. I think it's Ormand's mowers acting like radio antennas."

"Sure thing. And I've got Modesto coming in on my molar fillings."

"Ormand's mowers," my father said again. "Maybe it's the way he's ripped out their guts."

In spite of my reluctance, I listened out the door again. Maybe the sound was coming from the mowers, but it sounded far away and eerie. "Sons of the Pioneers," I said. "'Ghostriders in the Sky.'"

"It started out awhile back," my father said. "Give me the heebee-jeebies. Nothing but old tunes. He sat in his chair, then leaned back. His lips moved and I heard him sing just above a whisper.

I was surprised that he sang so well, and I recognized the words to "Blue Moon of Kentucky" by Bill Monroe. As Rudell sang the line, "Shine on the one that's gone and proved untrue," I wondered if he ever thought of the time he left my mother.

When Rudell finished the first verse, he frowned. "Your uncle Martin liked that one. He was singing it a lot before he got killed."

I nodded but didn't say anything. Martin is my first name, one I've never used, because my mother didn't want me to be nicknamed "Marty" and my father figured it was bad luck. Still, he had wanted to honor his brother when he named me.

The music had stopped. I waited for it to start again. Nothing. I checked my father's bedroom once more, then leaned out the trailer door. I heard only the usual night sounds.

"Someone turned off the switch," my dad said. "I don't care what you think. Ormand swears the mowers pick it up like antennas."

"What do you think?" I asked. An old memory stirred, but it was of my mother singing, not some night music in a two-bit town.

"I think we better hit the sack. Tomorrow we got to look at busted fence line."

"'Blue Moon of Kentucky.' I think Mom used to sing that, but never too loud. She almost kept it secret."

He cocked an eyebrow. "That's not like Hazel."

"You probably went dancing with her some when you were in the service."

"Hell. Everybody knew that song back then. Anyway, we was in Mississippi, not Kentucky. Hattiesburg."

"Mom told me it was so hot and sticky she couldn't get her dress over her head after work. It just clung."

"It was mighty hot. I don't remember any trouble with the dress."

"The army houses were small and full of cockroaches. She had to use a washboard for the clothes, and the tap water came out murky. Half the time the electricity was out." I was waiting for my father to say something more about those days with my mother.

Rudell stood and stretched. "Winky-blinky. Time for some serious shut-eye."

"You used to take her dancing on paydays. She told me all about it."

He looked at me straight on. "Your mother was never short on talk."

23

MARTIN

Reading about your death in the newspaper creates a strange sensation—a kind of chill similar to the one that comes from stepping on a grave.

My uncle Martin C. Lesley, the man I'm named for, was born in 1905 and killed in 1919, at the age of fourteen. It always struck me as ironic that his shooting and my accident both happened when we were about the same age. Maybe the name Martin has bad karma for the Lesleys. I'm glad I've always gone by Craig.

Cedric Scharff, an unstable citizen of Monument, killed Martin. Newton Lesley, my grandfather, had warned Martin and his friends to stay away from Scharff. Before the killing, Scharff had threatened town boys for trespassing on his land, stomping through his watermelon patch. Some he had chased off with a rifle.

Although sternly warned, Martin was "easily swayed," according to my aunt Sally, who was eight at the time of the shooting. Bill Elder, the brother of my father's friend Bacon Elder, convinced Martin to go duck hunting, even though it was August. The boys planned on doing a little swimming at the same time.

They started crossing Scharff's watermelon patch to get to the river. With that slight provocation, he fired on them. Bill and the other boys escaped, but Martin's legs shattered with Scharff's bullets. He lay helpless, bleeding in the field while Scharff chased the others.

Newton was away on one of his gold-mining excursions, but after hearing of the shooting, Martin's older brother, Hoot, seized a rifle and stormed into the yard, where he was intercepted by his sisters Clarissa, Dora, and Manila. The three girls struggled to take his rifle away.

Meanwhile, a group of men raced to help Martin. They managed to load him into a wagon and started off for Condon, the location of the nearest doctor. On the way, he died.

Other townspeople seized Scharff and hurried him away to the Grant County jail before my grandfather Newton received word and came to kill Scharff himself. Hoot managed to find another gun and went after Scharff, but by the time he reached Scharff's place, he and his captors were gone.

Given that no person in Grant County was ever found guilty of murder until 1998, after a logger beat a policeman to death with a table leg, I'm certain either Newton or Hoot would have been exonerated had they managed to kill Scharff.

As it was, Scharff received a seven-year sentence for manslaughter, serving only five before he was released. The *Blue Mountain Eagle* of March 24, 1919, recorded this strategy by the defense: *The defense was that the defendant shot more to scare the boy than inflict a wound, and further, that the wound was not necessarily a mortal one but was due to improper medical treatment.*

The paper further stated, *In view of the fact that the jury returned a verdict of 'Guilty' the points of the defense were not established.*

Shortly before the shooting, Martin had been measured for his first suit, one intended for weddings, church events, and school functions. The suit did not arrive in time for the funeral and my uncle was buried in a borrowed suit.

By the time of Scharff's conviction, both my grandfather and my uncle Hoot had settled down a little. The *Blue Mountain Eagle* carried this assessment of the trial and Martin's death, written by my grandfather:

> *I found the jury and all concerned to be composed of honest, sincere men whose only aim was to arrive at a conclusion that would uphold the sanctity of the law and administer justice fairly and impartially.*
>
> *As a father, I wish to say that my son Martin was a lad that caused me very little trouble. He was obedient, bright, and considerate and what I considered a very good boy. He was much interested in his schoolwork and popular and well liked by his companions.*
>
> *He was thrifty and industrious. And although only 14, by his own endeavors had accumulated $40 of which he had invested in thrift stamps and which he had refused to cash although tempted by his boyish desires.*
>
> *And so, permit me to say, deploring the homicide, as a father can, that I was greatly impressed by the honest efforts of able and sincere men to administer justice and to uphold the sanctity of the law. —Newton Lesley*

If anything, I was puzzled by the reasonable tone of my grandfather's letter. He was known for having a temper, and he had witnessed vigilante justice in Idaho and Alaska. In Monument, he served at times as Deputy Sheriff.

When I asked my father about the letter, he just shook his head and told me I didn't know anything about trapping. "That letter was a lure, bait to make Scharff think everything was okay and bring him in. The old man wanted to kill Scharff right up until the day we buried him.

"After they released him from prison, Scharff did come back. He hung around Boyer's store, acting right as rain. Said he found the Lord while in prison and was serving Him by preaching at a little church out of Salem.

"If the old man had been here, he would guarantee Scharff got to serve the Lord up mighty close, but the bastard's luck held. The old man was prospecting for gold in Alaska, and Hoot and I were off hunting. Scharff walked out of town. Any other time, they'd have carried him out."

"Why didn't your father track him down and kill him in Salem? Or you and Hoot could have done it later on."

"I'd kill the son of a bitch any day of the week in Grant County. But kill him in Salem, and you might wind up in the hoosegow."

24

LONG CREEK

My father sat thin-lipped when we came to the line of downed fence. He gripped the steering wheel and slowed after we had followed the fence line about a hundred feet, stopping where the tire tracks crossed the fence and continued past the big trees toward a clearing.

"Here's where the sons a bitches went in." Rudell drove forward, following the line another fifty yards until the posts were upright again, the fence intact.

We got out to take a look. Wade mimicked my father's grim look and stiff-legged walk. "Them sons a bitches." He thrust his hands in his pockets. "Them are sons a bitches, right?"

My father leaned down to examine one of the freshly sawed juniper posts. The earth was torn where they had run the chain saw into the dirt. "Piss-poor woodcutters."

From where we stood, we couldn't see the trees they'd taken off this section of Tom Slater's place. The woodcutters could get fifty dollars a cord in Baker or LaGrande, maybe more if they found a doctor with a woodstove. A doctor wouldn't want to wreck his hands sawing wood.

"This ain't the half of it," my father said. "This section's always been bad luck."

"Why did they drop so many fence posts?" I asked. "Five or six would let them take their rig in and out—no problem."

My father looked at me. His gray eyes had turned cold. "Just for meanness maybe. Or because they don't like Tom Slater. When you get big, you got enemies. But Tom and I go way back. I built him this fence, guaranteed. Now I got more work."

We were out there because Slater was in the hospital recovering from double hernia surgery. Mrs. Slater had called Rudell the day before when she heard chain saws and gunfire up on the mountain.

My father fingered some of the sawdust. "When the sheriff catches those boys, they'll probably claim elk rubbed down the fence."

The two of us got in the pickup and drove back to the tire tracks—Wade ran alongside the downed fence, shouting, "Sons a bitches!" My father left the pickup on the road so he wouldn't foul the tracks. He squatted beside them, studying the double sets of tread marks, light ones going in, heavier ones coming out. Something about the heavier ones caught his interest. A few dark spots stained the ground.

"Too thick for coffee." He took a dirty handkerchief out of his back pocket and dabbed at one of the spots. Then he stood and held it out for me to inspect.

"Blood."

"Well, it's not barbecue." He put the handkerchief in his pocket.

I was pleased because his tone told me I'd guessed right. Still, it had been fairly easy—because Virginia and Otto had showed me all the bloody spots from Sarge before he jumped through the window. "Somebody poached a deer, maybe an elk."

He squinted at me. "If you're wrong, will you buy dinner?"

"Why not?" I doubted I was wrong.

Wade picked up on the conversation. "Oh boy, oh boy! Somebody shot a deer. Where is it?"

"Follow these tracks," my father said, pointing to the tires'
trail.

"Careful there." I didn't want Wade running off, getting too
excited or lost, but he raced ahead—whooping like a wild man. I
heard magpies jabber and rise in the far clearing.

Wade screamed. The scream was followed by a deep blurbing
sound. Panicked, I started to run ahead. Maybe someone was up
there wounded, left to die—or murdered.

"The boy chucked his cookies. That's all," my father called after me.

I found Wade leaning against a small ponderosa, supporting
himself on the rough bark with his right arm. As I approached, he
threw up again. Tendrils of vomit hung from his mouth.

Three piles of guts; three black cow heads with gaping eye
sockets where the magpies had picked them clean; seven legs;
gouts of blood everywhere. The cow heads had yellow ear tags.

Olde English malt cans, cigarette butts, potato chips, and
bloody Cheez-It boxes littered the ground. A watering trough and
salt lick stood close by. Wade came over and threw his arms
around me. Some of the vomit wiped against my shirtfront.

"Hell of a party," my father said, studying the wreckage. "Those
bastards shot the cows when they came to water last night. They
probably read in the *Blue Mountain Eagle* that Slater was laid up."

Wade let go and staggered away. He spit three times to clear
his mouth.

I looked at the watering trough, but my father shook his head.
"They'll have it all bloodied from washing up. You don't want the
boy drinking out of that."

Wade spit two more times. "Bastards," he said. "Bastards." His
voice cracked.

My father studied the ground, but he didn't pick anything up.
"They took the shell casings so the sheriff can't match the caliber."

"He can get fingerprints off the beer cans," I said.

"I doubt it. They were probably wearing gloves."

At the edge of the clearing, lots of sawdust and bucked limbs
lay on the ground.

"They cut their wood, then waited for the cows. After they shot and gutted them, they sawed them into quarters, threw wood on top and drove out. The dumb bastards didn't bother taking the hide off the meat. Damn sorry butchers. Most of that meat will go sour."

"I feel bad for the old cows," Wade said.

My father pointed to the remains. "How many legs do you see?"

"I don't know," Wade said. He thinned his mouth.

"Can't you count?"

"I can count, almost to a hundred."

"Well, count the legs. Tell me how many."

Wade walked closer to the guts and legs. His mouth moved as he counted on his fingers.

I still counted seven. Maybe the others were under the guts. I didn't want to look real close.

Wade came back. "Seven. Six or seven."

"Seven legs," my father said. "How many should there be?"

"Seven?"

"For three cows?" Rudell chuckled. "They must be pretty crippled up."

Wade didn't say anything.

"Listen, Wade, how many legs does one cow have?" I knew he had trouble with abstract concepts, and without actually seeing a cow, he probably didn't know.

"Not seven?" He nodded for emphasis. "Not six, maybe?"

"Jesus, he's thick," my father said under his breath.

"Let him figure it," I said, warning in my tone. "There's a way to do this."

With a stick, I drew four lines underneath an oval, representing a cow's body. At one end of the oval, I drew a rough head, a small tail at the other. "Pretend this is a cow. Count the legs. One, two, three, four. Four legs. Two in front and two in back."

"Four legs." His face brightened. "A dog has four legs."

"That's right. Good." I drew two more ovals and sets of legs. "How many heads are over there?"

He turned and counted. "Three."

I drew the other two heads and tails. "Three cows. Count all the legs now."

When Wade figured out five legs were missing, he went to look for them.

"Those yahoos had a leg-throwing contest," my father said. "Sailed 'em into the woods."

While Wade was looking, Rudell walked over to the cow heads. He took a large Ka-Bar Stockman's knife from his pocket and cut off the ears with the yellow tags. "Slater can get the numbers off these. Figure out which beeves he's got missing."

Wade had found three of the legs and carried them back to the bone pile.

"Something's seriously wrong with him," my father said, eyeing Wade. "He's real retarded."

"He's got learning problems." I resented my father's using that word. "He's been slow, but he's improving."

"That boy don't know which nostril the booger's in." My father slipped the ears and tags inside his jacket pocket. "Couldn't you have any of your own kids?"

I jammed my hands deep in my pants pockets—so I wouldn't strike him.

■ ■ ■

By the time we ate dinner, I had cooled off. "How did you know they didn't shoot a deer or an elk?" I put more sugar in my coffee.

The waitress cleared our plates. "Did you save room for dessert, hon?" she asked my father.

"I never pass up something sweet, Connie. Cherry pie sounds fine. Unless you got banana cream."

"Not today," she said.

"I'll try cherry, too," I said.

Wade had gone outside the Long Creek Cafe to watch the pickups and trailers loaded with firewood gas up at the Texaco.

My father blew on his coffee. "Blood was coming out the

trailer, so the meat was loaded on the bottom, wood on top. That means rustlers."

"But if someone did some elk poaching, they'd hide the meat, too."

Rudell shook his head. "Not out here. Everybody poaches, and whatever law there is looks the other way. It's poaching or hungry kids. The wardens got that much figured. And no one but a block-head rustler would bruise up good meat by piling wood on top."

The waitress brought the pie and refilled our coffee cups. Out-side, a trucker was letting Wade try on his cowboy hat, but it was too big.

My father continued. "I knew that watering trough was there, so I figured rustled cows. Somebody knows the place." He took a bite of the pie. "The cook's name is Elegant," he said. "Out in this country."

I had a couple bites of pie. It tasted good. I wondered if Elegant was a first name or a last.

"Funny what you remember," Rudell lowered his voice. "Tom Slater washed the blood off his hands in that same watering trough thirty-five years ago."

"Was he butchering cattle?"

My father looked around the restaurant, but no one was pay-ing attention to us. One old rancher at the counter played the punchboard.

"I want that deer rifle you got," the guy told Connie. "I must've spent over fifty dollars punching this thing."

"This could be your lucky day, Raleigh," she said.

"Maybe. I've got something in my pocket," he said. "It's good for a punch."

"I don't want to see it," she said. "And watch your mouth."

My father wiped some crumbs off his chin. "Slater and his brother-in-law Archie Peck hated each other. In those days, that section was Archie's land, but sometimes Slater let his cattle graze over. No fences back then. Archie took the whip to them, once he caught on, drove them till they dropped.

"The bad thing was Slater's sister Stella. She married Archie—

liked his wild streak, I guess—but then he took the whip to her. Slater called him a downright coward. It was at a grange hall dance, so lots of people heard.

"That night, their fights kept getting broke up by other ranchers, but Archie was insulted. He challenged Slater to a duel and they agreed to meet a week later."

"A duel," I said. In my mind, duels were Southern.

"Slater had this Luger semiautomatic he'd taken off a German soldier he killed. For seven days, he practiced with that thing. Archie Peck drank and raised hell and blustered about killing Tom. Neither would back down.

"Slater asked me to be his second, and Archie got the Henderson kid. Well, he was a kid back then—another wild one. The four of us drove out to that same section where we found the cows. There's a nice meadow, just a crow's hop from where we were today. At dawn, red-winged blackbirds started singing in the cattails. While the sun came up and we saw a doe drinking with her fawn, I said to myself, 'No one's going to die today, if I can help it.'

"Slater and Archie stood back-to-back in that meadow. Each man had a rifle and a pistol. They could use either one of them.

"The Henderson kid's job was to make sure they didn't turn and fire too soon. He was counting paces. When they got twenty steps apart, I had this big rock to drop on the pickup hood. When they heard the clang, they could turn and fire. But I didn't plan on dropping the rock until they were a good stretch past twenty. That way, I figured one might just wing the other and that would stop the nonsense."

My father had finished his pie and the old farmer had gone outside and driven off without winning his rifle or getting any satisfaction from Connie. She brought the check, then stood gossiping in the back with the cook named Elegant. I wanted to order a to-go piece of pie for Wade, but I was so caught up in my father's story, I forgot.

"I guess they were counting paces themselves. The Henderson kid stopped counting at twenty, and the duelers each took about two more steps when Slater called out, 'Drop the rock, Rudell!' and Archie added, 'Drop it now, you son of a bitch!'"

"So I dropped it. Damn, but it was loud." My father took a sip of coffee, then set the cup down and studied his hands, as if he was wondering how he could have let the rock drop.

"Time slowed. It seemed a long while before I heard the first shot from Archie's thirty-thirty and saw Slater flinch and go down. He was on his knees, and then he dropped completely to the ground as Archie fired again. Dirt flew in front of Slater's face.

"'Shit. It ain't over yet,' the Henderson kid said.

"Slater lay out prone, a small target, steadying that Luger, and he started firing carefully. Pow . . . Pow . . . Pow. Archie pitched forward and lay still. Slater fired two more times, but he missed.

"'Tom!' Archie called out. 'Let's not duel anymore.' Something was wrong with his voice.

"'Goddamn you, Slater!' Henderson yelled. 'Hold your fire!'

"'We better go see about patching them up,' I said.

"Slater was moving toward Archie then, crawling low, like a crab. 'Don't try anything, you bastard!' he yelled. 'I got more for you here!'

"Archie just rolled away from his rifle and lay on his back, staring up at the blue sky.

"'Can you believe this shit?' Henderson said to me. 'I'll bet we have to take them both to Doc Wolff. He'll do some sewing and chew their ears off for this nonsense.'

"It bothered me the way Archie was just lying there, and when I got closer, I saw the hole in his shirt and blood bubbling as he breathed in and out. He had a hole in his thigh, too, but that one didn't matter much.

"Slater still held the pistol steady. 'You shot me in the ribs, Archie.' He was pumped, running on adrenaline.

"Archie opened one eye and smiled ruefully. 'I think you killed me, Tom.'"

My father turned toward the window and some truck's lights illuminated his face. He looked haggard. "I reckon we all knew then, when I saw Archie bleeding the same way I'd seen my buddies bleed in France. None of them made it. Lung shots just kill you a little slower.

"Slater stuck the Luger in his belt and dug in his shirt pockets for fixings and paper. He managed to roll a cigarette, get it lighted. He blew out the match and handed the cigarette to Archie.

"Henderson was propping him up then, trying to keep him from drowning in his own blood. Archie puffed twice on the cigarette but gave it up. 'You tell Stella I'm sorry about the whipping. Will you do that, boys?'

"We all nodded. Slater pushed Henderson aside and propped Archie's back against his knees. 'You can tell her yourself, later on.'

"'I'll do that,' Archie said. But it was just bluff. 'Listen, Tom. I want you to have this section. Go ahead and run your cattle. Feel free.'

"Archie was dead before that cigarette burned down, but I'll never forget his last words. 'Feel free.'"

My father continued the story after they locked the doors of the café. "When Archie's eyes had turned dry and pebbly, we carried him to the bed of the pickup and covered him with a tarp. Slater took off his shirt and folded it under Archie's head. At the trough, he washed off his hands and wet his T-shirt to use as a compress. He was oozing blood and his rib was broken, but it was bleeding clean. All the way to Heppner, Slater kept asking, 'What am I going to tell Stella?'

"When Doc Woolf dazed him with chloroform, Slater said, 'Archie and I seen our mistakes now. Neither one of us wants any more dueling.'"

After Rudell and I loaded Wade in the pickup, we drove toward John Day to tell Slater the news about the rustlers. On the way, Rudell explained that they had tried Slater for manslaughter, even though everyone knew a Grant County jury would find him not guilty. Slater told his version of events; Henderson and Rudell told theirs. My father had been surprised when Henderson claimed that Slater had shot first. After that, for thirty-five years, Rudell and Henderson passed on the street without speaking or looking at each other. Slater inherited the section later, after my father supported his version.

At the hospital, Rudell introduced Slater to me and Wade. The old man didn't look much like a killer. He seemed to be shriveled and carrying a lot of pain from his double hernia surgery. When my father handed him the ears and tags, Slater's face grew dark and somber. I imagine he was thinking about that section of ranch and the bad luck that dogged it.

Wade fell asleep on the seventy-mile trip back to Monument. Both my father and I had bought large coffees to go at the Sundowner. The coffee was bitter, tasting as if it had been brewed hours before.

"So what are you thinking about?" my father asked me when we hit Kimberly. "I know you're thinking something."

His features were visible in the dashboard's lights, but I couldn't read them.

"He's not a city boy," I said.

My father didn't answer at first. Then he said, "Who the hell is, except you maybe?"

"I was thinking he could stay here and help you out for a while. I've kind of hit a rough patch with my life."

Rudell checked to make sure Wade was sleeping. "I don't know why you went and bit off so much gristle. Life's tough enough."

"He didn't have anybody else," I said. Maybe that would give my father something to think about.

He drove by a small ranch and two sheepdogs came out to bark and snap at the tires. "I'm going to kill them one of these days. Donny Capon can't control his damn dogs."

We'd hit the outskirts of Monument and the farm machinery shop when my father said, "I guess the boy and I can try batching together—for a while."

I felt some relief. Even a respite from Wade would help me to clear my head, make some better plans. I was hoping he'd do okay in Monument, at least for a while.

When the pickup lights shone down the hill toward my father's trailer, I could see a bronze Ford Ranchero parked in front.

Someone had opened the broken gate and driven through. The Ranchero had painted flames surging from the wheel wells and a bumper sticker that read HOT STUFF. I DRIVE LIKE THE DEVIL. The cartoon devil held a pitchfork.

"Well, look who's here," my father said. "I must be pretty hot stuff myself."

No one had to tell me it was Brandy and she'd come ten days early, before my father collected his disability check. I figured she'd heard about me and was protecting her territory.

"Who is it?" I asked, even though I knew.

"You'll get a kick out of Brandy," my father said. "She's a real live wire. And she's crazy about kids."

"I look forward to meeting her," I said, trying to sound sincere. However, I feared that all my hope had come to bitter disappointment. Deep in the marrow of my bones, I knew nothing was going to work out, and I felt sorry for Wade, but mostly for myself.

25

BRANDY

"He's as handsome as you are, Rudell." Brandy laughed and hugged me in a too-familiar way.

Her breasts were soft and pillowy, but her arms were muscular, as though she was used to hard work. She smelled like beer, cheap perfume, and broasted chicken. The whole place smelled of cigarettes.

Turning to Wade, she tried to hug him, too, but he ducked away. "And who's Mr. Shyface?"

"Leave me alone!" Wade's mouth twisted and he edged toward the bedroom.

Brandy tried to sustain her enthusiasm, but her voice dropped a notch. "He must be Craig junior. Isn't he cute?"

"He's a foster kid that lives with Craig," Rudell told her. "He's an Indian."

"Well, isn't that nice?" She stretched her mouth into a wider smile. You'll get used to Aunt Brandy soon enough."

She gave my father a big kiss and hug. "So what have you boys been up to? A little road hunting? I got here and no one was around, so I just made myself at home."

Rudell hung his jacket on the elk-horn coatrack. "We've been looking at some country," he said.

"We saw four dead cows!" Wade said. "We saw their heads and their guts, and I carried some of the legs."

"Is that true?"

My father nodded. "Slater had some rustlers."

"And him all laid up like that. How'd he take it?"

"He took it kind of hard," my father said. "But he took it."

She nodded. "He's a tough old wrangler."

I thought she might be referring to his killing Archie. In these parts, I imagined everyone knew something about it.

"I'll bet you boys are hungry. After work, I stopped at the Grubstake and got some of their broasted chicken." She nodded toward grease-stained paper bags on the table. "It took longer than I thought, because they tried to give me all dark meat. Can you imagine! Here I am one of their best customers and they try and pull a stunt like that."

She was getting more agitated. "If they keep treating customers like dirt, there's no way they're going to get any repeat business."

"They are unless you're willing to drive to Baker," Rudell said.

She ignored him and looked at me. "I've been thinking about starting my very own restaurant. I can cook. All I need is a decent place and a little start-up money." She gave Rudell a hug. "When are you going to get me a little start-up money?"

He smiled slowly. "I'm working on it. I got a gold mine."

"That Big Creek place is all but give out," she said. "Kaput. Anyway, I can cook up a storm. Darrell, that's my first husband, we had a place in Boise called DB's. D for Darrell and B for Brandy. We were working like troopers but doing okay. Then Darrell went and got himself killed in a car wreck. And, see, we'd been so busy with the café, he never got around to taking out insurance." She spread her hands. "He left me high and dry."

"How'd he wreck up the car?" Wade asked. "Was he spinning out, doing wheelies?" He paused. "Do you like the *Dukes of Hazzard?*"

"Black ice," my father said, more to me than to Wade. "Just

north of Long Creek. Black ice is nothing to fool with in these parts."

"The strange thing is how slow he always drove." She shook her head. "The way he farted along so slokey-pokey used to drive me crazy. I wish I could take back some of the mean things I said to him. Why was I so impatient?"

Rudell put his arm around her. "Darrell knows you didn't mean it. Now you got me."

It surprised me to see my father show what seemed like genuine affection.

"I know I'm a lucky woman," she said. "I suppose this is what God wants for me."

In some ways, I couldn't imagine God wanting any woman to be with my father, but then I thought, here I was trying to get him to watch Wade for a while. That's what I wanted, whether God was for it or not.

"I'm really hungry," Wade said, and everyone turned to look at him. "I don't want stew. Is that chicken for me?"

"Of course it is, sweetie." Brandy put on a big smile for him. "I heard Rudell had company and I said to myself when I got off work, 'Brandy, you pick up some chicken and slaw before you head out to Monument.'"

"Who's Brandy?" Wade said.

"Well, I am. I meant I was just talking to myself."

"Do you have corn on the cob?" he asked.

"Honey, it's not summer. You can't get corn on the cob unless it's summer."

"Wade must think he's still in Portland," Rudell said. "Going out to someplace fancy." He raised his voice a little as if it would help the boy understand. "This isn't a restaurant. You better eat what you got and be thankful for it."

"He's not fussy at all about food," I said. "He just likes corn on the cob."

"You better wash your paddywhackers," Brandy told Wade. She took some plastic plates out of the cupboard and put them on the table.

Wade just stood watching her. "Well, go on," she said.

"She means go wash your hands." I took his shoulders and steered him into the bathroom. "Wash them good after carrying those legs."

"Am I going to get cow flu?"

"No one's getting anything. That's why you're washing your hands. Look, I'm washing mine real good." I demonstrated the hand washing, then gave him the soap, a yellow Fels-Naptha bar.

"Do you boys want light or dark meat?" she called. "We got lots of both."

"Wade wants a couple drumsticks. I'll go for light."

The little table was cramped when we sat down. We concentrated on eating. All of us were hungry. Wade finished both drumsticks and then two thighs.

"Eat your vegetables, too." Brandy pointed her fork at the coleslaw.

Wade made a face. "Too sour."

She sprinkled a little sugar on the slaw. "Try that. I never got my own boys to eat salad without sugar."

Wade tried it but spit most of a mouthful back onto his plate. "It's icky."

My father's face clouded.

I set down my fork, annoyed that Wade wasn't eating the slaw. Usually, he went for it. "Don't spit food onto your plate. It's bad manners. Now tell Brandy you're sorry."

He hung his head but wouldn't say anything.

"I'd cuff him," my father said.

"I know it's store-bought," Brandy said, "but it was hard-earned money that bought it."

"I'm full," Wade said. "I can't eat any more or I'll go pop like a balloon."

"Maybe you are full, but don't spit out good food." I gripped his shoulder. I hated it when he put me in this kind of position. "Tell Brandy you're sorry."

He twisted his bony shoulder, but I wouldn't let go. Wade squeezed his eyes shut. "Wade is sorry. Wade is a bad boy."

I released his shoulder, although little had been gained.

Brandy lit a cigarette and squinted at the boy. "Maybe he wants to be excused."

"Go ahead," I said. "Go outside and play a little before bedtime. Put your coat on."

As he took his coat off the antler, Wade looked out the window. "Dark," he said. Turning to Brandy, he asked, "Are you staying here all night?"

She blew out some smoke. "I thought I would. You got anything against that?"

"You don't have a bed," he said. "Hey. Maybe you can sleep on the floor with us. Do you got a sleeping bag in your truck?"

She laughed. "Honey, I forgot it at home, so I think I'll just sleep with your grandpa."

Wade seemed to consider this. His gaze moved from Brandy to Rudell. He cocked his head to one side. "You're going to sleep in the same bed with my grandpa?"

She put down her cigarette. "Sure looks that way. I forgot my sleeping bag."

"How come, if you guys aren't married?"

Rudell snorted.

Wade pursed his lips and started making loud smacking noises. "Oh, sweetie, sweetie. I love you, sweetie." He looked at me. "I'll bet they're too old to fuck, right, Dad?"

My father rose from his chair, but I was faster. I grabbed Wade's arm and yanked him toward the door.

"You better talk to that boy," Rudell said. "You better get that kid under control."

After opening the door, I glanced back at Brandy. "I'm sorry." She didn't answer.

"Don't let Wade near her truck!" my father said.

Thirty feet from the trailer, Rudell had a small shed with a broken door. Inside were his traps, tools, coyote stretchers, an old V-8 engine, and a couple of come-alongs. Outside were two empty wooden cable spools and a small stack of straight juniper trunks for fence posts.

"Sit right there." I indicated one of the cable spools.

Wade sat, head drooped, and kicked the bottom of the spool with his heels.

"You know better than to talk like that!"

"Them old people sleeping together—it's gross."

"It's their business, not yours or mine."

Wade shook his head. "Those cow heads were gross, too. Where were their eyes?"

"I don't know. I guess magpies picked them out."

Wade focused on the juniper. "What's he want all that wood for?"

"He builds fence. He'll cut those into fence posts."

"Where's his chain saw? You need a chain saw to cut posts."

I didn't know how Wade knew about the chain saw, but when he observed things and made connections, it gave me hope. "Maybe he loaned it to somebody. Maybe he borrowed one."

"He doesn't have a chain saw or any money. He's just an old fart."

■ ■ ■

I took Wade's bicycle from the back of the pickup. "You need to work off a little steam before you come back inside."

He blew small clouds of breath. "Look how cold it is. You can't leave me outside."

"Twenty minutes. And when you come back in, watch your mouth."

"Twenty minutes," he said. "That's better than an hour, right, Dad?"

"A lot better," I said.

Inside the trailer, I apologized for Wade's language.

"It's all right," Brandy said. "I hear worse every night at the Mother Lode." She lit another cigarette. "I used to work at a day-care center," she said. "I been around all kinds of kids. Right off, I could tell that boy has some problems."

"His mother's drinking affected him."

She nodded. "He's some retarded."

"Some retarded!" Rudell slapped his knee. "He's slower than molasses."

I winced at the word *retarded*. I tried not to use it when referring to Wade. At that time, the doctors believed that children like Wade were just emotionally handicapped and would catch up with lots of good nutrition and love. The Fetal Alcohol Syndrome diagnosis would come later.

Brandy looked out the window. Wade was doing his best to ride his bicycle through the snow, but he couldn't spin out or do wheelies. She smiled. "He's a regular little fireball, ain't he?"

"They say he's hyperactive," I said.

"I don't mind hyperactive," she said. "It's a lot better than the kids that just sit all day with long faces. At the day care, we knew which ones the parents beat on. A lot of times, they was sad cases."

"Did you turn them in to the authorities?" I asked.

She squinted at me. "What authorities? This is Grant County, not Portland."

Wade rode his bike down the hill and crashed into the stack of juniper posts, but he was going too slowly to do any damage. He got off the bike and rammed it into the posts three times, until he'd knocked two off the stack.

I got up and went to the door. "Put those posts back on the stack!"

"I hope you didn't pay full price for that bike," Brandy said.

"I got it secondhand," I said, even though I'd purchased it new at the Schwinn shop in Oregon City. I was afraid my father might hit me up for a loan if he thought I had money. My mother had said he was always tin-cupping somebody.

"We got good bikes at the pawnshop where I worked in Bend," she said. "I got first crack at lots of good merchandise. Bikes, guitars, record players, chain saws. We even had a saxophone for a while. I liked working in the pawnshop. I'd just pretend I owned all that stuff."

"There's no point in paying out top dollar," Rudell said. "I bought good rifles at that pawnshop. A Penn reel. I had me a chain saw, but someone ran off with it. Now I use Bacon's."

She leaned back in the chair and put her arms around her knees. "I sort of miss the pawnshop, except when the cops came sniffing around for stolen goods. What a hassle! How am I supposed to know if something's stolen or not?"

"Do you get much stealing around Bend? I thought it was full of doctors, architects, and business people."

"Honey, there's some that would grab your underwear, if you took it off for half a minute."

Wade wheeled the bike up to the pickup and put it in the bed. Then he went down to the pile of posts and began kicking the snow off.

Twenty minutes was up.

When Wade and I went back inside the trailer, Brandy and my father were smoking cigarettes and drinking beer.

"Rudell and I were talking while you were outside." Brandy tipped her beer can toward us. We think both of you should come up to elk camp next fall. I'm the cook, so the trip is worth it—just for the grub."

"You'll come back with meat," my father said. "Now there's no guarantee it'll be from a bull, but cows are might tasty."

Wade looked at me. "Can we go, Dad? I want to shoot an elk."

I didn't trust Wade around guns and was surprised my father even brought up elk camp. "We'll see," I said, remembering the promise I'd made to my mother about not hunting with my father.

" 'We'll see' means we won't get to do it," Wade said. "I know that."

"You're not supposed to shoot an elk until you're fourteen," I said. "A couple years from now." Even though it wasn't the truth, I figured it was a good stall.

"He could stay in camp and help me cook," Brandy said. "You and your dad could go hunting."

"Hoot and I will show you the ropes." My father studied the boy. "We could have old Wade here hike through the canyons and chase the elk right to us."

"Wade can help chop firewood," Brandy said. "We always need big fires up in elk camp to keep us warm. If a cold front comes down from Canada, it might drop to twenty below."

"Your piss freezes to your pecker," my father said with a laugh. "Anyway, Wade would probably get scared out in those dark woods."

"I'm not afraid of anything," Wade said.

"Big talker," my father said. "What if you ran into Bigfoot?"

I didn't think Wade knew about Bigfoot, but he surprised me.

"Hell, I'm not afraid of any ape," Wade said. "I'd shoot it deader than a doornail."

"Tell him about that time Bigfoot came to your camp," Brandy said.

I was curious about this. My father had lived out in the woods all his life. If anyone ran into Bigfoot, it would be him.

My father smiled at the attention. "I admit I was some spooked, especially when Jackrabbit John's big dogs crawled under the cots in the tent, shivering and yelping. The way that critter made cowards of those big dogs was something to see."

"What kind of dogs?" Wade asked.

"Two Dobermans," my father said. "John thought he was a good dog handler, and he was training those two to be guard dogs, but I think they were ruined after that night. Rock and Roll. That's what he called them.

"Anyway, me and John was up Cupper Creek building fence. We did it right—split the juniper posts, dug the holes, looped and stapled each strand of barbed wire.

"Some nights we went down and fished. Caught supper. We coated them in Krusteaz and fried them in bacon fat. Nothing tastes better than fish cooked right out of the stream like that, unless it's fresh elk liver with Walla Walla sweet onions."

"Rudell can cook," Brandy said.

Rudell brought his beer can to his forehead as a kind of mock salute. "Anyway, we'd been up there about a week when we moved onto a stretch of land that just felt funny. It made my skin tingle. The dogs got jumpy, too. Each time John took Rock and Roll for a walk, they put up a fuss, whined all the time, and wanted to go back to camp.

"Then one day, while we were fishing, we run across trees that were broke off funny. A bunch of them. Hell, we thought it was just blowdown or a big bear knocking over trees, looking for grubs and honey. That's what we tried telling ourselves.

"But finally, John said, 'Don't look like no bear done this.'"

"Sometimes Bigfoot knocks down trees to mark his territory," I said. "Was that it?"

My father squinted at me. "Who's telling this story? Me or you?"

"You are."

"Then don't go rushing me."

Sometimes my father's slow way of talking made me impatient, but I had to remember he'd lived in Monument most of his life. There was seldom any hurry.

He lit another cigarette. "So about two in the morning, we woke up with a start. Something was stomping and shaking the tent.

"'We might have us an earthquake,' I told John. See, Mount St. Helens was acting up and there were lots of earthquakes, although not usually around Monument."

"'Rock slide,' John said. 'A huge boulder banging downhill.'

"That didn't sound exactly right, but we were tired and went back to bed."

"Bigfoot was stomping around," Wade said. "Bigfoot was trying to scare you off."

Rudell nodded. "That's what we think now. The next night, we heard the thumping again. John jumped out of bed and grabbed his thirty-thirty. He just kept it around for camp meat. The rifle was so old, there was more blue than barrel."

"I'd shoot that Bigfoot," Wade said. "I'd shoot it right in the face for waking me up."

"I didn't want John to shoot," my father said. "I was afraid he might wound a bear or a big ol' cat with that thing and we'd get attacked.

"'Don't get too excited, John,' I told him. I got a big lantern out and shone it around the camp. That's when I saw these yellow eyes, nothing like a bear's. Big yellow eyes, larger than a cat's eyes or anything else I knew. And right then, I smelled a horrible stink. Even my rotten fish coyote bait smells better."

"That's hard to believe," Brandy said. "I've never smelled anything worse."

"'That's a damn Bigfoot,' I told John. 'If you fire that peashooter at him, you'll just make him mad.'

"John didn't say anything, but I think he was kind of glad I told him not to shoot."

"I would have shot," Wade said. "Then I'd get out a knife, if I had to. I'd carve old Bigfoot up like a pumpkin." He made fierce stabbing motions.

"Settle down, Wade." I was thinking about Sarge.

"I'd carve him up like those cows."

I took his shoulder. "We get the idea. Now let Rudell tell the story."

My father chuckled. "I guess we should have had you along, Wade. But if you're so brave, how come you threw up when you seen them cow heads?"

"Those were icky. That's different."

I wondered what real evidence my father had. I had always wanted to see Bigfoot. "Did you see it again?"

He shook his head. "We built up the fire. Huge. We piled wood on because we wanted to keep that thing away. We kept that big fire stoked up all night.

"In the morning, we found places where the ground was all tore up, but we couldn't find a distinct track—nothing like those plaster casts you hear about.

"I found a tuft of hair hanging from a strand of our barbed-wire fence. Maybe Bigfoot stepped right over that and snagged his crotch. The hair was dark reddish brown, with a little black and yellow thrown in. I wrapped it in wax paper. Later I gave it to one of the forestry guys in John Day. He promised to send it to the wildlife boys at the college by where you live."

"What did they say?"

"I never heard back. That forestry guy moved down by Roseburg someplace. Got a promotion."

"So what did you think?"

"It could have been off a grizzly bear, I guess, but I never saw a grizzly around here. And I never saw that much ground tore up. A bear will tear up a few trees looking for grubs, but not half the damn woods."

"I'm sure it was Bigfoot," Brandy said. "Your father doesn't exaggerate when it comes to animals."

"Did you ever go back and try to find it again?" I asked.

He shook his head. "The weather turned sour on us. We finished the fence and hightailed before we got snowed in." He studied his hands as he turned the beer can around. "I wish I had seen it again, or had me a camera."

"I can't believe you didn't shoot it," Wade said. "You got no proof."

"We built the fire up to chase it out of camp. That was the best we could figure at the time."

"Maybe it wasn't Bigfoot at all," Wade said. "Maybe you got scared of an old cow."

"Wade, you're getting rude," I said.

My father thumped his beer can on the table. "I know damn well what I saw."

■ ■ ■

Once the woodstove had burned down, the front of the trailer grew cold. Wade burrowed so deep in his sleeping bag, I couldn't see his head. My father's snores came from the bedroom. It seemed odd that his snoring was such an unfamiliar sound. Most children grow up with their parents' night noises. I heard Brandy snoring, too, but softer than my father.

When I'd first started out for Monument, I didn't even know Brandy existed. At first, I thought she had come only to protect her territory, to make certain nothing got between her and Rudell. To be sure, she was rough around the edges, but it occurred to me that she might support Wade's staying with my father. She had seemed genuine in suggesting that Wade come up to elk camp. Somehow, I hoped that all of us might grow closer, in spite of our differences.

26

SNIPERS

"Get up!" Rudell nudged me with his bare foot. He was in his underwear. "We've got trouble."

For a groggy moment, I couldn't remember where I was. Monument, I thought. My father's trailer.

He crossed to the window, and flickering light from outside played across his face. He stood to the side of the window, holding a pistol.

When I looked outside, the stack of fence posts was burning. Fiery sparks rose into the night sky.

He pushed me away from the window with his free hand. "I don't want you getting shot."

"What's it about?"

"Somebody's out there behind the Jeep. Maybe Quint, Brandy's old boyfriend. That gutless chickenshit!"

She appeared in the bedroom door, a towel draped across her front. "What the hell's going on?"

"Someone lit up the place. Maybe Quint."

"It's not Quint. He doesn't have the guts. Anyway, I'd skin him alive." She stepped into the front room, but he waved her back from the window. "Where's Wade?" she asked.

"I forgot he was here." My father squinted at Wade's sleeping bag.

"Right here," I said. "He's so skinny he doesn't make much of a lump." When I threw the top of the bag back, he wasn't there.

"I guess it's not Quint," Brandy said. "I guess it's the boy set the fire."

"Wade doesn't set fires," I said, hoping he hadn't set this one. He had started a few small ones before. I wanted the arsonist to be Quint, but my stomach felt sick when I realized Wade's clothes and boots were missing.

"Son of a bitch," my father said. He picked up a three-celled flashlight and shone it out the window. "I can't spot him. I've got to go outside."

"What's wrong with that boy?" Brandy said. "He's retarded and mean."

"Bring me my boots," my father told her. "I don't want to cut up my feet on Ormand's shit."

I hurriedly slipped on my clothes and boots while my father got dressed. "Do you have a gun in the pickup?" he asked.

"No." I wondered what he was getting at.

"Are you sure? I don't want to step outside and get shot."

"I'm positive. He doesn't have a gun."

"All right." Rudell opened the door a crack and shone the light around the Jeep.

"Wade, I'm coming out," I said. Turning to my father, I said, "You can leave the gun."

"If he doesn't have a gun, I won't shoot." My father stepped out the door.

I was right behind him and tried to grab his arm, but he jerked it away and moved quickly toward the Jeep, playing the light around the tires.

A dark figure jumped from behind the Jeep and ran past Brandy's truck. I grabbed Rudell's gun arm with both hands, but he didn't try to aim the pistol. Instead, he tried to catch the running figure in the flashlight beam, but couldn't. Still, there was no question. I could recognize Wade by the flapping, scarecrow way he ran.

"Like a scared rabbit," my father said.

Closer to the fire, we found the dog's water bowl. My father picked it up and sniffed, then thrust it under my nose. "Gasoline."

A couple of the mowers had been tipped over, so I could tell Wade had drained their tanks, then taken the gas to the pile of juniper posts.

Rudell flung the bowl. It clattered off the empty doghouse. "You got yourself a damn firebug!"

I didn't have anything to say, so I thrust my hands into my coat pockets.

"I'll bring the wieners," someone called from the road. The man was carrying a flashlight.

"There's Bob Wells," Rudell said to me. "His wife is a big gossip."

Bob came down the hill. "You guys got buns and pickles?"

"We was toasting us some marshmallows and it got away a little," Rudell said.

"I can see that," Bob said. "We got a sick cat, and when Jamie got up to put her outside, she saw the burning and woke me up."

"It's not much," my father said. "Just some more cutting and splitting."

The three of us stood watching the fire. Although the heat blistered the paint on one side of the shed, the damage wasn't too bad. Still, I knew what my father was thinking. Wade was a firebug, and if he stayed in Monument, he'd set more fires.

"How do you think it got started?" Bob asked. "Say, don't I smell gasoline? You think someone lit you up on purpose?"

"Spontaneous combustion," Rudell said. "I should have known better than to have a bunch of greasy rags hanging around."

I slid a sideways look at my father. Him covering for Wade was hard to believe.

"Quint Harris has set some fires," Bob said. "It could have been Quint's doing." He scuffed at some of the ash with his boot.

"Everyone knows he lit those fires in Mount Vernon, but they couldn't get anybody to testify."

My father stared at the fire. "I thought it could be Quint at first, but now I don't think so. He knows I'd shoot him if I caught him messing around my place." He turned to look at Bob square on. "It was them greasy rags. Ormand's always fiddling with them mowers, tossing the rags into a pile."

Bob seemed disappointed that my father told him it wasn't arson. He probably wanted to bring some gossip home to his wife.

"Well, if you don't need any help, I think I'll try to sleep awhile before it gets light." Bob turned on his flashlight and started back up the little hill.

"Thanks for checking it out," my father said.

"I thought the whole place might be going up in smoke."

"Sorry to disappoint you," my father muttered. He turned to me. "If Bob had a lick of sense, he would have spotted Wade's tracks. I tried trapping with him one year. He can't find his butt in a bathtub."

"Thanks for not mentioning Wade," I said.

"I don't want the town to know I got a son stupid enough to take in a shitheel firebug."

I kept a flashlight behind the seat of the pickup, and I figured I could use that to track Wade. At least I'd be saved the humiliation of asking my father to use his light.

"Let's go have some coffee," my father said. "I expect Brandy's made some."

"I want to look for Wade," I said.

"Suit yourself, but if you wait for daylight, we can track him better."

I shivered. My father's tone suggested Wade was a convict or a wild animal.

"I need to find Wade now."

"Don't know what for. There's no bounty on him."

"He'll bolt when it gets full light." My father sipped his coffee. "Right now, he's holed up trying to stay warm."

I warmed my hands on my coffee cup. I had flailed around in the dark for an hour but hadn't found Wade. I was disgusted at my inability to find him, the folly of bringing him to Monument in the first place.

"Maybe he'll just come back here."

My father shook his head. "He'll bolt."

When the light became full, we drove into town in my father's Jeep. It was snowing hard and I was concerned that Rudell wouldn't be able to track Wade, but I didn't need to worry. We picked up fresh tracks near Boyer's Cash Market. Wade had spent the early hours hiding in a pickup parked there. Now he had started down the road toward Long Creek.

Oscar once said my father could track a one-legged midget through a shopping mall, and he was probably right.

"He's running," my father said. "See how far apart his tracks are."

The tracks were still distinct but filling with snow, and I was afraid we'd lose them. My father didn't seem to be in any hurry now. He had the Jeep in second gear and kept watching to see if the tracks veered into the fields or woods, but Wade had kept to the middle of the road.

"He didn't get much of a jump on us," Rudell said. "Maybe an hour."

"What if he catches a ride?" I asked.

"We're the first ones on the road," my father said. "If someone comes along, we'll flag them down and tell them not to pick him up."

I checked behind but there were no cars.

"I can pay you for those posts," I said.

"Let's snag the boy first thing."

"I'll make it good," I said. "Wade should know better."

It seemed strange apologizing to my father for Wade's behavior. His own behavior had been plenty shabby. Why had he run off and not ever shown up until I was fifteen and lying at death's door?

"I don't understand people that go looking for trouble," Rudell said. "Trouble is a part of things. You don't need to crawl through the brush, banging into more."

I knew what he was talking about. "You mean Wade?"

"That boy is going to come after you," my father said. "And if you ever have kids of your own someday, he'll come after them, too."

"Thanks for the advice," I said.

He ignored my sarcasm. "Sometimes you get a coyote or a lynx in a trap and they'll go for you—pull that chain right out to the end, snap at your hand or leg—try to give you some real hurt."

He stopped the pickup and opened the door, then studied tracks that led into a field. Climbing back in, he said, "Big dog. Probably Lee Olex's black Lab, Cola. I caught that dog once way up Resurrection Creek." He chuckled. "Cola was sure glad to see me. He'd been in that trap about four days, I figure. Had crapped himself out."

He shut the door and shifted into first, then second, and held it steady. "The thing is, you can tell when one of those critters will come after you. It's how they hunker, the turn of their head, maybe a flat meanness in their eye. They got one notion. To bring you hurt." His eyes cut toward me, then back to the road. "You got to keep your distance—stay back farther than the chain reaches—and nail them between the eyes."

I didn't say anything. Bringing Wade out to meet my father had been a horrible mistake. There was a good reason he'd been in nineteen different foster homes before he'd come to live with me and Payette. Nobody could handle him. Why had I thought I could?

The abandoned buildings of Hamilton came into view. They looked sad and weather-beaten. Who had lived there, I wondered, and why had they left? Barns that had once held cattle and sheep now tilted at odd angles, the doors open like gaping mouths. Most of the windows on the houses were broken out. Disrepaired tractors and farm implements lay scattered across the snowy fields.

Rudell stopped the truck. "He's in that place with the faded green paint. Or maybe he went out the back door and holed up in the barn behind it."

I could see a faint set of tracks leading to the front door of the green house. I wondered why people didn't keep the old places padlocked. No reason, I guessed.

"Why did he stop here?" I asked.

"He's winded. He stumbled a few times."

I started to open the door. "I'll go get him. He's probably scared to death."

My father put his hand on my arm. "He might have a gun. I don't want you walking out there in the open if he has a gun."

Suddenly, I knew where Wade might get a gun. Every rancher and farmer carried at least one in his rig to shoot coyotes or to poach. Wade had spent part of the night holed up in someone's rig. We should have checked. Even if I hadn't thought of it, my father should have. He fouled up, I thought. Both of us fouled up.

"Sit tight," Rudell said. "Maybe he'll come out on his own." He honked the horn four times, blasts that disturbed the silence. "He knows we're here."

"I hope he hasn't frozen to death."

"Now that he's quit running, he'll start to chill," Rudell said. He reached into his jacket pocket and took out a cigarette. When he offered me one, I took it, cracking my window just a little. My father lit his first, then offered me the match. After lighting mine he turned his face straight ahead as if he were watching the road.

"Did your mother ever tell you about shooting the Germans?"

"No," I said. "She told me you saw horrible things in the war." Perhaps she had been right. Maybe the war haunted him.

He spoke slowly, as if trying to get the story right. "Weather like this. Snowing all day long. Woods and fields, everything covered with snow. The Germans sent ski troopers covered in white, and they knew their stuff. I'll give them that.

"The day before, they had killed three guys from the next outfit. A bohunk from Milwaukie and a wop. I never heard about the third guy. Nobody saw the Germans. All of a sudden, three men dropped dead, and everybody else took cover. Nobody saw a thing. That outfit sent a messenger to our camp, giving us a warning. When I heard about the shootings, I thought the Germans might be sending ski troopers.

"I can see shades of white—snowshoe rabbits, ermine. Once I shot an albino deer in the dead of winter. The venison tasted the same as other deer. Anyway, I set up a tripod like a sniper and watched the fields the same way I look for game. I used snow goggles because the sun was bright. I was looking for white against white, but not quite the same shade.

"In late afternoon, when the light got tricky, I saw something white, but a different texture than the snow. It might have been a slant of light, so I kept watching, and after awhile it was closer."

He stopped the story to honk the horn again. "That kid should figure out we got heat in the truck. He's got to have brains enough for that, don't you think?"

I resented the remark but didn't say anything. I looked out the passenger window at the green house and garage, but there was no sign of Wade. "Was it the Germans?"

He flipped his cigarette butt out the window. "Three of them. No one could see those Germans except me. They wore pure white. Even their boots and rifles were white. I squinted through the peep sights and fired a clip at the closest one. Then I slipped in another clip and went for the second." My father's voice was calm.

"The lieutenant came running over, chewing me out for wasting ammunition, but right then, the third sniper started shooting and our guys took cover fast. Most of our outfit was city boys who couldn't tell shit from Shinola, and they couldn't see that German, even though he was right out in the open.

" 'Where is he? Where is he?' they shouted, and fired blind into that big white field.

" 'I'll get him,' I said, working on the third clip, but my rifle jammed. I grabbed another fella's. The sights were off, and I could see the snow spit to the left, so I tried to adjust, but the third sniper got away clean.

"The others were stone-dead. Three of us went out to check. We took their chocolate and cigarettes but left all their ID and family pictures. One looked just like a blond rancher I knew from Dayville, except that his face was painted white. With all that white, he already seemed like a ghost."

"Did it bother you a lot?"

He thinned his lips. "It was something I had to do. After that, all the guys acted like I was Audie Murphy and bragged me up to the other outfits."

"But did it give you nightmares or anything?"

He shifted, half-turning toward me. "Not really. One thing seemed strange, though—eating their chocolate and smoking their cigarettes." He paused. "The smokes were better than ours. Turkish, the lieutenant said."

My father fiddled with the defroster's control. We were fogging up. "Too much blab," he said.

I rolled down my window and studied the green house, the barn behind. I couldn't see anything. "Maybe he went out the back."

"Could be." My father nodded. "Maybe he's just waiting for us to walk out there closer so he can get a good shot."

"Wade's not like that," I said.

You said he didn't start fires. I knew what my father was thinking. *Trouble. A crazed animal caught in a trap.*

"I'm going after him," I said.

"He's your boy," my father said.

Opening the door, I started to slide out. Then I felt something cold press against my hand. When I looked, I saw my father's pistol.

"It's double-action," he said. "But it shoots straighter if you cock it, then squeeze."

I shook my head.

"If you go in from the right, you can keep that gray house between you and the upstairs windows. If anything happens, duck behind the gray house."

"Nothing's going to happen," I said. "Wade's just too scared to come out." A part of me, my father's blood, wanted to take the pistol.

Maybe it was foolhardy, but I wasn't going to give in to fear. Once Wade came out, how could I explain having a pistol in my hand?

My father held out the pistol. "If I were you, I'd take it, just for emergencies."

"No," I said, wondering if that was the right decision.

"You're a damn fool," he said. "Watch yourself."

■ ■ ■

In my hometowns, more men hunted opening day of bird season than shot off fireworks on the Fourth of July. All the wheat fields filled with pickup trucks, bird dogs, fathers and sons, uncles and nephews. Carl Bragg took his fifteen-year-old son, Dwight, one bright October morning. Dolly, their six-year-old Springer spaniel, stood poised, eager for birds.

Carl carried his Winchester Model 12, an inheritance from his father, and Dwight hauled a Mossberg pump with a thirty-inch barrel. It was a little heavy for the boy.

During the morning they shot four pheasants, two each, and after lunch they decided to hunt the ditch bank leading to the stock pond. Over the years, it had proven good for two or more birds each opening day, before the birds scattered into the marginal land and junipers beyond the fields.

Dolly froze over a bird, and both men fired when the rooster rose, cackling as it climbed. Tumbling to earth, the wounded pheasant raced down the ditch. They could hear its feet crackle the dry leaves and they could catch glimpses of Dolly as she raced along the bank. Both men chased the bird, each keeping to his side of the ditch bank. Carl panted from the run.

When the bird left the ditch and ran onto the pond's bank, Carl sluiced it, taking care not to shoot the pursuing dog. Dolly retrieved the bird, and after admiring the pheasant's bright plumage for a moment, Carl wrung its neck and waited for Dwight.

As the boy approached, his father tried handing him the bird, but Dwight shook his head. "You ruined it," he said. "That bird's full of shot."

Carl still offered the bird. "Here. Now you've got your limit."

"Dolly would have caught him. You had no cause to shoot it on the ground."

"I was just making sure. Go ahead. Take it." Carl stepped toward the boy.

Dwight claimed he couldn't remember shooting Carl, but somehow he raised his shotgun and filled his father's chest with number-four shot. From the number of pellets the coroner dug out, he testified that Carl was shot at least twice.

Dolly was shot only once—up close. Gunpowder burned her side.

For the first two hours that the police questioned him, Dwight tried twisting the event into an accident, but he couldn't account for two shots fired accidentally from a pump. And there was no story to explain Dolly.

Half the town thought Carl was a hard, stubborn man, and those people might have been sympathetic to Dwight. However, they couldn't get past the dog.

Six years later, the state released Dwight, but the town had turned its back. He went to Alaska for a new start and crewed for a fishing boat out of Dutch Harbor. After that, I lost track of him.

That tragedy and similar dark tales flashed through my mind as I got out of the Jeep and took a few steps toward the green house. If Wade had stabbed Sarge, claiming he had seen a monster, he might shoot me, I thought, then pushed that thought away. No, I've been good to Wade and he loves me. *But he loved Sarge, too.* Surely he didn't have a gun. *Or if he did, Wade didn't know how to use it.*

Suddenly fear gripped me. Otto might have shown him how guns work. Who knew what the hell Otto did?

My eyes slid from one window to the next, looking for movement.

"Wade, come on out," I said. Or had I just thought those words? I concentrated on speaking out loud. "I don't want you to catch a cold. Let's go back into town and have some breakfast."

My voice sounded strained and phony. Words hung dead in the air, muffled by the falling snow. As I walked, I kept track of places I could duck for cover—a rusted International Harvester farm truck, empty fuel barrels, a blue sofa with a missing cushion, five tilted fence slats, a doorless car with fuzzy orange dice still hanging from the rearview mirror.

Surely I wasn't going to be shot here, I thought. Two Martin
Lesleys shot dead near Monument by disturbed people. Lightning
doesn't strike twice. Anyway, I didn't really belong here. My
mother had raised me and I wasn't one of these people. All this
would be over soon, and I'd be taking Wade back to Portland for
more rounds with psychologists and counselors.

No cover was available while I walked across the thirty feet of
snowy yard. As I reached the front door of the green house, my
chest ached and I took quick shallow breaths. Stepping to one side
of the door as the actors do in police movies, I knocked.

"Hey, Wade. Are you in there? I'm hungry. Let's go eat."

Opening the door, I peered into the dark interior, but couldn't
see him. Then I heard his teeth chattering. He sat in the remains
of a stuffed chair, with a piece of rat-chewed oilcloth draped
around him for warmth. He had a lost and helpless look that reminded me of the first time I'd seen him in the small bedroom at
Payette's parents'.

"You look cold," I said. "The Jeep has a heater."

"Are you going to send me away?" he asked in a thin voice. He
seemed forlorn and hopeless.

"No," I said, but I didn't know what I was going to do.

"You and Grandpa are really mad at me."

"Yes, we are. You burned up all his fence posts. That was a terrible thing to do." Somehow, those words didn't cover it. I felt like
a petulant second-grade teacher.

Snot ran from Wade's nose. He brought his arms out from under the oilcloth and wiped the snot on his coat sleeve. His hands
held nothing. He was not armed.

"Bigfoot came," he said. "Dad, I heard Bigfoot."

Wade sat between my father and me, holding out his reddened
hands to the Jeep's heater. "I smelled Bigfoot, too." His face was
turned toward Rudell, trying to convince him. "I heard the big
thumps, just like you said. Then I smelled him."

Rudell looked across at me. "He should walk back. A little
more fresh air might clear his thick head."

I gripped Wade's shoulder and he turned. "Listen. I didn't hear anything. Why do you think that is?"

"You were asleep. All of you were asleep and snoring."

"You could wake me up."

"I knew what to do," Wade said. "Bigfoot hates fires. And he was getting closer. I saw his yellow eyes."

"The little shitheel can't open his mouth without lying," my father said. His hands gripped the steering wheel. His jaw twitched.

Wade stared at the Jeep's floor. Drool hung from his mouth.

My father was right. Wade lied every time he got in trouble. Crazy lies that no one would believe. I had learned to get my mind around that. But not fire.

When we got back to the trailer, Rudell flung open the Jeep's door and jerked Wade out by his coat collar. After dragging the boy over to the ash pile from the burned posts, he demanded, "Do you see that—all the trouble you caused? Well, do you?"

Wade lowered his head but didn't answer.

"You burned up a hell of a lot of my work, and now I've got to go cut posts all over again."

"Maybe Wade could help you cut some more," I said, even though it sounded stupid. The counselors were always talking about giving Wade consequences for his actions. I wished they were here for this.

Rudell glared at me. "I don't know which one of you is the biggest fool. I sure don't want any help from him. I can burn the place down myself."

I wish I could say that something profound happened then. When Lesleys get together, they usually fight, and certainly we might have fought then. I sure felt like pounding somebody, mostly myself for ever half-hoping, half-believing that some event involving both my father and Wade could lead to a reconciliation. Getting them together under any circumstance had been a harebrained, forlorn hope from the start. My father wasn't about to accept any responsibility for me or for Wade, and Wade had deep, serious problems that had tangled my life.

I realized I couldn't get free of either one.

Rudell released Wade, giving him a hard shove sideways. Then he pointed at me. "You get him out of here or I'll whip him. Maybe whip you both."

I was frustrated and angry enough to fight my father, but I turned away.

"Get in that truck," I told Wade. "And don't you dare mess with anything."

Wade shuffled toward the truck and my father remained by the burn. I headed for the trailer to collect our stuff.

Brandy wasn't around and I figured she'd gone back to bed. Not much point in telling her good-bye anyway. I didn't bother rolling the sleeping bags because it would take too much time. I hung them both over my right shoulder and grabbed the duffel bags with my left hand.

My father waited outside the trailer. "If you got any dry wool socks, put them on the boy. Warm his toes some. No point in paying a doctor to treat frostbite."

His anger had cooled some, so I tempered mine. "I can send you a check for those posts, if you tell me how much." As I offered, I realized I'd already given any extra money to Otto and Virginia. "First of the month."

"I don't think so." Rudell shook his head. "If you come back sometime, don't bring that boy."

"You got it," I said, even though I believed my father had no business telling me what to do. I wasn't likely to come back. Still, my father's words stung because they reminded me of other times when friends and relatives had told me to keep Wade away.

The toll kept mounting. Wade's face belonged in the post office on an unwanted poster. Mine, too, as his accomplice.

27

EFREM

When my aunt Judy died, I tried to see my father again in spite of the episode with Wade; however, Rudell failed to show up at his own sister's funeral. I could tell how disturbed Aunt Sally was by his absence, and she seized on me, steering me around by the arm to meet relatives I didn't care about and didn't plan to see again. I pasted on a smile, exchanged pleasantries, and listened to family stories I had no part in. I felt like a phony because I'd never been close to Judy, and although everyone acted friendly enough, I was disappointed and angry Rudell hadn't shown.

Of course Aunt Sally introduced me as Rudell's son, and I grinned like a fool, but my ears burned from the sham of it. He wasn't really my father, nor was I his son, yet at least for the funeral, I kept up appearances. The truth was, Wade and I were much closer, even with all his faults and in spite of lacking a bloodline.

A few months after the funeral, just before New Year's, Sally called to tell me that Rudell was going to visit his nephew Ernie out in Molalla, not too far from the community college where I worked. "I thought you might like to go and see your father," she said.

At the mention of my father, my head started ringing and my stomach twisted. I just couldn't accept the idea that I meant so little to him.

In a pig's eye, I thought at Sally's suggestion, but as the time for his visit grew closer, I began to consider driving out to Molalla. It was only twenty miles, nowhere near the investment required by a trip to Monument.

Also, Molalla and Ernie rang bells.

Years before, my mother had told me Rudell went deer hunting with Ernie after he returned from the war. Back in The Dalles after hunting, Rudell realized he'd forgotten his flashlight, so he told my mother he was driving to Molalla to get it.

She felt that was odd, but she added that he did some peculiar things after the war. My father never came back or got in touch again, unless you counted the divorce papers served on my mother in The Dalles. I never saw him until the mint chopper accident.

Thirty years later, I felt strange seeking him out in Molalla. I found Ernie's address and followed the winding driveway to the mobile home. The Dodge pickup in the carport had a Molalla Buckaroo sticker, so I figured that was Ernie's. No sign of my father's rig, if he'd brought one.

A familiar-looking man answered the doorbell. I smelled cooked roast, and potatoes, and beer.

"Are you Ernie Packard?" When he nodded, I said, "I'm looking for Rudell. I'm his oldest boy, Craig."

"He's here." Ernie held the door open so I could step in. He took my coat and hung it on a coatrack made from elk antlers.

My father sat in the front room watching TV, a rerun of *The FBI* with Efrem Zimbalist, Jr. Rudell had aged well. He remained lean and his face resembled good leather.

At first, he just glanced up, then went back to watching TV and eating supper from a tray in front of him. I imagine he thought I was one of Ernie's friends stopping by.

"This here's Craig," Ernie told him. "He come a-looking for you."

Rudell squinted at me. "Doesn't look like you've been missing any meals."

I grinned awkwardly. I weighed two hundred pounds, twenty more than when he'd last seen me. Since he didn't seem to be getting up, I crossed the room and we shook hands. "How's it going? Aunt Sally said you'd be out here."

"I got a creak or two but keep pretty limber. You still doing all right after that hay baler?" He turned to Ernie. "He played chicken with a hay baler. Got all crippled up."

"I was run over by a mint chopper," I told Ernie.

"He was a slow healer," Rudell said. "We had guys in the war like that."

That remark angered me.

Ernie asked, "You been in the service?"

I shook my head. "They wouldn't take me because of the accident."

"Ernie got two Purple Hearts," my father said. "He was like you, kept getting hurt." He turned back to the TV and his food.

"You want supper?" Ernie asked. "I got elk roast and spuds. Beer, or I could make some coffee."

I wasn't hungry, but I thought if I ate, it would give me the opportunity to start talking with my father. "Sounds good."

Ernie dished up the food. "I don't have another TV tray," he said apologetically. "Do you mind sitting at the table?"

"The table's fine."

When a commercial came on, Rudell turned my way. "Did you get your elk this year?"

"No. I had to teach."

"Nothing's worth staying out of the woods during elk season."

"I have to make a living."

My father turned back to the television.

"This elk tastes good," I said.

"Your dad shot it. I put my tag on it."

"Ernie might starve to death if it weren't for me," my father said. "I got three of them halfway legal this year. Hoot tagged the other one."

"You ready for another beer?" Ernie asked Rudell.

My father nodded. When Ernie took him the beer, my father said, "You'd make someone a good wife. Hell, I might marry you myself, if you weren't my little brother."

Actually, Ernie was my father's nephew, but they were raised like brothers. Ernie's mother, Dora, was my father's oldest sister. After Dora died of cholera, my grandmother raised Ernie and his two siblings, along with her own eleven children.

For the next few minutes, the three of us didn't speak. I had trouble following *The FBI* plot. I wanted to talk with my father, but I didn't know where to begin.

At the next commercial, Ernie got everyone another beer. Seven empties lined up beside my father's chair. "This is a good time to be drinking," Ernie said. "The cops caught their quota of drunks already, so they're off drinking coffee and keeping out of the rain."

"You should come out and trap in the Owyhee Desert," Rudell said. "I'd buy a case of Heidelberg in Rome and have it half-drunk by the time I got back to camp. I never saw a cop all winter."

It seemed to be my turn to say something about drinking, but instead I told Rudell, "I didn't see you at Aunt Judy's funeral. Were you sick or something?"

"Too crowded." He tipped his beer can toward Ernie. "He went."

Then I knew why Ernie had seemed familiar when he opened the door. At Judy's funeral, he had been wearing a brown sport coat.

"Judy still looked good, in spite of everything." Ernie turned toward me. "That woman was long-suffering."

"Was her kid there?" my father asked. "The weird bald one?"

He meant my cousin Freddy, who had been a Hare Krishna. "He was there," I said.

"Your uncle Emmett should've knocked more sense into him." Rudell pointed at me. "Just like you should whip that firebug."

"You notice I didn't bring him with me," I said.

"Good thing," my father said. "Ernie kind of likes this place."

Fuck you, I thought.

Rudell went back to watching television. Efrem was closing in on some counterfeiters.

"You want a piece of cherry pie?" Ernie asked. "It's good for store-bought."

"Sure." He handed me a piece and I ate slowly, wondering if I could suggest turning off the TV when *The FBI* was finished. However, to my disappointment, another episode of *The FBI* followed the first.

Rudell was tickled. "That Efrem Zimbalist, Jr., sure can act," he said.

When the second program started, Rudell turned up the sound. "I can't hear with all this gabbing."

I stood.

"There's more pie," Ernie said.

"I have to go to work early."

"Craig's got to go to work tomorrow," Ernie almost shouted.

My father shifted in his chair. "Drive careful."

Ernie took our coats off the rack. "That driveway's tricky to back out of." He grabbed an old flashlight out of the drawer.

I thought of my father's trip years earlier. Had there been a flashlight? Or was there something else?

"I'm helping him back out," Ernie said to Rudell. "You want to see him off?"

"This is a rerun," my father said. He pushed back the TV tray and stood, wobbling a little. "What are you driving?" he asked me.

"A '68 El Camino."

"You got a three twenty-seven in it?" Ernie asked. "Three on the tree? I had me a '65. Wish I still had it."

Outside, it was drizzling. "I should have put on my cap," Rudell said. "I hate this rain."

I didn't like it either. Growing up east of the Cascades in the high desert, I couldn't get used to all the wet.

"Why don't you open her up?" Ernie asked.

When I popped the hood, he leaned over, shining the flashlight on the engine. "Hardly leaks any oil. How many miles?"

"Eighty-two thousand."

"Just breaking her in good." Ernie shone the light on the exterior. "I like the maroon."

"The salesman called it 'Black Cherry.'"

"Let me see that light," my father said. After Ernie handed him the flashlight, Rudell squatted, shining the light under the chassis. "Not much clearance," he said. "You couldn't take this up to elk camp."

"I drove it to Oscar's camp last year," I said.

"If you could drive this rig in, then you're hunting in the wrong place."

And you're full of bullshit, I thought.

Ernie said, "Hang on a minute," then went into the trailer.

My father stepped back under the carport. "Damn rain."

I followed. "Listen," I said. "Do you remember leaving The Dalles and coming here to get a flashlight?"

"What are you talking about?"

"You went to get a flashlight when you left The Dalles."

"A flashlight?" He didn't say anything else for a while, and I tried to read his expression.

"Why would I drive all that way for a damn fool flashlight?"

"When you left The Dalles, didn't you come here?"

The question hung between us. His jaw tightened.

Just then, Ernie returned and handed me a package wrapped in white butcher paper. "Take these steaks with you," he said. "Your father shot it."

I felt the weight. "Thanks."

My father handed Ernie the flashlight. "You can help him back up. Too wet for me."

"Down here, you got to get used to it," Ernie played the beam onto the gravel drive behind my pickup. "Just follow my light and you'll be okay. This driveway is more crooked than a dog's hind leg."

All my questions remained unanswered.

Perhaps I should have stayed longer, but I didn't see the point. Most likely, my father wouldn't have any answers; certainly nothing he could say would narrow the wide chasm between us.

I climbed in, setting the elk meat on the passenger seat. I looked in the rearview mirror and saw Ernie's flashlight.

My father stepped forward and tapped the hood of the car twice. Then he headed for the trailer.

Fuck the old man, I thought as I backed up, concentrating on Ernie's wavering light. No point in turning to look for my father. He would be inside the trailer, watching Efrem.

28

ORMAND

I met my wife Kathy in graduate school at the University of Massachusetts, where we were fellow students in fiction writing. At first, we seemed to be opposites. Kathy had never been to Oregon; I had never visited her home state, Delaware. Her parents had left Kiev to escape Stalin and she was first-generation American, the daughter of a doctor and a chemist. No one in her family hunted, fished, or trapped coyotes.

Kathy had grown up with a mother, father, siblings, and grandparents—all living together. She couldn't imagine a life not knowing her father and suggested that I get in touch with mine. Maybe she was curious, too. She knew Wade, my mother, Ronna, Oscar, and Mac, but Rudell was still a mystery to her.

After convincing Hazel to watch Wade, one spring break Kathy and I went on a trip to see Eastern Oregon. Although we lived in Oregon City near Portland, I wanted her to see the country where I had grown up. When we drove over Mount Hood and reached the long stretch of high desert on the Warm Springs Indian Reservation, I felt that I could breathe again. I wasn't hemmed in by houses or trees.

To the west, Mount Jefferson, Broken Top, Three-Fingered Jack, Mount Bachelor, and the Three Sisters shouldered into a cloudless blue sky.

"Now we're in God's country," I said.

"It's really beautiful."

The tone of Kathy's voice pleased me because I could tell how awed she was by the vast country surrounding us. Growing up in Maryland and Delaware, she had never seen anything like this.

"You've got to look twice to see the horizon," I said, borrowing one of Uncle Oscar's phrases. "Open country."

Two nights later we stayed at a snug motel in Heppner. The next morning, it rained. When I peered out the motel window, the sky stood gray and gloomy.

"It's not supposed to rain in sunny Eastern Oregon. The travel brochures boast three hundred and sixty clear days a year."

"We're having a good time."

"But I hate the rain, especially out here. Unless it's a thunderstorm with lightning. I like that because it's passionate."

"Don't get any ideas. It's time for breakfast and I'm hungry."

While we ate in the café, Kathy studied the map. I had planned on hiking in the John Day Fossil Beds, but I hadn't prepared for rain.

"We're not too far from Monument," she said. "Maybe we should go visit your father."

"I don't think so. Why spoil this trip?"

"It was just an idea."

"Did you want to meet him?"

"I think you should see him."

"When I've tried that before, nothing happens. We don't have anything in common."

"But you do come from here, this country."

"He's got nothing to do with it."

I resisted seeing my father. I always had wanted him to say something I could understand about his leaving, about the choices he had made. And I wanted him to acknowledge me in some way, instead of that half-mocking moniker he gave me—The Professor. But every time I approached him, I got nothing. The trip to Molalla was the perfect example. His indifference had made me indifferent and angry.

Still, as I considered taking a detour to Monument, I thought, why not? We were already pretty close, and the rain spoiled any chance of hiking. Why not drop in on the old man and let him know I was doing okay without his help? I had married a beautiful, talented young woman from the East. Both of us were taking care of the hard-luck Wade and planning a family of our own. I even had a good four-wheel drive pickup, only two years old. If nothing else, Rudell would appreciate the truck.

■ ■ ■

My father's forlorn Spartanette single-wide trader looked worse than before. Two bullet holes pierced its aluminum skin near the back bedroom. His wheel-less Olds stood jacked up on blocks, and he had the old Jeep pickup loaded with trash. A pile of beer cans, mostly Heidelbergs and Olys, sat thirty feet from the front door, about the distance you could fling an empty can on a windless day.

A dozen juniper posts occupied the spot near the homemade utility shed where Wade had started the fire. Half a dozen mowers showed above the high weeds. Weed eaters, hedge trimmers, various rusted tools spilled out of the shed onto the dirt doorsill. Two large spools of barbed wire rested against the front of the shed, along with three coyote stretchers.

Maybe Kathy had seen worse places in the Maryland woods. She told me that the hillbillies from West Virginia came to small-town Maryland because the social services were better. But if she had seen worse places, they couldn't top Rudell's by much.

"Surely he doesn't live here."

"Country living." I felt smug that the place had caught her off guard.

"You think this is the right place?"

"Unless he sold it and moved to the Heights." Smoke rose from the chimney, so I figured he was home. "We drove all this way. Are you going to back out?"

She opened the door. "I wouldn't miss it for the world."

We stood together on the leaning porch. When someone answered our knock, I was surprised to see Ormand. His bulk filled the doorway. He had to be at least six five and weigh three hundred pounds. Ormand held a .357 Magnum in his right hand and a cleaning brush in his left. I could smell the solvent.

"Well, Craig, we haven't seen you in a while. Come on in. Is this the little woman?"

His tone suggested that I'd been there a week ago, but I hadn't seen him since Rudell had brought his second family to Madras twenty years earlier. "This is my wife, Kathy." I touched her shoulder just to make sure she was really there. "My brother Ormand."

I don't think anybody shook hands. Ormand turned sideways. Kathy kept staring at the pistol as we squeezed past him into the small trailer.

"I was just cleaning Dad's Colt Python," Ormand said. "He carries it with him at the gold mine. You can't be too careful in these parts. Later, you can try shooting it, if you want. It's got just a little burr in the trigger pull. A Colt shouldn't have that hitch. This gun is the standard by which all other three-fifty-seven revolvers are measured."

Kathy nodded but kept her distance.

Inside the house, my old man sat huddled in front of a small woodstove. He had on thick wool socks, two wool shirts, a wool vest, pants, and a stocking cap. "Hey there," he said, looking up from a Louis L'Amour book he was reading. "It's the Professor."

"Hello, Rudell. I wanted you to meet my wife, Kathy."

He grinned and shook her hand. "Well, if you hang out with such beautiful women, I wish you'd stop by more often." He gestured toward the old sofa. "Take a seat. Ormand, get these folks a beer."

"Do you want an Oly or an Oly?" Ormand asked.

"I'll take an Oly." Turning to Rudell, I asked, "Are you feeling sick?"

"I'm plumb cold all the time."

"We took him to the Vet's, but they couldn't find a damn thing wrong with him," Ormand said, handing us the beers. "They got piss-poor excuses for doctors in Walla Walla."

"I got the chills and these blisters on my back. Ormand thinks I'm making it up, but I took off my shirt and showed him the red sons of bitches all over my back."

"Maybe you've got shingles." I hoped he wasn't planning on taking his shirt off to show Kathy.

"I think something's chewing on him," Ormand said. "All the mites and fleas that jump off those coyotes and cats when Dad skins them."

"Kathy's father's a doctor," I told Rudell. "Too bad you can't see him."

"Is he a chiropractor?" my father asked.

"He's a real doctor," I said. "Pop runs an emergency room."

"Well, I'm turning into an emergency right quick."

"Dad might be getting reactions to all the stuff he takes—a bottle of Geritol every day, potassium tablets, Saint-John's-wort. All that might give you a reaction, don't you think?"

"Next thing, you'll want me to cut out beer," Rudell said.

"Like I keep telling you," Ormand said, "anything can be bad for you when you take too much of it."

"Especially women," Rudell said, and we all laughed.

"Well, you can't have too much gold," Rudell said. "Get that bottle of gold out for them to see."

Shit, I thought. The old man is going to start telling "stretchers," trying to show off for Kathy. Well, she wanted to see him, and now she's getting an earful.

"I expect she's never seen real gold straight from the creek."

"Dad and his partner are running a gold mine up on Big Creek," Ormand said. "I'd like to help them some, but this right arm is giving me fits."

"Most likely, you'd just get in our way," Rudell said.

Ormand went into the back bedroom to find the gold. I knew

there had been a lot of gold in Eastern Oregon. The U.S. Bank in Baker City had a huge display with one nugget the size of a small fist.

"How did you find the gold?" Kathy asked.

"My dad. His dad showed him. Back in the 1870s, grandpa was mining somewhere up Big Creek on one of the tributaries and found a really rich vein. But the Indians got to acting up and run him out of there. He left a sledgehammer as a marker, figuring he could go back and find it, then know where the gold was, but he never could find it again. My dad looked, too, and I've been looking."

"What Indians were they?" I asked.

"Damn mean ones. They burned a lot of ranches around Long Creek and tried to get over into the Monument country, but my grandpa and three others killed their scouts. They were trying to follow the trail the settlers took when they left Monument high tailing for Heppner."

Ormand came back with a good-sized prescription bottle. It contained flakes and a few pieces of pea gold. Maybe the entire bottle had ten ounces, not much for a season's work, I thought.

When Kathy looked at the bottle, she asked, "What are you going to do with all this gold?"

"My partner and I keep about half of it for a stake. That's what you're looking at. Then we always have enough to start the next year. With the other half, we take off for Nevada and a little vacation."

"Do you head for Las Vegas?" I asked, knowing damn well he was too cheap for that.

"The money goes farther in Winnemucca. Ralph and I found us a good Basque restaurant there with a hotel attached. We eat good, drink a little, tell lies, and chase the women."

"Do you ever catch the women?" I wondered if he would say *whores* in front of Kathy. As an Easterner, she wouldn't know Winnemucca's reputation for houses of ill repute.

"Only if they're slow."

Ormand finished cleaning the gun and gave it to Rudell. "Here, Dad. Keep it handy."

"A couple fellas came up one night fixing to rob me," Rudell said. "They walked right up to the trailer door, acting like they needed directions. I kept them outside and the gun within reach. After we talked a minute and they figured I was alone, the thin one pulled a knife and threatened to stab me if I didn't produce a poke.

" 'I heard all about you getting rich from some guys in the next camp, so hand it over, old man,' he said. I grabbed the Colt and pointed it right at his belly. When I pulled the hammer back, he just stared into the bore.

" 'I'm shooting you right in the belly so you can die slow. Then I'm shooting Fatty the same way. You'll both have time to think about it.' "

Ormand slapped his knee. "Oooh-wee! I love hearing Dad tell about it. You should see all the medals he won for marksmanship. No one could outshoot him in the army or at the Umatilla Army Depot."

Rudell nodded. "Fatty ran so fast, he beat Skinny getting out of there. I never did see either one of those drifters again."

"They made a big mistake," Ormand said. "They brought a knife to a gunfight. He'd have shot them, too."

"Quicker than I'd shoot a damn snake." Rudell stood and walked over to the refrigerator.

"No one's ever been found guilty of murder in Grant County," Ormand said. "And since that fella had a knife, Dad would get cleared on self-defense."

Peering inside the refrigerator, Rudell said, "We need some fixin's for lunch. You boys get something at the store. I'll keep Kathy company. I got some good coyote pelts out in the shed. It was a hard winter, and they really come into thick coats."

"Dad, I don't know if we can trust you with Craig's woman."

■ ■ ■

A sheet-metal grasshopper about the size of a horse rested on a trapwagon across from Boyer's Cash Market. "The Mormons wouldn't like that," I said, thinking of how the grasshoppers had eaten their crops when they settled in Salt Lake. Ormand missed the reference.

"What do they do with that thing?" I asked.

"That's the mascot for the Grasshopper Festival. It's in the big parade every year. Then it presides over the fireworks and jackpot rodeo. The grasshopper gets featured in all the other town parades, too. Heppner, Spray, Condon, John Day. We go all out to advertise the Grasshopper Festival."

"It's sure big." The sheet-metal grasshopper reminded me of the ants and bees you sometimes see on exterminator trucks. "How'd the festival get its name?"

"Well, Monument needed to get some kind of celebration, so a bunch of people gathered in the park to swap ideas. While they were talking, a grasshopper landed on Paul Jewell's plate. Halfway in fun, he said, 'Let's call it the Grasshopper Festival.' No one could come up with a better name, so they went with that. Paul got put in charge of the festival and he made that old hopper in his machine shed. That's his place you saw coming into town. He's the only mechanic, fix-it guy Monument has."

When we came out of the store carrying fresh oysters for stew, ham, beer, and a bottle of white wine, Ormand looked at the grasshopper. "That silly old grasshopper broke up a lot of marriages."

I couldn't imagine why, unless it made people realize how desperate they were to live in a place like Monument. "How's that?"

"See, you go to a parade in John Day or the rodeo in Spray and you're in charge of pulling the grasshopper behind your pickup. You start to get the swelled head.

"And you have to watch it close at night, so no goof-off from Condon comes and paints 'DDT' on it or the peace sign or other hippie stuff. Then some of the local girls come around batting their eyelashes and asking about the grasshopper and how you got to be in charge of it. Pretty soon, one gets flirty-skirty and you go for it. You get her into the pickup, and of course your wife or sweetheart finds out about it, because everybody kind of knows everybody else out here. That grasshopper has busted up more than one marriage."

I bit my lip to keep from chuckling. The grasshopper looked innocent enough, and it was difficult to picture it as a kind of serpent in the Garden of Eden. The grasshopper leading us into temptation. Half of me wanted to believe that Ormand was just putting me on, but I realized he was on the level.

"Thinking of bad behavior, I wouldn't exactly trust Dad around your wife."

"I think she can handle him."

"You remember Brandy? She was here when you brought the boy out?"

"I remember."

"She was my girlfriend before Dad took ahold of her."

His voice hitched and I realized that the betrayal still bothered him. That's kind of curious, I thought, but I said, "I'll watch out for him."

"Dad can't help it. He just likes women. Young or old, rich or poor, fat or skinny, spoken for or not. Most of the time, he flat-out asks them to sleep with him. If they get mad, he just shakes his head and says, 'All you got to do is say no.'"

"If it comes to that, Kathy will say no, but thanks for the tip." I was a little surprised Rudell still had steam in his pipe. I figured age and bad luck had cooled him by now.

"Whatever happened to Brandy, anyway?"

"Oh, she still comes around—regular as payday."

■ ■ ■

After Kathy and I left Monument, we drove to a wayside park and made love by the John Day River. As we rested, listening to the rushing water, she asked, "What would you want to name our son?"

"Rudell Newton," I joked. "We could call him 'Rudy' or 'Newt.'"

"I'd like to call him Steve, after my brother."

"What about Ormand, after my brother?"

"It takes a little getting used to."

"Maybe we'll have a girl." After all the trouble Wade had given me, a girl seemed better. "Hazel is a terrific name for a girl."

"I like Helen, my mother's name. Ellen, Alaine, Elena. I like all of those. Like Helen, they come from the Greek word *helios*, for 'sun.'"

"That's kind of highbrow. I'm holding out for Hazel."

"Well, it sure beats Rudell."

29

PROSPECTING

"Prospecting runs in the Lesley blood," my aunt Lela said. "My father, Newton, headed to Alaska three times with dreams of striking it rich, and Momma had to run the ranch by herself. I remember how she always sang while she worked. She missed him and wanted to buck up her spirits."

Lela always picked up rocks herself, especially on the Middle Fork of the John Day, where prospectors mined for gold.

"I'm always putting interesting rocks in my pockets. Your uncle Bob scratched the gold itch, too. After he retired from logging, he and his wife spent two years in Ruby, Alaska. Now, that's remote."

Rudell tried his hand at mining several times. His most successful attempt occurred when he and two other partners staked claims on Big Creek, near Prairie City. One nugget he uncovered weighed over an ounce, and his brother Bob bought it for a thousand dollars.

The company my father kept was always a little shady, and he had trouble with Arvel Shaniko, an unscrupulous character and scam artist. Shaniko was the "paper man," the partner who filed the mining claims at the courthouse in Canyon City.

"He hopscotched the claims," Ormand told me. "Dad got pissed at Arvel for being so greedy." *Hopscotching* refers to the practice of cheating your partners by taking every other claim. Arvel staked a claim for himself, then one for Rudell, then another for himself, then one for Ralph, another for himself, and so on. In that way, he controlled much more land than either of the other two.

Arvel also tried to sell shares in the operation that already belonged to him and his partners. Around John Day and the rest of Grant County, people were wise to his scams, but he took the "claim deeds" to Nevada, where he sold them to gamblers for three or four thousand dollars apiece.

More unsavory characters started showing up at the tiny travel trailer my father kept near the claims. Concerned about trouble, he started carrying his .357 Magnum Colt Python. He made certain no one knew where his claims were or followed him. During one quarrel with Arvel over his dealings, my father held the gun on him. Ralph broke it up.

"Dad got to hating Arvel so much, he'd walk off whenever he came around," Ormand said.

Their quarrel became a mystery when Arvel disappeared. Because he had so many enemies, no one tried too hard to locate him. Many believed he had gone to Nevada to pull another scam. Some thought Arvel met his fate there at the hands of people he'd cheated. Whatever happened, Arvel never came back to Grant County, even after his father died and he stood to gain an inheritance.

The IRS couldn't locate him, either. They came looking because he hadn't paid taxes in years.

Some speculate that Rudell killed him and buried him in the Malheur Forest or dropped the body into an abandoned mine shaft. "If your father did it," one informant told me, "he did it for the right reason. Rudell had a strong sense of what's right and what's wrong."

While that didn't apply to his marriage to my mother, if he was the injured party, Rudell went after the culprit, seeking his own payback. Maybe an elk hunter, trapper, or miner will stumble onto Arvel's remains. If the authorities discover a .357 Magnum slug with the body, my hunch is that it will match my father's Colt Python.

30

RUSTY

Kathy and I managed to brace ourselves for the big crises with Wade, but the day-to-day pressures were as corrosive as acid. Schools were a series of disappointments. He couldn't stay in a program for long before the directors would place him in a different program, usually resulting in other schools and classmates, inconvenient bus rides or taxicabs.

Mainstreaming never worked, nor did programs for the Emotionally Handicapped, Learning Disabled, or Trainable Mentally Retarded. An Indian woman with the Multnomah County Educational Service District wanted to place Wade in her program, which was especially for Indian children. She said it would be stable, permanent, and culturally relevant. Wade lasted a month before she took him out.

Conferences with teachers, administrators, psychologists, counselors proved futile. Medication, diet, therapy were useless. Some ideas bordered on the idiotic. One expert hypothesized that Wade hadn't been toilet-trained at the right time. Retraining him would help him develop, she claimed. I doubted it, because Wade never wet the bed or had accidents.

The schools' psychologists believed that Wade hadn't crawled and walked in the right sequence, so one doctor spent several sessions crawling with Wade on the floor while making certain the boy came in contact with children's toys—plastic blocks, wooden animals, Legos, and finally pull toys—during the walking stage. However, rather than walking, Wade insisted on returning to crawling, and the accommodating expert complied, joining him in crawling around the playroom until Wade slipped into his dog routine and bit the good doctor. Those sessions concluded with a tetanus shot and a hefty bill.

One counselor at work heard about Wade being in the school's day-care program and sought him out without my knowing. He believed the boy had not experienced enough touching as a baby, so he spent part of Tuesday and Thursday afternoons wrestling and roughhousing with Wade. When I picked Wade up after those sessions, he was particularly wild. Once I was informed what was going on, I burst into the counselor's office and threatened to punch him out.

Nothing worked.

In the ensuing two decades, the experts have learned more about Fetal Alcohol Syndrome and Fetal Alcohol Effect, but a diagnosis isn't a cure. I've attended conferences sponsored by the Centers for Disease Control, the March of Dimes, the state of Alaska. At those events, I've seen the same desperation that I had felt on the faces of parents, grandparents, and other caregivers. Twenty years later, they ask the same unanswerable questions. They hold on to the fragile hope for a somewhere near normal life and believe any strategy or program is worth trying.

People want breakthroughs (frequently promised by the "experts"), where the affected child will learn to read, tell time, do simple math problems, make change. And the caregivers hope hardest that the children will change their erratic behavior and understand that their actions have consequences, often severe enough to land them in the criminal justice system.

Still, many of these children cannot learn abstract concepts or understand cause and effect, in spite of love and the caregivers' best efforts. During his later teen years, Wade stole over seventy cars, joyriding until he was caught each time. He never seemed to comprehend that a theft would lead to an arrest. Fortunately, the prosecutors and judges eventually realized that he had a diminished capacity for understanding and was unable to stand trial or assist in his own defense.

The many times I visited Wade in the county jail, I tried explaining time after time why he couldn't steal cars.

"But Dad," he said. "People leave their keys in them."

Until he reached puberty, Wade remained good-natured. That quality was his saving grace. However, by the time he turned fourteen, Wade had become more sullen, sneaky, and unpredictable.

Kathy and I got him a dog for companionship and to help him learn responsibility. Rusty, a small mutt, became his inseparable pal.

Wade also idolized Elvis Presley, listened to his music, hung up his pictures and an Elvis calendar. He got a guitar and tried singing Elvis songs while banging the strings. "Hound Dog" was his favorite.

One fall evening, Kathy and I took a walk with our baby daughter, Elena, in her stroller. Wade stayed behind with Rusty to watch television. When we returned, we could hear Elvis blaring all the way down the block, and we knew that he had the tape player outside someplace, cranked up to full volume.

"I hope the neighbors dig Elvis," I said as we neared the house.

We stood as if frozen in the driveway. Through the open garage door, we saw Wade's wiry figure silhouetted against the wall. He was kneeling beside Rusty, seeming to hold her down on the garage floor, his hands around her neck. He was so intense that he failed to notice us coming up the driveway.

Alarm swept across Kathy's face. "What is he doing? Wade, stop that!"

I got to him first, seizing his shoulders and pulling him away from the dog. Rusty limped to the corner of the garage, gasping for air.

Wade jerked away from my grip. Something wild flashed in his eyes before he lowered his head.

"What in the hell were you doing?" I seized his shoulders again. "You were hurting Rusty." I was angry, but inside, my guts twisted with fear.

Looking up, Wade's face was full of confusion and defiance. "I wasn't doing nothing. Shit! I was playing Elvis for Rusty, but she wouldn't listen. She kept trying to run away, so I put her head by the player."

"Damn it. Don't lie to me. You were hurting the dog!"

"No I wasn't. I just wanted her to listen to Elvis with me."

Kathy grabbed my arm and I released Wade. The baby had started crying, and Kathy held her with her other arm.

"Go to your room right now!" I said.

Wade had started to cry. "I wasn't doing nothing bad."

After he had gone into the house, Rusty came over and put her front paws on my leg. I scratched behind her ears. "It's okay, girl." I didn't want to look at Kathy. I didn't have any explanation.

Desperation gripped her face. "He was trying to strangle the dog, wasn't he?" She rocked the baby back and forth, as if trying to comfort herself.

I couldn't say anything.

Kathy relaxed a little. "I don't know." She shook her head. "His explanation makes sense in his own weird way of thinking. But it sure seemed like he was strangling Rusty, whether he meant to or not."

I squeezed my eyes shut. Sarge, Yukiko, Bigfoot, Rusty, and Rudell's warning all raced through my mind.

"What are we going to do?" Kathy asked. "How can we even explain this sort of thing to anybody?"

I touched her shoulder. "Listen, we'll figure it out." She wasn't convinced, and neither was I. I could no longer figure out anything.

Uncertainty can break the camel's back. Uncertainty followed uncertainty. When Wade went into the crying baby's room to take her a pillow, we were uncertain of his intent. If he stuck her with a diaper pin, we didn't know if it was accidental. When I told

Wade not to leave hunks of fried chicken near the baby because she might choke, I found pieces within her reach. He wanted to feed Elena, to hold her and play with her, like a "normal" big brother would. We weren't sure.

We could never leave him unsupervised. Day and night, we listened to every footfall, every creak of the floorboard, each small sound. And we doubted.

The time came when I couldn't listen or doubt anymore. The decision to give up Wade was the most difficult decision I ever made and remains so. Through a psychologist, we found a family whose mission in life was taking care of troubled and handicapped children. Because they had so many kids, it wasn't an ideal situation, since Wade wouldn't have as much personal attention as he needed. But we believed in the Swancutts and admired their devotion. Besides, we had gone far beyond the search for ideal. Our lives had become desperate.

Letting go was necessary, I knew, but I regarded it as a failure. "You're like your father," mocked the nagging devil on my shoulder. "Getting a divorce and giving up Wade. You're just like your father."

Even today, I look at photos from those days with Wade and my heart hurts. Wade as a skinny kid holding up a fish he caught, his excitement palpable. Wade looking pleased and proud, standing with Kathy and baby Elena on the day we first brought her home from the hospital. On his birthday, Wade, Elena, and my mother standing behind her signature lamb cake with its blazing candles, all three of them grinning. After that birthday, the photos of Wade stop.

31

GREYHOUND

Outside the Portland Greyhound terminal, Rudell stood as straight as a lodgepole pine. Unlike the other disheveled passengers, he appeared crisp in his stiff new Levi's, polished dark brown cowboy boots, a sheepskin vest over a denim shirt with white snap buttons. Beside him were a small suitcase, an Emporium Department Store shopping bag, and a tightly rolled sleeping bag.

Doorway winos shared a bottle. Hustlers and whores strolled past, but no one bothered Rudell. Comfortable in his own space, he seemed to have brought a section of Monument with him.

"Hop in," I said, reaching across and opening the passenger door.

"I was looking for your pickup." He threw his gear into the backseat.

"I had to sell it. With the baby, a car works better."

He offered his hand and we shook awkwardly. "You put on some weight, Professor. Easy city living."

"I walk a lot," I said, even though I didn't. The sleeping bag had me worried. Was he planning on spending time with us? He had called out of the blue and asked me to pick him up.

Rudell squinted at the dashboard. "What kind of a rig is this?"

"It's a Honda Accord." I patted the dash. "Almost thirty miles to the gallon."

"You stopped buying American?"

The implication angered me. "It's a great car. Responsive steering, even braking."

"Made in Japan, huh?"

"The parts are. It's put together in Ohio."

"After the war, they made junk. I guess it's changed."

"That's right."

"Not many Hondas in Monument. You got to head to Boise to get one fixed. Ormand says they're hard to work on, but he can fix any Ford or GMC."

"These cars never break down," I said. "Hondas and Toyotas have the best repair records."

He didn't say anything. The sleeping bag still concerned me. "Are you in town to get checked out at the VA hospital? Do you have some personal business?"

"No. I'm just here to see my granddaughter. You sent me that card. Did you know she was born on my birthday?"

I nearly lost control of the steering. What a cosmic joke, I thought. Here I don't even see the old man until I'm fifteen, lying half-dead in a hospital, and Elena's born on his birthday.

"That's some coincidence," I said.

"March eighteenth is a good day for Lesleys," he said.

"You live kind of far from the bus depot. I guess that's why it took you so long to pick me up."

I had been slow. After Rudell's call, I had talked with Kathy. "I'm not wild about seeing him," I said.

"I think it's good he came. He's taking an interest."

"He was never any part of my life."

"But his genes are. Like it or not, he is part of things now that we've got Elena. She's one-quarter your father. Anyway, don't you want to know something about your family?"

I knew my family all right, and it didn't include him. I had sent the birth announcement on a whim. Now, I thought I had made a mistake.

As we approached the house, Rudell watched the people on the streets. "Quite a few coloreds."

"We like this neighborhood." I thought Rudell might find the mixed neighborhood unusual. We had purchased a modest but solid house in Northeast Portland, which reminded Kathy of the ethnic Eastern neighborhoods and of the home she knew as a child.

Also, we had hoped that Wade wouldn't be very conspicuous, given the variety of people living here. At the time, we expected him to continue living with us.

"A trolley used to run down this street," Rudell said.

"That's right. How did you know?"

"I was stationed for a while in Vancouver," he said. "Out at the Barnes VA Hospital."

"I never thought of you around cities." Still, I knew that he must have met my mother in Vancouver when she worked there in the courthouse.

"I've been to Paris and Berlin," he said. "Snipers were trying to pick me off. That's hard to forget. I don't care much for cities."

Elena sat in her high chair, wearing lime-green bib overalls with a bright orange ladybug design, a white T-shirt, and red tennis shoes. Kathy had pulled her straight brown hair up in a topknot.

Rudell grinned when he saw her and held his hand out so she could grasp his finger. "Stout. She's got a grip like a blacksmith." When Kathy came in, he shook her hand. "You've got a beautiful baby," he said.

"Thank you. I think she's got your nose," Kathy said. "Ours are big. And now I see where those gray eyes come from. People are always stopping us to comment on her eyes. They're such an un-usual shade of gray."

Kathy studied him, and I could see she liked what she saw. Dressed up in his best Western gear, he looked sharp. After all these years, women were still giving him a second look.

"Elena was born on his birthday," I said. "What do you think about that?"

"Really?" Kathy laughed. "Amazing. What are the odds?"

"I'm not likely to forget Elena's," my father said. "Come to think of it, she looks exactly like my sister Clarissa when she was a baby. Spittin' image."

During dinner, Rudell told stories of hunting, coyote trapping, Monument. Kathy offered to let him feed Elena. He grinned and set about the task with a silver baby spoon that had been mine. Elena kept reaching for his glasses. She smeared apricots, carrots, and liver around her tray.

"I wish I had some venison liver to feed her," he said. "We chopped it up fine for my kids. Nothing tops venison liver except elk back-strap."

"I don't know what that is," Kathy said.

"It's the good meat along the backbone. Sort of like T-bone."

"It's delicious," I said.

"Did you get your elk this year?" Rudell asked.

"Oscar gave me some." I didn't mention it had been three years earlier.

"It tastes better if you shoot it yourself."

I didn't reply, so Kathy said, "Do you cook a lot?"

Rudell nodded. "I just get by in the kitchen. Mostly, I cook deer and elk." He looked at me. "I'm leaving you my rifle when I go. A bolt-action thirty-ought-six Winchester. You just have to remember—it shoots a matchstick high at a hundred yards. At two hundred, it's dead-on."

"I'll remember." I doubted I'd ever see the rifle. Anyway, I already owned a .30-06 Remington I'd bought from Oscar with money people had sent me when I was in the hospital. I wouldn't part with that rifle because it reminded me of how Madras people had been so generous. I'd also thrown in the five dollars Rudell had left for cigars.

After dinner, my father took a large package out of the Emporium bag and handed it to Kathy. He waited for her to open it. The package contained a bright pink dress with an enormous bow in front and an equally garish pink bonnet.

Kathy examined the dress with a perfectly straight face. "This is really nice. Elena's a little small for it now, but she'll grow into it."

"Maybe by summer," Rudell said. "She's a bruiser, like her uncle Ormand."

"It's a lot and a half," I told my father when he and I went into the backyard. "The guy we bought it from used to raise chrysanthemums in the side yard. He entered the best ones in flower shows and always won a few prizes."

Rudell studied the flower bed. Now the stalks were withered and the blooms rotten. "It takes all kinds."

"I like that big maple." I pointed to the enormous tree. "The leaves turn gold and crimson in the fall. Last year, we raked six bags of leaves. When she gets older, Elena can press leaves for her scrapbook."

Rudell seemed bemused. "Out my way, the leaves just blow into the next county. The tumbleweeds pile against the fence."

He concentrated on the maple's trunk. One portion had a large crack two inches deep. Digging his thumbnail into the crack, he pulled out a wriggling grub. "Beetles start working a crack like that. Pretty soon, you have to take the tree down."

He thumped the trunk with his fist. "Five or six cords. You can buy a wood-burning stove. That fireplace you got sucks the heat straight up the chimney."

"I'm not ready to take that tree down," I said, even though I knew my father was probably right. In the summer, I enjoyed lying under the tree in a lawn chair and watching the robins and squirrels.

"Suit yourself, but when maples get old, they start to crack like rotten ice. If you're afraid to do it by yourself, I could ask Ormand to help you buck it. He's fixing chain saws now. Got him a Stihl with a twenty-six-inch bar."

"I'll keep Ormand in mind."

"You and him and the boy could make short work of it. Keep the wood stacked away from the house. No bugs that way—or fires." He glanced at his watch. "When does Wade get home from school? He's probably all grown up."

Flush rose in my neck. I didn't want to tell Rudell we'd had to give up the boy.

"He's not with us anymore, but I see him at least a couple times a week."

"Is he with his mother? She was a stunner."

I knew he meant Payette. "She wasn't his mother. No, he's with a family that works with difficult kids."

An awkward silence crept between us. Then my father said, "All my kids went off to hell and yonder. The wife, too. But now Yuba-Jean's back with her mother and Ormand's with me."

"That sounds good," I said, even though I didn't know what it meant.

"I hope this woman sticks with you," he said. "The girl, too."

I resented the superficial comparison that I felt he was making between us. Somehow, I'd always thought I'd done better than my father. "They'll both stick, and, like I say, I keep in touch with Wade." Like you never bothered to do with me, I thought.

"Maybe now that the boy's gone," he said. "That boy was a spark in dry grass."

■ ■ ■

Wade was getting by with the Swancutts. No breakthroughs, but he kept busy with school, chores, a weekend job as a janitor's assistant at the Valley River Mall. He liked that job because he wore a blue uniform with his name on the pocket and carried the janitor's toolbox.

He fixated on cars. An avid fan of *The Dukes of Hazzard*, he planned on buying a car exactly like the General Lee and marrying a girl resembling Daisy. Wade told me that he and some of the other Swancutt boys were fixing up a Toyota pickup they had salvaged from a wreck. He was eager to get a learner's permit. I didn't have the heart to tell him he'd never pass the test.

One Saturday night, I received a call from a very angry man in Eugene. "Are you the father of Wade White Fish?" he demanded.

His tone made me glad I wasn't. "I used to be his foster father. Now he's got a different placement. Is something wrong?"

"This is Sergeant Cody of campus security at the University of Oregon. We caught Wade directing traffic at Autzen Stadium for the Oregon-Washington football game. Now we've got twenty-seven cars bogged down in a muddy pasture."

Relieved that I was no longer responsible for Wade's misadventures, I laughed.

"This is very serious, sir," Cody said. "It's too muddy to even get a tow truck down there. We've got one sunk up to its axles."

"You'd better round up some horses, then," I suggested. "Or call Oregon State and tell them you need someone smart enough to drive a tractor."

Later, I learned that Wade had worn his blue janitor's uniform, set up orange cones, and directed the cars into the field with a flashlight from the janitor's tool kit. The towing charges topped a thousand dollars. I didn't pay them, and neither did the Swancutts. I imagine the university raised tuition, as they always do when faced with financial exigencies.

Not all of Wade's escapades turned out to be as humorous. While he was sixteen and seventeen, he stole over seventy cars in the Springfield-Eugene area. If a driver left his keys in the ignition while he went into the 7-Eleven for a pack of cigarettes, Wade took his car. He'd joyride a while, then abandon the car someplace remote. Although he scraped the sides and crumpled fenders from time to time, he never injured anyone. Even so, the Swancutts and I were terrified that he would.

Much of those two years he spent in the Lane County juvenile facilities. When he was incarcerated, I drove down on visiting days to see him and leave twenty-five dollars (the maximum allowed) for the commissary. By the time they got him from his cell to the visiting room, we could talk for only about twenty minutes. We had little to say to each other, but I hoped my presence would pick up his spirits.

Out in the back yard, I was glad that my father didn't mention Wade again. And I was relieved when he asked me to drive him out to Ernie's place. Before he left, Rudell kissed both Kathy and Elena goodbye. On the way to Molalla, he said little, but noted that the country was becoming too crowded with new houses.

Before he closed the car door, my father said, "Thanks for the lift."

"You bet."

"For made in Japan, this rig rides pretty good." He paused. "That's some granddaughter. And she was born on my birthday."

I nodded but didn't say anything. Nothing but chance, I thought.

"Well, so long. Don't take any wooden nickels."

That night when Elena was almost asleep, I laid her in the crib as gently as if she were a hollow, painted egg. Illumination from the street lamp entered the window, and the swaying tree branches cast flickering patterns across her smooth white forehead and curved cheek, the sweet bow of her mouth.

A *miracle*, I thought. I felt that her small life was on loan, somehow, to Kathy and me, entrusted to us. One day we'd be called to account for her, and nothing else we did would matter when that day came. As I watched her sleeping, one arm stretched above her head as if reaching to heaven, I wondered, how could anyone throw away the life of a child? How could my father?

A car passed, and I could tell from the sound its tires made, rain was falling. A world existed out there, but it didn't concern me. The only world I cared about was here, in this house, right now.

32

SMOKERS

My father's reputation as a boxer and brawler was legendary in Monument and throughout Grant County. Most of the Lesley brothers fought after school, during dances, nonstop at parades, rodeos, and festivals. They wore black eyes like badges of honor to school plays and sporting events.

Later they fought at "smokers," amateur boxing events sponsored by the local granges and rural fire departments. When the Civilian Conservation Corps had a major work force in Monument employing three hundred young men, the CCC held over twenty smokers. My father went undefeated. In his prime, he stood six two and weighed 190 pounds. From fence building and bucking bales, he was tough as whang leather, hard as juniper.

Speed set my father apart from his opponents. A lot of the men were tough. Most did manual labor—logging or ranching—and only the hardiest qualified for the smokers. But being tough wasn't enough to win twenty matches. Speed kills, and speed is a gift—a quality in a fighter no coach can teach.

Rudell had lightning-fast hands and a fast head that enabled him to duck and dodge the opponents' blows. He could strike quickly with the right or the left fist, and his opponents seldom touched his smooth, tan face.

"Your father had a wicked left hand," his brother Bob told me. "A nasty hook, and he loved to rabbit punch an opponent behind the ear. He was so fast, he could knock you out and nail you three more times during the drop."

Bob would know, because Rudell had used his younger brother for a sparring partner and punching bag the same way Rudell's older brother Huston had used my father until he couldn't whip him anymore. According to relatives, my father's first item of business anywhere he went was to put up a punching bag.

"That saved wear and tear on the neighbors," Bob noted.

As with many family stories, it's difficult to tell the true ones from the "stretchers," but some stories stand out with the consistency of their detail and repetition.

In Long Creek, my father whipped three cowboys because one complained he smelled of coyote bait and they tried throwing him out of the bar.

"I did have a bottle of bait in my pocket that had leaked a mite," Rudell said. "I was used to the smell." Then he grinned and said, "I only knocked one of those fellas out, I think. The others fainted from smelling the skunk glands and rotten fish in that bait."

Today, the Long Creek tavern where Rudell fought the three cowboys has been converted to a Christian youth center, although it's difficult to picture clean-cut cowboys sitting on the former bar stools, singing religious songs and holding prayer meetings.

Some might call it progress.

"I'm hoping I'll be able to buy a drink in Long Creek again one of these days," Ormand said. "Right now, the nearest bar is in Dayville. You've got to drive eighty-six miles round-trip to get beat up."

Remarkably, sometimes my father didn't fight. "He always behaved himself in Winnemucca," Ormand said. "We'd come in from a trapping season out on the Owyhee and head straight for the houses. You know girls are legal in Nevada. Dad was sweet on a Hawaiian girl, and he'd be powerful mellow around her. When she went back to the islands, he acted like his dog died, but he'd find somebody else and behave okay with her, too."

"Your father would rather fight than fuck," Bob told me once. And it seemed to be true. While he might have behaved in Winnemucca, he never passed up a chance to fight in Grant County.

Perhaps my father's most remarkable fight occurred at the Grubstake in John Day. He had turned seventy-three the week before. "The doctors told him to give up drinking for a while," Ormand said, "and that really soured him. When he pushed past seventy, he turned meaner than a three-legged badger."

Columbia Power Co-Op, which provides much of the electric power for the rural West and Alaska, publishes a monthly pamphlet called *Ruralite*. In 1987, at age seventy-three, my father appeared in a *Ruralite* profile written by Rick Steber. In the profile, Rudell comments on the fight in the Grubstake and adds:

I suspect my fighting spirit comes from Dad (Jasper Newton Lesley). He never backed away from a fight—I don't either. I don't profess to be tough, not anymore. Not at my age. My last fight might be behind me. Again, it might not.

According to all the family sources, Rudell and Brandy went to the Grubstake for drinks and dinner to celebrate her birthday. My dad was drinking beer and she was tossing back Whiskey Ditches.

A bigmouthed local tough named Hines sat at the bar, glowering. His girlfriend's car had broken down as she was driving over from Burns, and he thought he'd been dumped.

Suddenly, he rose from the bar, strode over to my father's table and said, "What are you doing with this bitch, old man?"

Hines was thirty-eight and Brandy had just turned forty-two. Most likely, he thought he could take her away from Rudell. Hines clenched his fists, waiting for my father to stand.

However, Rudell didn't rise. He tensed, and from a sitting position, struck Hines in the neck with his left hook. Stunned, Hines stumbled back two steps.

"Then I was out of my chair and in the middle of him," Rudell would say later when he told me the story. "I got my hands in his hair and beat his head against the floor a few times. After that, the fight pretty much leaked out of him."

The bartender cursed and told them to take it outside. When my father let up for a moment, Hines started crawling for the door, scuttling on all fours and staying under the tables so that Rudell couldn't pounce on him again.

"In the old days, I would have booted him some," Rudell told me. "I hit him hard. I can't understand why I didn't knock him out." My father seemed genuinely puzzled that Hines had crawled away.

In their rush to clear out before the cops showed, Brandy left her coat in the bar. The following morning, Rudell called his brother Bob from the motel.

"They had a little fracas in the Grubstake last night," Rudell said in his slow, hungover voice. "Could you go and fetch Brandy's coat?"

Over the years, Bob had received many similar requests. He expected the call. Along with everyone else in John Day, he had heard the story of an old man beating up a bully.

"I figured Rudell was back in town," Bob said.

As I was growing up, my mother had called my father "lazy" and "shell-shocked." But she would hasten to add, "Your father never had a mean bone in his body." My aunt Sally seemed equally deluded. "Rudell was always so gentle while we were growing up," she said. "The army wrecked him. Can you imagine being such a quiet, gentle man and seeing all those horrible sights in France? He had to stack frozen bodies on trucks. Both Germans and our boys."

No one else ever called my father gentle. "He was a pugilist," Bob said with a kind of awe. In fact, most of his smoker victories occurred before he ever entered the service. Once enlisted, he boxed for his unit and went undefeated. In boot camp, a drill inspector, fed up with my father's laziness, challenged him to a fight behind the mess hall. Rudell kicked his ass.

When he lost a fight, he admitted it. "After I got out of the service, I fought a few more times in the ring. One fight over in Pendleton, I got the hell beat out of me. Never was knocked out, but boy, what a beating!"

When I was in my early fifties, after I had talked with my father a few times, I pointed out to my mother that Rudell was always beating people up. "Your version of things is wrong," I said. "How could you tell me he wasn't mean?"

"He just didn't give a damn about me or you," she said. "He was lazy. To tell you the truth, I never thought he'd waste enough energy to be mean."

33

ELENA AND KIRA

It's difficult to say what I wanted from my father those times I saw him at the Monument trailer, in Molalla, and later on in the convalescent centers. Nothing could have made up for his absence during my childhood or the fact that I'd had to deal with my stepfather, Vern. I know that I wanted Rudell to say that he was sorry for abandoning me, but I also wanted more.

When my father was in the Blue Mountain Convalescent Center in Prairie City, the staff posted a sign on his door featuring his picture in his army uniform and offering a brief biography. One line read: "Rudell is the father of Oregon writer Craig Lesley."

The wording struck me because in most ways he had never been my father. We had only the sketchiest history. At the same time, I realized that I longed to have a relationship with him, some moments of intimacy and connection.

Once, in Monument, shortly before his death, Rudell wanted to sing the Western classic "Strawberry Roan." By then, his voice was weak and quavery, but he got most of the verses.

"Boy, I love to hear Dad sing that again," Ormand said. "We al-

ways asked him to sing that at bedtime because it took so long. All
those verses. Was that your favorite, too?"

Of course, Rudell had never been around to sing anything
when I was a kid, so I had no recollection, no fond memory. As-
tonishingly, Ormand didn't know that, but he believed Rudell had
been present during my early years. Apparently, my father never
mentioned his limited time with me and my mother to my half
siblings. I suppose this isn't uncommon with second marriages.
Still, I wondered if Rudell kept quiet out of shame and guilt or just
plain indifference.

I do know that when I sang (poorly) to my own children, or
read books, or told Captain Mike pirate stories, we were building a
history. I had nothing resembling that with my father.

He wasn't there for bike lessons, ball games, play perfor-
mances, or graduation speeches. Given her work schedule, my
mother came when she could.

Much later in life, I wanted Rudell to tell me why he had left
and if he was satisfied with his decision. Did he believe that he
had made the right choice? However, even more than that, I
wanted him to give me solid advice on how to live my own life,
the way I imagined caring fathers did. What college, which career,
which woman, which belief? Without that, I always remained
foggy, trying to test the wind and follow the faint trails the best I
could.

My mother always supported me, but if it came to practical advice, she offered little. "Well, there are good times and bad," she
was fond of saying. "Overall, I believe the good outweighs the bad."

From my uncle Oscar, I learned that silver flatfish work better
than gold ones most days on the Deschutes, and that when hunting elk, I should avoid the ridgeline and keep a third of the way
down the hill. When Payette left, I went to see him for advice on
how to get her back. After opening the door and seeing my face,
he said, "You've got trouble. You've got *big* trouble." He took me
inside and gave me a glass of whiskey. After finishing the drink, I
asked him what I should do.

"Maybe you're too good to her," he said. "Some women don't
like good men."

I was so short on guidance, I listened to any source. John Wood, Oscar's cousin, sold me a life-insurance policy when I worked in Oscar's guide service. After he picked up my check, John said, "Let's hope you live a long time. What are you going to do?"

"I'd like to be a teacher," I said. "But teachers don't make any money."

"They change lives," John said. "If you want to be a teacher, be a good one."

My father never met me without asking how many elk I'd killed. I resented the question because killing elk wasn't important to me. Doing well in school, teaching successfully, writing books, taking care of my own family and Wade—all of that meant far more to me than killing elk. If putting meat on the table was his test of manhood, I found other ways to do it.

Still, if I had accepted my father's invitations to join him at elk camp, I might have learned something more about him. However, I stayed away. Part of the reason was my job and family responsibilities. Even so, I managed to visit Oscar's elk camp during the five years I spent writing *Winterkill*.

A small part was trying to honor the promise I'd given my mother to stay away from Rudell and his backsliding. Harsh as it is to say, I was ashamed of my father. I considered him a failure. Like my mother, I wanted to keep my own children away from him, because they were so filled with joy and promise. Rudell had made crippling compromises. He was dogged by bad luck, frequently the direct result of his own decisions. I saw no reason to entangle my children in his limitations.

But the biggest reason for staying away came down to anger and pride. That anger carried me forward for many years, and I was afraid to let it go. Also, I wanted to show my father I could succeed where he hadn't. That was pride.

I'm doing all right by myself, I thought. I don't need any of your help.

One spring break, Kathy and I took the girls to the John Day Fossil Beds. Elena didn't have decent hiking boots, so we went to the Emporium Department Store in John Day to buy a pair.

While they shopped, I waited in the car. A beater pulled up

beside my car and an old geezer stepped out. He had taped glasses and wore a faded red-and-black hunting coat. As he opened his door, a cascade of beer cans clattered to the ground.

"That old fart looks kind of like my father," I muttered.

My first thought was that he was in Monument, seventy miles away. However, when I looked closer, I determined the man was indeed my father, looking much older. The woman with him must have been Brandy. I hadn't seen her in many years.

I didn't call to him. I turned away, then glanced back to see the two of them go into Chester's grocery.

When Kathy and the girls came back, for some reason, I told them I had seen a man who resembled my father.

"Maybe it was him," Kathy said. "Aren't you going to find out?"

"Naw. It's just some old guy," I said. I didn't want the girls involved with him, and I didn't want him to tin-cup me for money.

"I want to make sure it's not Grandpa," Elena said. "I'd like to see my grandpa."

"Me, too," Kira said, even though she'd never laid eyes on him.

While we were talking, Rudell and Brandy came back outside.

"I believe that is your father," Kathy said. "He's really aged."

"It's all that good living," I said.

"Well, go say hello to him," she insisted.

Reluctantly, I stepped out of the car. He didn't recognize me. "Hey, Rudell. It's me, Craig."

He studied me for a minute through his taped glasses, then slowly smiled. "I haven't seen you in a spell." He peered in the car window. "Still hanging on to the same wife?"

"That's her. Elena's nine now, and that's Kira. She's six."

He tapped on the window and Kathy rolled it down. "You're feeding him too good," Rudell said. "The Professor has put on a little weight."

She took his hand. "Good to see you again, Rudell."

"I got beautiful granddaughters, don't I?" he said. "Elena, do you remember you were born on my birthday?" When she said yes, he nodded. "That's really something."

■ ■ ■

Skiffs of March snow surrounded the yellow pine stands near Monument. A cold wind scoured the basalt hillsides. The late-winter sun shone with a hard white light. Gray smoke rose from the shabby single-wide at the frayed edge of town. My father's place was strewn with even more junk than I remembered. For some reason, he had added dozens of grimy house windows to the trash around his place, and their splintered casings leaned against the front and back of the trailer.

In spite of my doubts, the girls had a pleasant afternoon. Rudell entertained them with the Bigfoot story, and Brandy laid out ham sandwiches and store-bought peanut butter cookies. As usual, Rudell asked me how many elk I'd shot. My answer hadn't changed. Later, everyone put on coats and went outside to see the coyote traps and fence-building equipment. Now the side of the shed was so weathered, the charred wood from Wade's fire had faded.

Toward dusk, we got ready to head back to the motel in John Day. Both Rudell and Brandy kissed the girls good-bye.

"I got a phone now," he said. "You could call." He might have been talking to any one of us.

"I'll call you on my birthday," Elena said.

"It was my birthday first," he said, and she giggled.

After that visit, both girls received a five-dollar bill from Rudell each year a week or two after their birthdays. The worn bills came in yellowed envelopes addressed in pencil and sealed with masking tape.

Looking back, I was glad we drove out to Monument. On the drive back to John Day, the girls speculated about Bigfoot and believed they spotted several furtive coyotes in the shadows of the woods. I realized that they had experienced something I never would—a childhood memory with my father.

Not long after, Ormand called to say my father had suffered a stroke. While he was in the hospital, Brandy had cleaned him out. She even took his books, including the signed *Winterkill* I had sent him.

34

BLACK ICE

In 1988, Robert Stubblefield enrolled in my fiction-writing class at Clackamas Community College because he had read *Winterkill* and wanted to write about his region in a similar way. To my amazement, Robert had graduated from Monument High School and knew my father well. His father, George, and Rudell had been lifelong chums, and Rudell frequently helped George build fence. Oftentimes, he stayed for dinner at the Stubblefield place. "Venison and sourdough biscuits was his favorite meal," according to Robert's mother, Cora. "But he'd eat most anything."

As time passed, Robert and I became fast friends, and I joined him in Monument to go steelhead fishing or bird hunting. Sometimes the two of us visited my father in his trailer. Having Robert along gave me a kind of ally and helped ease the strain of seeing Rudell. I didn't expect any revelations or answers—just stories about hunting, prospecting, and my father's prowess as a boxer in his earlier days.

Robert loved to tell the story of George, Rudell, and Ormand building fence on a particularly ornery and steep hillside on the Stubblefield place.

"Rudell had poor old Ormand packing the heavy spools of barbed wire, the posts and posthole diggers. He was scrambling across the hillside wearing broken-down boots when my dad said, 'Rudell, you need to get you a horse.'

"Rudell considered the idea for a moment, then said, 'George, I don't need a horse. I got Ormand.'

"We all laughed, and Rudell said, 'The only horse I ever owned was old Hammer. He could pack a whole elk, including the head, out of the Hell Hole.'"

At times, Ormand was around. For a while, he had a job and wife in California, but he came up on holidays and for hunting season. When he lost his job and wife, he moved back permanently and once again helped my father with his trapping and fence building.

Between Thanksgiving and Christmas in 1996, I got a call from Ormand. I listened to his slow voice telling me that Rudell had suffered another severe stroke. Ormand had moved him out of the trailer into a small rented house he shared with Opal, and they took turns watching my father.

"If you want to see Dad, you better come on up, Craig. He's stopped eating and he won't take his medicine. At this rate, he won't last long."

■ ■ ■

Rudell lay in the back bedroom. Although he had lost a lot of weight, he still stretched out long under the cheap blanket. He wore an orange-and-green stocking cap pulled down to his ears.

"Look who's here to see you," Ormand said.

Propping up on one elbow, my father tried a smile. "It's good to see you, Huston."

"This is Craig," Ormand said, raising his voice so my father could hear. "Huston's still in California."

"Craig," my father said, as if trying to remember. Then he smiled. "The Professor."

"Listen," Ormand said. "He brought a tape recorder. If you get up and tell us some stories, we'll break out the brandy."

"Deal," my father said. "You've got to celebrate company." A sly look came over him. "Maybe I need a slug to get out of this bed."

"I'll try to rustle some," Ormand said.

After my brother left, Rudell nodded at me. "Hand me a robe or something, would you?"

A blue robe hung on a chair. When I handed it to him, I saw it had a white patch, as if someone had spilled bleach on it.

When Rudell stood to put on the robe, he teetered a little, and I put my hand out to steady him.

"I'm getting awful puny, Craig."

Helping him put on the robe, I felt the bones under his thin flesh. His skin was dry and scaly. "Not so good, huh?"

"I've gone nine rounds with the devil. One still to go."

"Maybe you'll knock him out."

Grinning with mock ferocity, he jabbed with his right. "I'll smack Old Scratch right on the kisser."

Sitting back down, he asked, "Can you put my slippers on? I get woozy when I bend over."

"Sure thing." His toenails needed clipping and the yellow calluses on his soles had started peeling away. I wondered if they had toenail clippers or if Ormand trimmed them with his knife.

Rudell lowered his arm. "Nobody goes ten with Old Scratch."

"Who'll put up with an old buzzard like you?" Ormand was back with the brandy.

My father smiled. "You got me there."

Rudell sat at the kitchen table, staring at a calendar from the Les Schwab tire store in John Day. The pictured showed a pickup at the edge of a pasture. Two deer, a doe and a buck, grazed in the field.

Ormand forked a chicken breast out of a cast-iron frying pan and set it on a cracked plate. "Can you cut that up for him?" he asked me. Raising his voice, he said, "You might as well eat something, Dad."

My father held his left hand in front of him. It resembled a twisted claw. "Not worth a damn," he said, but there was no self-pity in it—just a statement of fact.

"There's applesauce in the refrigerator," Ormand told me. "Dad likes applesauce."

I found it behind a can of dog food.

"You should have seen the applesauce at the Vet's hospital in Walla Walla," Ormand said. "Pitiful. Moldy and sour. They should be shot for how they treat the vets. The rolls were hard as bricks. They feed better at the state pen than at the Vet's."

"I don't want to go back to the Vet's," Rudell said. "Fucking horse doctors."

Ormand grinned. "We should check you straight into the pen, Dad. It feeds good and you'd be among friends. Anyway, you should probably be there for all the game you poached."

Rudell smiled. "All those years, they never caught me. A couple times, the wardens came awful close."

"You were slippery." Ormand tapped his forehead with his finger. "Smart, too."

"I was downright lucky," Rudell said. "When you take all the chances I took, you have to be lucky."

"Tell Craig about the time you and Bacon got them beavers after the season was over."

"First I want to know how Bacon got his name," I said.

Rudell smiled. "He was always a ham in the high school plays. After that, everyone called him 'Bacon.'"

I didn't know what to say.

"Now tell him about the beavers," Ormand said.

As Rudell began to tell the story, his voice gained strength.

■ ■ ■

"Well, we let beaver season run out on us a little. Not much, just a few days. We had our traps set up on Cupper Creek, but the beavers had outsmarted us for a couple weeks.

"Bacon had this bright idea to take up a little dynamite and blow their dams. That way, he figured, they'd have to move around more. Chances were they'd hit the traps."

"Did it work?" I asked, leaning forward a little. The dynamite had me interested.

"Surefire! We caught two—both good-sized. The female had reddish brown fur, kind of unusual, and we knew she'd bring top dollar.

"We had stout gunnysacks—double sewn—and usually we tied the beaver pelts up under the truck real good so the wardens couldn't find them unless they got down in the snow and mud and belly-crawled." He grinned. "Get their spiffy uniforms mucked up.

"But this day was strange. I was feeling a little skunky, like a pup that catches a whiff of roadkill on the wind. Bacon stayed jumpy, too. Both of us kept looking over our shoulders.

"So we decided to keep the gunnies in the back, covering the dynamite, and Bacon stuffed the beaver pelts way down inside his waders. 'Kind of keeps my doofus warm,' he said.

"Neither one of us said too much coming down the two track from Cupper Creek, but just as we got near the spur, a white Dodge pickup came out from a thicket of jack pines."

"The fuzz drive white pickups in Central Oregon, too," I said. "Fergus Keep—the game warden out of Madras—nailed me for jumping the trout season down on Willow Creek."

My father nodded. "This was Orville Pogue out of John Day and his partner, Gus Rhodes. Gus was a pretty good fella, for a warden, but Pogue had a pinecone stuck where the sun don't shine.

"Bacon made a little noise, halfway between a sigh and a yo-del. 'Here comes trouble,' he said.

"Pogue walked straight to the back of the truck. Gus stayed in the Dodge. 'You boys wouldn't have a little venison under these sacks would you?' Pogue asked. 'Maybe the hindquarters from a dry doe?'

" 'Not unless one jumped in while we were snoozing,' I told him. 'Go ahead. Take a look.'

"When he flipped back them sacks and saw the dynamite and caps, he jumped away quick, like he'd spooked a rattler.

" 'Dynamite! Jesus!'

"He hustled around to the front of the truck. After getting his wits back, he asked, 'You boys been blowing fish up the creek?'

" 'Fish is for Catholics,' Bacon said, rolling down his window. He took out a thin cigar and lit it, cool as can be. 'I'd rather be gnawing on some tender venison.'

" 'I'll bet you would at that,' Pogue said. 'Maybe I'll come out and poke around your place, make sure everything's tagged proper.'

" 'It's a free country,' Bacon said. 'I'll fix you some coffee, if you don't mind instant.'

" 'Drink it yourself,' Pogue said. He walked back to his rig. Gus handed him a flashlight and Pogue returned to us. Then he dropped to his belly and crawled way under the truck. That took me by surprise, because I'd seen wardens squat before and have a quick peek. Nothing more. Right then, I figured one of the neighbors must have tipped him off, because I couldn't imagine him getting all muddy unless he had a surefire pinch.

"Bacon blew a bunch of smoke in the cab, then rolled the windows up tight. He opened the door and shuffled a few steps from the pickup. With them beaver pelts stuffed down his waders, he looked plenty awkward, but Gus couldn't see him because the truck blocked his view.

" 'How's that U-joint look?' Bacon called to Pogue. 'I think it's past due for a lube.' He shuffled toward a lone juniper.

"Pogue didn't answer. He stayed under the rig for along time. I'm sure he thought gunnysacks with illegal game might appear at any second.

"Finally, he crawled back out. He was a mess. 'I know you boys are up to no good, way up yonder, packing dynamite.'

" 'I got a land claim up there,' I told him. 'Taking out a little gold from a side creek. The dynamite saves a lot of hard-rock mining.' I pulled a small bottle out of the glove box that had some pea gold and half an inch of flakes. I carried it around in case I met anybody fool enough to buy that claim.

"He inspected it, holding it to the light and shaking it so he could see the pea gold better.

"'If you know anybody who's interested, I'm thinking about selling.'

"He handed back the bottle. 'I'll let you know when I meet a fool.'

"'I think I'll take a look behind your seat,' he said. I leaned forward and tilted the seat. Pogue squinted at the jumper cables, oil cans, tools, and tow chain. No fish, no game.

"He sniffed the cab. 'It smells kind of gamey. You boys must've packed something out within the last couple days.'

"'It's an old pickup,' I said. 'Anyway, Bacon buys them cheap cigars.'

"Then I about had an attack. Up by the juniper, Bacon slipped the suspenders off his shoulders and dropped the waders damn near to his knees. I thought Pogue would see those pelts for sure. Bacon just stood there, pissing downhill and puffing the cigar. When he was finished, he shook his doofus and pulled the waders up. I nearly wet myself thinking of him waddling back to the rig.

"But Pogue figured he'd been licked this time and started back to his truck. It was a good two-hour drive to John Day and they'd want to get there by supper.

"Bacon waited until the Dodge was out of sight. Then he dropped his waders to the ankles, took out them pelts, and came back. We put the pelts in a gunnysack and covered the dynamite.

"'The smell almost gave us away,' I said.

"'That's why I lit the cigar,' Bacon said.

"'Old Pogue's muddy and chilled for nothing. He won't let us rest.'

"'A fool's born a minute and only one dies a day,' Bacon said. 'Pogue will have better luck messing with someone else.'"

■ ■ ■

After he had finished the story, Rudell stopped smiling, and suddenly he seemed very old and tired.

"Maybe you better get Dad to bed," Ormand said. "I'll slick up the dishes."

"Give me a hand here," Rudell said as he slowly stood and clutched the walker.

I put my hand on his bony shoulder to help steady him.

"Don't tuck the covers in at the foot of the bed," Ormand told me. "He doesn't like to feel cramped."

On the way to the bedroom, Rudell stopped in the bathroom. "Don't need no help here. I can still hold it myself."

Once he was in bed, slippers off, he closed his eyes. I couldn't hear him breathing. I studied the hair in his nostrils, the scaly skin around his eyes. A friend of mine back in Michigan once told me about washing his father's face and shaving him after he died. I didn't see myself doing that. Maybe Ormand could do it, if he wanted.

Outside, coyotes howled. From the sound, they were close to town.

I started to rise, but Rudell reached out with his clawlike hand as if to stop me. "You ever shoot a coyote?" he asked.

"I shot a couple when I was out deer hunting."

"How much did you get for the pelts?"

"Nothing. I just hung their bodies from the barbed wire."

"That's kind of a waste," he said. "A good pelt will bring sixty dollars."

"I was hunting deer," I said. "The coyotes were a nuisance." My uncle Oscar and I had been hunting on Harvey Rhodes's place out near Hay Creek Ranch. Harvey's land was surrounded by Hay Creek, a big outfit, and he had to get a key from them just so he could unlock the gate across the road and get to his own cattle. The coyotes had been killing his calves. "Any coyote you see, shoot the son of a bitch," Harvey had told me.

Now my father lifted his head off the pillow and turned toward the window. "Every night they get closer. Soon enough, they'll be on the porch." He settled back down. "Ormand shot one last week just outside of town. He's got the pelt stretched out in the garage. Thick fur this time of year."

He turned toward me. "You sticking around long enough to let your heels cool?"

"I have to head back tomorrow," I said. "But I'll come see you in the morning."

"If you see a coyote on the way back, shoot it. Pays for your gas and grub."

"Okay," I said, even though I didn't have a rifle in the car. When he didn't answer, I said, "Well, I'm heading out for Stubblefield's."

"George and I go way back," he said. "The last of the old-timers."

George was dead. Maybe he'd forgotten that.

He turned toward the window. "Is it clearing out there?"

I crossed to take a look but couldn't see anything because the window was all steamed up. Wiping away some of the steam, I could see better. "It's freezing rain."

He seemed surprised. "I figured it was clear, the way you could hear them coyotes."

They did seem close. I looked out the window a few moments; then turning toward the bed, I realized my father had fallen asleep.

Where the window was still steamed, I wrote his full name, Rudell Newton Lesley, then added Ormand, Yuba-Jean, Opal, and Huston. I didn't add mine because I didn't really belong to this place or to these people. We were connected by blood—little else.

I knew the roads were bad, and I doubted Opal would be back tonight. I understood her staying away, getting a little respite while she could.

"Craig, I love you."

At first, I thought I had imagined my father's voice, but when I looked at the bed, Rudell's eyes were open. "You came a long way to see me," he said.

I hesitated, then stepped closer to the bed. His good hand edged out of the covers. When I took it, he squeezed twice.

I didn't think I really loved him. Still, he meant more than some old geezer I'd meet on the street. And I had driven a long way.

Bending forward, I kissed him lightly on the forehead. "I love you, Rudell." My voice was pretty steady. I couldn't call him "Dad" the way Ormand did. He wasn't my real father by any stretch, and I didn't feel anything toward him like I felt for my grandfather or my uncle Oscar. Still, he was my natural father. We didn't have much history, but we had blood, like it or not.

His hand relaxed and he was asleep again, so I stepped quietly into the front room. Ormand dozed on the couch.

I nudged his shoulder and his eyes opened. "I'll come back in the morning," I said.

Outside, the sleet snicked against the single-paned window by the porch. Crossing the road to the Honda, I slipped on the black ice. Then, thinking of the studded tires on the car, I smiled. Three miles to Robert's turnoff, then a quarter-mile drive on two-track through juniper and sage. I figured I'd park the car on the highway and walk in.

I wished my father hadn't told me that he loved me. That complicated things—got in the way of the deep coals of anger I kept banked against him. Love might carry you a long way, but anger carried me further. My anger for my father's abandonment, a deep burning anger that glowed like a signal fire in the dark woods, had carried me over many tough years.

Two coyotes slunk across the road just past the Elkhorn bar. They're getting bolder, I thought, snatching cats off the front porch, luring innocent dogs out into the sagebrush and killing them.

Maybe my father saw Death as a pack of coyotes. Certainly, he had killed enough of them; in turn, he had seen all they had killed—sheep, deer, cattle, pets—even each other when they were starving or became rabid. Now, he might imagine them slinking closer each day, approaching the house. Soon they would grow bold enough to enter and snatch him from the bed, then tear him to pieces.

Turning to face the house, I realized how squalid and pathetic it seemed. A worn blanket served as a drape; broken-down bicycles cluttered the porch. Two bald tires lay at the bottom of the worn steps. Closing my eyes, I thanked God for my mother.

Still, the old man's saying he loved me had blunted my anger a little. My heart had started to thaw. I walked two short blocks to the little park in the center of town and whisked the snow from the bench with my hat. Then I sat, feeling the cold. I took off my Filson mackinaw, staying quiet until the cold chilled my chest. It seeped into my flesh and bones. I shivered and calmed, shivered and calmed, until I became rigid and numb. Eventually, my heart refroze to black ice, invisible and deadly.

35

PRAIRIE CITY

The last time I saw my father was at the Blue Mountain Convalescent Center in Prairie City. Darkness had settled by the time I arrived, and the stars blazed in the black sky.

I felt odd inquiring about Rudell at the nurses' station. I figured their peculiar glances resulted from their curiosity. *And why haven't you visited your father more?*

He was always cold, they told me. He wasn't eating. What's the point of telling me this? I thought. When I reached Rudell's room, he was asleep, the orange-and-green stocking cap pulled low on his head. A heavy blanket lay over the bedclothes. On the wall opposite the foot of his bed, a calendar featured two Siamese cats playing with a blue ball of twine.

I sat, waiting for him to awaken. Out in the hall, a woman sang "Blue Eyes Crying in the Rain." The voice cracked, and an old woman in a cowboy hat and white plastic boots leaned into the room. Bright lipstick slashed across her mouth.

"I'm looking for Dugan," she said. "Have you seen him?"

"Who's Dugan?" I asked. "Your son?"

Her bright eyes gazed right through me. "I'm wasting my time. You don't know anything."

"Do you want me to help you look?" I asked, longing for a task that would take me out of the room.

"Be quiet. He'll hear you." She wandered to the next room. "Have you seen Dugan?" she asked someone in a stage whisper.

In fifteen minutes, a cafeteria woman arrived carrying a tray of food. She set it on the rolling cart beside my father's bed. "Are you related?"

I nodded. "I'm his son."

"I met another son."

"That's my brother Ormand."

"Well, I wish one of you could get him to eat." She pushed the cart over the bed, where Rudell could reach the food. "With no nourishment, he's drying up—withering away." She studied my face. "You got the same eyes and mouth."

"You think so?"

She nodded. "Make him eat some of that chicken."

All the food on the plate was pureed to the same texture. Green, gray, and orange. "Is this gray one chicken?"

"Honey, that's what they call it."

After she had left, I gently shook my father's shoulder. "Hey, Rudell. It's time for supper."

Opening his eyes, he shouted, "What the hell are you marines doing here? You're supposed to be crossing the bridge!"

He leaned back, his eyes slowly focusing on me. "I'm not in France," he said.

"No. This is Prairie City. You're still close to Monument."

"Are you the doctor?" He touched his neck. "I can't swallow. My throat's gone narrow."

"I'll tell the doctor," I said. "I'm Craig, your oldest boy."

"Where's Ormand?"

"He's back in Monument."

"You're the Professor." He seemed pleased that he could remember. "How's Hazel?"

I was surprised, because he'd never asked about my mother before. Maybe he wanted to know if she was still alive. "She's getting along okay. She lives with my sister Ronna and her husband, Dermot. He's Irish. She's crazy about her grandson, Ciaran."

"Is she hearty?"

"She's fine. She gets around in a walker. Deaf as a post, but she's fine."

"Too damn deaf to hear myself fart." He smiled. "I'll bet Hazel still talks plenty."

I chuckled. They had been divorced over fifty years and he still thought of that. "She likes to converse. The trouble is, anymore you have to shout so she can hear."

He didn't say anything.

"The nurse wants you to eat." I put my arm around his bony shoulders and helped him sit, propping his back with a pillow from the empty bed across the room.

"They expect me to sit up and take nourishment," he said.

"That's the idea."

He raised his hand, then let it drop. "Waste of time."

"Try some of this chicken." I held half a spoonful of the gray stuff in front of his mouth. "You got to open up."

"My throat's gone narrow. I can't swallow."

"Just try," I said.

When his mouth opened, I fed him the chicken. After moving it around in his mouth, he seemed to swallow. "Limberneck," he said.

I didn't understand but held out another spoonful of chicken. "Here we go."

"Don't rush me."

I thought of Lenna Chester, my high school girlfriend. At a reunion, she had told me about going to a Catholic rest home and feeding her father. Another visitor was feeding his father at the same time, and after talking, the two realized they had been classmates.

"In high school, none of us would ever think we'd wind up like this," Lenna had told me. "Feeding our parents. But I guess they fed us, so now it's our turn."

As I gave Rudell another bite of chicken, I thought that the responsibility was clear to someone like Lenna, who had a father present in her life. However, I felt like some kind of imposter. He had never been a father to me. In turn, I didn't feel a son's responsibility toward him.

How much am I supposed to do? I thought. I had shown up in Prairie City. Was that sufficient, or was there more?

Rudell burbled, and most of the gray chicken I thought he had swallowed ran down his chin and onto the bib. Shit, I thought. I wiped his chin with the small washcloth that came with the tray.

"Are you trying to swallow?" I was irritated. "The nurse says you have to eat."

He coughed and more goopy chicken ran down his chin. The anger went out of me. Nothing had gone down. Somehow, I felt as if I had failed.

"Limberneck."

"What are you talking about?"

"Our chickens got the limberneck," Rudell said. "Back when I was a boy. All of them died because their necks went rubbery." He put his hand to his neck again. "Now I've got the limberneck. I can't swallow. My throat's gone narrow."

I didn't know the first thing about chickens, although I had read Sherwood Anderson's story about them. In that work, they all died. I tried to determine if my father couldn't swallow or if he was being stubborn.

"Do you want your juice? It looks like cranberry."

"I'll try it," he said. "Apple juice gives me gas."

I got him to drink half of it. How long could he live on juice? I wondered.

When the cafeteria woman picked up the tray, she scowled at both of us. "I don't know why I bother," she said. "Next time, I want you to do better."

I couldn't tell which one of us she meant.

"Blue Eyes Crying in the Rain" echoed from the hallway. The woman with the cowboy boots came in and stood beside my father's bed. "How was dinner, Rudell?"

"I hate chicken," he said. "But I'm still sitting up and trying to take nourishment." He adjusted his stocking cap.

"You need to get out more. Come and watch TV with us. They have *Bonanza*." She clapped her hands. "I almost forgot. Dugan's coming to see me. I want to introduce you."

"Okay," my father said. "Bring him by."

"Dugan loves *Bonanza*," she said.

After she left, Rudell pointed to his head. "Missing some marbles."

"Who's Dugan?"

"He's been dead for ten years," Rudell said. "She was driving."

"That's tough on her," I said.

"If I see Dugan, I'm in the wrong place."

"Whatever happened to that firebug?" Rudell asked. "I should have whipped him."

"He's all grown up," I said. "He'd whip you now." I didn't tell him about all the cars Wade had stolen or the DUIs or any of the other problems. He was healthy and had a girlfriend. He wasn't in jail. Getting by, I thought. "Wade's getting by."

"Does he come to see you?"

"Sometimes." We saw each other a couple times a year but talked on the phone more often.

"No one comes to see me," he said.

"The nurses told me Ormand was here three days ago."

"No he wasn't. He was checking the traplines."

After asking permission, I got Rudell into a wheelchair and took him outside. The evening had turned cool and the air smelled of woodstoves and burning pine.

"Am I missing elk season?"

"No," I said. "It's still coming up."

"Hoot's getting the wood. I've got to bring up Hammer from the Stubblefield place. He's just an old plug, but he loves to pack elk. George Stubblefield might come up later on."

"You'll all have a good time," I said. Both George and Hoot were long dead.

"Are you still eating on that elk you shot last year?"

"It's about finished," I said. Maybe he had confused me with Ormand. "How many elk do you think you've killed?" He had told me ninety-four and I wondered if he could recall.

Rudell didn't answer for a moment. When he looked at me, he seemed confused. "I've lost track. I don't know."

"You've shot a lot of elk. You needed the meat."

"I killed a lot of chickens, too," he said. "They're good eatin' on Sunday, the way Mama bakes them."

"I don't want you to catch cold," I said. "But let's look at the stars before we go in. Can you see them?"

He tipped his head back. "Maybe a little. My eyes are shot."

"Well, I'll tell you about them. The Big Dipper is right above your head." I knelt on one knee and pointed so he could sight along my arm. "And there's Ursa Major." I shifted and tilted his head a little, then pointed again. "And Orion's straight up there."

He leaned a little, following my finger. "It's all a blur."

"Maybe there are too many lights."

"Out in Monument, you can see better."

■ ■ ■

Once he was back in his bed, Rudell stayed more focused. "You're Craig, aren't you?"

"Yes I am."

"Your daughter was born on my birthday."

"She sure was. Do you remember the birthday? What day it is?"

After a moment, he said. "Three, eighteen. I can't remember what the month is called."

"March," I said.

"Like a soldier."

"Just like that."

"You've got another girl, don't you?"

"Kira," I said. "I've got two great daughters."

"Ormand's got two boys and a girl. All of you can come up to elk camp. Ormand knows right where it is."

"I'll talk to Ormand," I said.

Rudell touched his fingers to his throat. His Adam's apple bobbed. "My throat's gone narrow. It's hard to swallow."

"I'll leave a note for the doctor," I said.

"Ormand can fix it." His voice grew quiet and his eyes closed. "I don't need a horse," he whispered. "I got Ormand."

36

PECKER

"That son of a bitch won't eat a grasshopper, the little pecker. 'Pecker,' that's what I call him. The son of a bitch catches yellow jackets and eats them. That's why he's so mean. Look out there! Pecker will draw a blood blister."

Sam Howell had hatched the chukar from an abandoned nest he found, but the bird never returned to the wild. "Son of a bitch thinks he's family," Sam said.

The chukar pecked at my shoe, leg, and shoelaces. He didn't let up as we moved around the house. When Sam wasn't looking, I kicked Pecker but the bird came right back, more feisty than before.

"These are Kenny Depew's spurs," Sam said, holding up the silver inlaid pair. "He drowned on horseback below Spray. I give your dad two hundred dollars for them. They're worth more, but I won't part with them."

He brought out my father's old elk rifle, a Winchester 54 .30-06. "It shoots a matchstick high at a hundred yards," Sam said. "Dead-on at two hundred." He handed me the rifle. I recognized it as the one Rudell had said would be mine.

The government-issued rifle had a tapered stock, a nickle steel barrel, and a peep sight. "It's got a new barrel," Sam said. "Rudell shot the old barrel out of it. I give him six hundred for it, and worth every penny."

"Would you sell it?" The stock seemed a little long for Sam, who was short and wiry. The rifle felt good in my hands.

"Not on your life. A deal's a deal. You can drive a gnat's ass with that thing. I'm saving it for my grandson."

After I handed the rifle back to Sam, we sat at the kitchen table, going through a photo album. He took out a half-gallon bottle of Monarch Canadian whiskey, and we passed it back and forth. Harsh stuff, but cheap. Rudell drank Monarch whiskey, vodka, brandy.

I examined a photo featuring dozens of coyote pelts, too many to count. "Over a hundred?" I asked.

"Ninety-six. I sold those son-of-a-bitching hides and bought me a brand-new Chevrolet pickup. Four-wheel drive. January thirty-first, 1981. Coyotes went for about sixty dollars then. Throw in a few cats, a fella could buy something."

Sam pointed to the pictures of his other trophies: a six-foot cougar weighing 180 pounds, huge elk, deer, bobcats, and bear. In some photos, Sam posed with his daughter; in later ones, his grandson grinned from the pages.

One photo passed without his comment but caused me to catch my breath. "What the hell is this?"

"That son of a bitch is a Bigfoot track. I found it when I was logging up on Arbuckle Flat."

The picture looked exactly like the Bigfoot tracks shown in all the literature. Someone had written below the photo: *17" long, 10" at ball of foot, 5" at heel*. Suddenly, my father's Bigfoot story seemed more credible.

"Did you find any more tracks?"

"No. But I found a dump the son of a bitch took. I scraped it into a paper bag and turned it over to that Bigfoot outfit on the Columbia. You can't believe how bad that dump stunk."

I remembered that the British big game hunter Peter Byrne

had set up a Bigfoot clearing house in The Dalles during the seventies and eighties. I had visited it at least three times and talked
with Peter, who believed the creature existed.

"Did you leave it with Peter Byrne?"

Sam's head bobbed. "I couldn't remember the name."

I grew excited. "What did he say?"

"When I checked back, the son of a bitch didn't have it.
Somehow he lost the dump."

My excitement drained. Another dead end.

"How far is Arbuckle Flat from Cupper Creek?"

"Twenty miles. Your dad saw the son of a bitch all right."

Sam's garage held more trophies. First he showed me the antlers
and skull of a buck that had become tangled in barbed wire and
then was eaten by coyotes. "I won't sell that either, but I've had
offers. Had to rip out a section of fence."

He pointed to hundreds of traps hanging from the walls and
ceiling. Victors and Triumphs in sizes three and four. "You got to
use fours for cougars, and half the time they drag those off."

His bait came from a five-gallon jar of rotting fish. To this he
added skunk musk, coyote urine, and Taunton scent he purchased
from Union City, New Jersey.

"Your dad liked Acidophia. I think Taunton's a little better."
Taking one of the traps, he demonstrated how he set it, burying it
in dirt, laying out the toggle rock, placing the scent stick four
inches behind the trap, a little to the side.

While Sam explained the process, Pecker kept going for his
hands, and he had to knock the bird away so it wouldn't get
caught and kill itself or spring the trap on his hand. "Son of a
bitch," he said, cuffing Pecker a good one.

"Your father and I kind of kept track of each other," he said. "I
caught more coyotes, but then I set out more traps. I got three
hundred and fifty. Rudell set out a hundred maybe. I used a motor-
bike to cover the sets, but Rudell never went modern. He just kept
walking those sets himself. That's awful slow."

Or he made Ormand do it, I thought. I figured Sam checked his traps more than once a week, too.

After he sprang the trap and hung it up again, Sam said, "I got a bear trap I want to show you. That son of a bitch has two rows of steel teeth. It's illegal now."

As the three of us made our way into the woods, Sam tugged at my sleeve. "I didn't mean to insult your dad back there. I mean he just never went modern."

"You didn't insult him," I said.

"Anyway, he killed more elk than I have. Ninety-four. I got seventy-one and I'm still working on it."

"That's a lot of elk," I said.

"It sure is," he said. "You know us old-timers only count the bulls."

37

SUNFLOWER FLAT

There years after my father's funeral, I called Ormand to suggest that we move some of the dirt containing Rudell's ashes from Easter Point on Monument Mountain to his old elk camp on Sunflower Flat. We had intended to scatter his ashes in camp following the funeral, but the raging forest fires had closed off the roads to the Flat.

The old elk camp where Rudell had taken Marion Stokes and his other clients had been sold four times since Hoot had won it in the lawsuit. No one seemed to know the current owner, but he had slapped up big NO TRESPASSING signs everywhere.

Even so, we figured he'd let us spread some ashes on the grounds. By our reckoning, as Rudell's offspring, we had that right. Both Ormand and I agreed that our father would like the idea.

A tall wooden cross towered above Easter Point, where townspeople held sunrise Easter services. Once vandals had ripped down the crossbars, but Ormand replaced them, fastening the heavier

new bars with twisted steel nails. If vandals still wanted to get the
bars off, they'd have to climb up and use a chain saw.

Ormand put a shovel full of dirt into a white pail. After putting in another, he handed the shovel to me. I picked up the pail
and walked down the hill thirty feet.

"I was right here by this mountain-mahogany tree." The earth
was soft for the first three inches, then hardpan, so I took small
portions of dirt. I remembered that I had been lower on the hill
than Ormand when we spread Rudell's ashes after the funeral service. Delayed by the fires, Huston had arrived at the funeral late,
but he had helped spread the ashes below Easter Point.

Now, Ormand studied the mountain mahogany. "I'm going to
cut me more limbs for walking sticks. Trouble is, the carving hurts
my right arm too much. I work one day and get stoved up for three."

Ormand carved Bible verses into each stick, then darkened
them with a wood-burning pen. John 3:16 and the Twenty-third
Psalm were favorites, along with the passage from Hebrews where
Jesus says, "I will never forsake thee." He sold them at Boyer's
Cash Market and had special requests for Matthew 6:33.

When I climbed back to Ormand, he grinned and squinted at
the pail. "How much of Dad do you think we got in here?"

"Enough to count."

He wiped his forehead with a large blue bandanna. "Let's leave
the rest for the Resurrection."

"Sounds good to me." The late-afternoon sun beat on the hillside and we had beer in the truck. Even moderate grave digging
proved hot work.

"I don't think Dad will mind being split up all that much," Ormand said. "Not the way he loved going to elk camp."

We put the shovel and pail in the back of my pickup.

"Do you think your mother would like one of my walking
sticks?" Ormand asked. "It might help steady her after that hip
replacement."

"Sure." I appreciated his offer, even though the doctor had ordered her to use a walker. "She likes natural stuff, things made out
of wood."

"What verse would she like?"

"'In my Father's house, are many mansions,'" I said, because my grandfather had that verse on his funeral program, and I quoted it at Rudell's funeral.

"Dad didn't come to Jesus for a long time," Ormand said. "He was stubborn that way. But he finally came, and that's what counts. He wouldn't budge when I tried talking to him about it. I guess it just wasn't time yet."

"So when did he convert?"

"Just two years before he died. One Sunday morning, Ben Grisham, the minister from church, went over to see Dad in the convalescent center. When I showed up for service, Ben had a big old smile on his face.

"'Ormand, this morning your father got saved. And it's genuine.'

"That meant so much to me, I busted out in tears. All through church, I kept weeping and blubbering like a baby. Being moved to tears like that was my personal witness. That's how I know Dad's conversion was genuine."

"Is Ben Grisham still around?" I thought I might talk with him about my father and see if Rudell ever said anything about me.

Ormand shook his head. "Ben had a weakness. He was a good man, but he stumbled when it came to women. He left town with the church secretary."

"Well, a lot of people have stumbled on one thing or another."

"The main thing is, Dad was saved. This time we have on earth is as brief as the dew in the morning. Then we have an eternity in heaven. Think of it. We can all be together for eternity."

"That's right," I said, even though I remained doubtful that I wanted to spend eternity with Rudell. And I was certain my mother didn't.

■ ■ ■

On the way to Sunflower Flat, we stopped at the upper meadow on Donny Capon's place because Ormand wanted to show me some fence and gatepost jacks our father had built. All of

Rudell's range fence had burned up in the forest fire, but some sections of his pasture fence remained. Donny was out in the field checking on his cattle. When he saw us, he walked over to the pickup.

"You boys up to any good?" he asked.

Ormand told him our plan and Donny nodded. "Rudell did love the elk camp."

"I wanted to show Craig some of the gate jacks and fence Dad built."

Donny smiled. "Rudell worked kind of slow, but he built the best fence in these parts. He cut junipers for the anchors and gateposts, and he was the first one to put four legs in the fence jacks. Everyone else used three, but he insisted on four. And he wrapped each leg with wire. No one else did. When Rudell got through, you had a fine fence. Husky."

"I helped him a lot," Ormand said. "Until I got shot."

"That was a sour deal," Donny said. "Still, the Lord is in it. We just don't know why."

Donny turned to me. His eyes were innocent blue. "Take a look at that gatepost on the left. Check out the size of that rock Ormand packed."

"It's huge," I said.

"You bet," Donny said. "One day Ormand and Rudell showed up with the biggest rock in the county sitting in the back of the pickup. I couldn't budge that rock, much less carry it to the fence jack.

"I told your dad, 'Rudell, let me go get the tractor and a sled to carry that rock.'

"'Don't need no tractor. I got Ormand.'" Donny laughed at the memory.

I shook my head and smiled. My dad had worked Ormand like a mule, breaking him down, but there was no use in pointing that out.

"Your dad built stout fence. He told me his jacks and posts would last fifty years. Here it's been thirty-two now. They might go fifty at that."

Fifty years was a long time, I thought. Now Rudell and Donny's wife were both gone. Ormand and I had taken some rough wear. At fifty, who knew what would be left standing?

"How many miles of fence did Rudell build for you?" I asked.

Donny leaned his head back, closing his eyes. "Well, there's two hundred and sixty acres of alfalfa. Then I wanted fence up Cupper Creek and along Rail Canyon. And we had to fence Wildcat to keep the cows off government land." He opened his eyes. "Of course, when someone leaves a gate open, the fence won't stop them, and I get a reprimand from the Forest Service." He held up both hands, fingers extended, then closed them and showed two more fingers on his right hand. "Twelve or fourteen miles, I guess. And it's all stout."

"That's a lot of fence," I said.

"He even tried saving me money on the wire," Donny said. "But it made more work for him."

Donny had wanted to buy new wire, but my father claimed the old wire was better quality than new. He could save Donny money by mending the old wire's weak and rusty sections, then using it again with the new fence posts. On some sections they put in new wire, but in others, Donny let Rudell keep the old. "All of it's still husky," Donny said. "Your dad was right about that wire."

Ormand and I got out to examine the jacks more closely. "Dad used red-hearted juniper," Ormand said. "It's tougher than the white-hearted. You can't tell the difference until you cut it." He explained that my father found the red-hearted growing from the rockiest hillsides he could find. Only the hardiest of trees survived there.

Until he was shot, Ormand dug most of the fence-post holes with a shovel and bar to break the hardpan. Sometimes, my father used dynamite to dislodge the donnikers, large rocks embedded in the hardpan.

"Dad loved dynamite," Ormand said. "He was always looking for an excuse to blast a stick or two."

At the gateposts and attached jacks, the four legs were wired to the joints with both baling and barbed wire. I tried moving the legs, but they wouldn't budge. The quality of fencing, even after thirty-two years, was impossible to believe.

During those years Ormand had been in the service, my father had hired ex-cons to help him build fence. In the state pen at Salem, a Monument convict told the others that the town sat seventy miles from the nearest law-enforcement agency, and many had gone there after finishing their sentences, staying only until they found out how difficult it was to make a living.

"Dad always took in strays," Ormand said. "Cats and cons."

Aside from the cheap labor, Rudell hired the cons because he wanted someone to look up to him. At least that was Ormand's theory, and it made sense. Not everyone in Monument considered Rudell an asset to the community. They didn't like his run-down trailer, the company he kept, his drinking and fighting. Some regarded him as a throwback to rougher frontier times, a man living in the past.

However, no one questioned his ability to build fence. And no one crossed him. The incredible strength he gained from manual labor, combined with his speed and boxing skills, made him formidable. Even the ex-cons stayed on his good side.

■ ■ ■

The forest fire had scorched the ground in patches and blackened the west side of the pines. The wind had pushed the fire through fast, sparing the buildings. No sign of burn marred the bright NO TRESPASSING signs that had been nailed up since the fire.

The elk camp at Sunflower Flat consisted of a main cabin, a broken-down shed, a small bunkhouse, and a one-hole outhouse. Five stacked bedsprings rusted fifty feet back from the bunkhouse.

"That's where Dad sat on the porcupine." Ormand pointed to the bunkhouse. "All the adults were drinking in the cabin and old porky crawled onto the sleeping bag for a snooze. Dad got ready for bed and sat square on him. He didn't stay settled for long."

I laughed. "How bad did he get hurt?"

"Mom picked quills all night."

Ormand explained how Rudell and Raylene brought the children to the cabin for a week in summer. Twice, my father took the kids fishing on Wall Creek. Most of the time, he went by himself, scouting for elk. I wanted to know more about my father's winter elk camp, what I might have experienced had I accepted his invitation before he lost the place to Hoot. My uncle Oscar's elk camps had provided some of my fondest memories.

"When you got older, what did you do in elk camp?" I asked.

Ormand shook his head. "Dad didn't like mixing kids with hunting. He wasn't real involved with us in that way. I guess you could say he was not real involved as a father."

"Not real involved" might be the understatement most relevant to my father's entire life, I thought. How would Rudell have treated me if I had taken up his invitations to join him and Hoot?

Ormand unlatched the door to the broken-down shed. Inside were tools, cans of yellow-jacket spray, a deer leg hanging from the rafters.

"Dad kept Hammer in here when he wasn't packing elk," Ormand said. "I was six or seven the last time I rode that old plug around the place."

"So he died?"

"He must have." Ormand and I stepped outside and he closed the door. "After elk season, Dad turned him loose."

At first, I thought Ormand meant my father had turned the horse out to pasture on one of the Monument ranches. Then I realized he'd left it to starve or be eaten by coyotes and cougars. I didn't want to believe it. Still, I asked, "You mean Rudell turned Hammer out on Sunflower Flat in winter?"

Ormand nodded. "Maybe somebody else took him in. We never found any bones."

"I guess he was counting on you to do his packing for him after the horse was gone." I tried to make it sound humorous, but I was seething at his turning out the horse. My uncle Oscar had told an elk camp story about a frozen horse that had wandered into their camp one late November. Starving and shagged with ice, the horse stayed close to the fire, eating the apples, carrots, and canned corn the men offered. In the morning, they made inquiries about the horse at local ranches. Although no horse was missing, one of the ranchers brought a trailer up and moved the horse to his place while he advertised for the owner.

The least my father should have done was walk Hammer a mile from camp and shoot him. I heard my mother's voice: "He never gave the slightest damn about anything."

At times like this, I believed she was right. He never gave a damn about the horse. He never really gave a damn about me. He seldom put himself out for Ormand and his other kids.

The moment tasted bitter. Any sentiment I had for spreading the ashes faded. Let's just get this over with, I thought. I had shown up and I'd go through with it for Ormand.

"Where do you want to do it?" I asked.

"Let's spread the ashes around the main cabin first," Ormand said.

"Might as well."

We took turns pouring dirt and ashes from the bucket, saving a couple inches for the final place we'd talked about.

"Do you want to say a prayer?" Ormand asked.

"You go first." Anger gave me a headache. All my father's faults glared—his indifference, his laziness, his weakness. Why wouldn't he buy Ormand shoes that fit? Why didn't he contact me until I was near death's door? Why would he turn out an old packhorse?

Ormand was finished praying, waiting for me. I hadn't heard his prayer.

I picked up the pail. "Let's spread the rest of these." Ormand didn't say anything as we headed past the spring and toward the canyon that lay beyond. Maybe I could pray later.

"Do you think there are any elk in heaven?" I was trying to lighten my mood by teasing Ormand a bit.

"No doubt about it. The Bible says it will be more glorious in heaven than anything we can imagine down here."

"So maybe there won't be any elk, since we can imagine them now. There might be something else. Maybe we'll go pelk hunting."

His brow furrowed. "God made elk. They'll be in heaven all right."

"And the devil will make you pay for the tags," I said.

Ormand bumped against my side. "You think like a crazy

man. Speaking of crazy, sometimes I get myself into trouble for thinking too much, but I took this notion that maybe we should go over to France. Dad's army experiences had a big influence on him."

"The French really love what we did in World War Two," I said. "If I just mentioned that my father was in the war, they wanted to know all about it."

"You've been to France?" Ormand had never heard me talk about it before.

"Just once. When they brought out French editions of my novels. The French love books about the West."

"Did you see where Dad fought?"

"I didn't have time. We were on a tight book-signing schedule."

Ormand seemed disappointed. "Dad came back with two boxes full of medals and souvenirs. Somebody stole them. I wish I had them now."

I nodded. "You got to listen to this, Ormand. I was in Saint-Malo. That's on the coast of Normandy, where the soldiers hit the beaches on D day. Anyway, I was signing the French edition of *Winterkill*. They call it *Season of the Hunt*, which I think works pretty good.

"Suddenly, this tall, athletic man carrying a thick wooden staff stopped at my table. You should have seen that staff; it was much bigger than your walking sticks—a regular lethal weapon. This character dressed in fringed buckskin from head to toe. He wore a hat made from deer hide and matching high-topped moccasins. He looked like a French movie version of a mountain man. All gussied up. Lots of ornate jewelry, including a belt buckle shaped like a boar's head.

"Picking up the book, he tapped the cover, then shook my hand furiously. 'Ah, you must be a brave, brave hunter!' He was practically shouting.

"'I enjoy hunting a lot,' I said.

"He pounded his chest. 'I, too, am a very brave hunter.'

"'Good for you,' I said. 'What do you hunt?'

"'Monsieur, I hunt the wild pigeon!'"

Ormand laughed. "That's mighty dangerous game. Do you ever think you'll go back?"

"I'd like to." Who knows? I thought. I never got there at all until I was past fifty. Too busy working, raising my daughters, writing.

"I'm not ever getting to go," Ormand said. "Not on a disability pension. But I'd like to see those places where Dad fought."

"If I ever get rich, we can go there together," I said. "Terrific food. Beautiful women. Pigeon hunting. We can feast on the wild pigeons after a dangerous hunt. If we survive."

"Dad loved the French women," Ormand said. "Sometimes, he talked about them. I don't go for adultery now that I'm a Christian, but that was during the war."

War or no war, I figured that Rudell hadn't taken his wedding vows too seriously. "French women are lovely," I said.

"What about the country? Is it beautiful, too?"

"Nothing like this."

Hell Hole, the rugged canyon where Rudell had killed the five elk, dropped off Sunflower Flat half a mile behind elk camp. Wildcat Canyon came in from the west. Red fir, tamarack, and juniper covered both canyons' steep granite slopes. Tall ponderosas stood on the canyon floors.

We had hiked one-third of the way down the Hell Hole and spread the remainder of the ash and dirt. Oscar always said elk favored the country one-third downcanyon, and neither Ormand nor I wanted to descend farther. Walking was too tough.

"I wish I knew the exact places Dad killed those five elk," Ormand said.

"Marion knew."

"Those old guys are gone." Ormand took a package of Roi-Tans from his pocket and offered me one. "Dad left me some bad habits. I guess you never smoked."

Taking the cigar, I said, "Still trying to start."

We lit the cigars, dropping the ashes into the pail because the country was so dry.

"That must have been a helluva hunt." I kept thinking about the five shots. The elk would have spooked after the first one or two. How could anyone kill five elk with five shots? Oscar had shot two with one five-shot clip, but only once. An elk was difficult to bring down with only one shot. No matter how many awards Rudell had won for marksmanship, the feat seemed impossible.

"Dad didn't tell stretchers about hunting," Ormand said, as if he had been reading my thoughts. "Even so, I wouldn't have believed him except that I got the story straight from Marion and Clara. They were really steamed that Dad cut the hunting season so short."

"Well, they should just sit back and enjoy the view," I said. Studying the canyons, I understood why my father had loved this country. Perhaps the Cascades seemed more glamorous, and the Wallowas stunned you with their rugged beauty, but this was spellbinding, too. Even so, all this beauty hadn't been able to scour the dark places from my father. I realized that darkness crept into me, too, especially when I nursed the anger I held against my father. Later on, I would try to pray, I decided.

"There are more elk in this country now than there used to be." Ormand stubbed his cigar butt in the pail. "But no one could kill five, even now."

"How many elk have you killed?" I asked Ormand.

"You mean legal?"

"Both ways."

"You're not going to put this in the book, are you? I don't need game wardens checking on me."

"Like Rudell always said, 'The law's a little slow getting to Monument.' " I smiled at the recollection of my father's slow drawl, the way he would have said it. "Anyway, the game wardens stay too busy handing out tickets to read my books."

"Two and a half," Ormand said.

I nodded, but I was still pondering the fact that Rudell hadn't taken Ormand up to elk camp. I considered how he had used my brother for packing fencing material into harsh country and checking thousands of traps in steep canyons. Damn hard work. Taking Ormand hunting should have been a little reward.

"Why the half?"

"With the spotlight on them and a couple other guys blasting bullets, you can't take full credit."

"No legal ones so far?"

He shook his head. "Stove up this way, I need a fair advantage."

"If I come out in November and we hike out to this canyon, do you think we could bag an elk?"

"Legal?"

"We'll try legal first." I smiled and shrugged. "They taste the same."

Ormand shook his head. "You've got a lot to learn, Professor. Illegal always tastes better."

"I believe it. The Bible is very clear about the appeal of forbidden fruit."

"Meat's different than fruit." Ormand squinted at me. "Craig, you've never shot an elk, have you?"

"Not yet."

"We'll come out here just like Dad and Hoot, before the trouble." Ormand seemed excited at the prospect.

"But we won't fight," I said. "Fighting doesn't get you anywhere."

The canyon shadows grew longer and dusk settled on the slopes. Along with the scents of pine and juniper, I smelled wood smoke. Archery season had opened and the deer hunters were setting up camps.

Ormand spotted another route out of the canyon that appeared to offer easier walking, so we headed toward Wildcat before climbing. By the time we reached Sunflower Flat, the sun balanced above the horizon.

On the way back to the truck, we came to an old blackened barbed-wire fence. Following the fence line were new steel posts and rolls of shining barbed wire. Someone was closing off the country tighter.

Ormand looked up and down the fence line. "Don't see a gate."

"We can make it through." I put my foot on the lowest wire and pulled the one above it high. The old wire had a lot of play. My father wouldn't have built a fence like this, I thought.

"Go ahead, Ormand."

He started through but snagged his pants. "Just keep the damned wire stretched," he said.

With my free hand, I worked the cloth away from the barb. "You didn't have to grow so big." I tried stretching the wire more. Helping my brother seemed like a good thing. My father was gone, but Ormand was still here.

He cleared the fence and stood for a brief moment. Then he stretched the wire wide, and I started across.

38

LESLEY FAMILY REUNION

My aunt Lela hosted the Lesley Family Reunion over the Fourth of July weekend at her cabin located on Granite Boulder Creek, near the Middle Fork of the John Day River. The festive announcement boasted: FIREWORKS, FISHING, GOLD PAN-NING, VOLLEYBALL, AND SOFTBALL. It concluded with: FAMILY BARBECUE. FOOD PROVIDED!

I had never seen my Aunt Lela's cabin but everyone said she had plenty of room.

Elena and Kira insisted that we attend. "It's the reunion of the millennium," Elena pointed out. "This only happens once in a thousand years."

"Yeah, Dad," Kira said. "I want to meet more of my relatives. You took Elena with you to Monument more than you took me."

"I want to pan for gold," Elena said. "You told me I have to help pay for college. Finding gold beats being a waitress in the dining hall."

I knew she didn't really expect to find gold, but the whole prospect of the trip excited her. Kira, the more sports-minded of the two, planned on playing volleyball and softball with her cousins.

"Your dad had eleven brothers and sisters. "There'll be lots of cousins." Kira picked up her soccer ball. "I'm going to play soccer, too."

"Prairie City is a long way," I said. The ride would take at least six hours, and Elena couldn't spell me because she only drove an automatic.

"What do you think, honey?" I asked Kathy. She usually had a good read on things.

"I'm not driving all that way to see a bunch of rowdy Lesleys. Besides, you'll be gone too long. I can't get off work."

"It wouldn't be the same without you."

"I'm perfectly happy to stay here," she said. "All of you can go, and I hope you have a good time." She looked directly at me. "Do you think they'll have guns? I remember the first time I met Ormand. He was holding that pistol. I don't want the girls around any guns."

"Don't worry about guns," I said. "They won't bring guns to the reunion." I had crossed my fingers. Most of the Lesleys, especially the rural ones, packed firearms at all times. Ormand never even rode the Greyhound bus without a pistol in his pack.

In spite of the girls' enthusiasm, I wasn't wild about going. The fifth of July was my birthday—this year the double nickel. I had counted on a quiet time at home punctuated by neighborhood fireworks, then a birthday barbecue with my mother, sister, and her family. And I didn't want to drive. I was teaching at Willamette University in Salem, a one-hundred-mile round-trip commute each day. That was enough driving.

I studied the Oregon road map, groaning at the three hundred miles between Portland and Lela's cabin forty miles outside Prairie City, the nearest town. The reunion was at least ninety minutes beyond Monument. Kathy had hit the nail on the head: Why drive that far to see a bunch of rowdy Lesleys?

Worse, the girls would want to play their music in the car. Eminem, Snoop Dogg and Lil' Bow Wow, Britney Spears. If I had to

drive almost as far as Prairie City, I wanted to listen to Hank
Williams and Patsy Cline. Some Jerry Lee Lewis if I got drowsy.

"Matt will be there," Elena said. "Matt and I hit it off."

Elena had been fascinated by Ormand's boy, my nephew, since
she'd first met him during a trip to visit my father. When Matt
opened the door, Elena was astonished to see her male counterpart. Both were tall, slender, and gray-eyed, with small noses and
delicate features. Matt and Elena took after Rudell. On that
visit, Matt taught her to play pool, and the fifteen-year-olds hit
it off.

When Elena was filling out her college applications, she wrote
about the experience:

*Monument lies in the center of Oregon's dry, sage-brush filled re-
gion east of the Cascade Mountains. Bordering on ghost town sta-
tus, it houses a small network of trailers, a "cowboy" bar, and a
general store. No tourists visit Monument. Unlike more trendy ar-
eas of Oregon, where out-of-town windsurfers and laptop-carry-
ing rock climbers congregate, Monument has no attractions. The
nearest bank, restaurant, or barbershop is seventy miles away,
and an ambulance will take an hour and a half to reach you after
you call 911. With an unemployment rate of over twenty percent,
Monument's 134 residents scrape by, some chopping wood, others
trapping coyotes or building fence. My dad and I ventured into
this desolate setting the summer of 1996 to visit his ailing father.*

*After a six-hour drive (from Portland) we arrived at my
grandpa Rudell's "trailer"—a wheel-less contraption, sunk into
the ground, with a makeshift wooden lean-to. Wondering if we
had found the right trailer, I hesitantly knocked on the door. As it
opened, the residence's smells struck me—cigarettes and chicken-
fried steak grease common to rural homes. Even more impressive
than the smell was the figure who stood, slightly hunched, in the
narrow doorway. Although a soiled red baseball cap partially ob-
scured the boy's face, his gray eyes and delicate features unmistak-
ably resembled my own. Examining his tall, lanky frame, I
realized that my male counterpart stood before me.*

*After numerous introductions, the boy (who I had learned
was my cousin Matt) and I sat down next to the trailer's heater—
a small, rusty device patched with aluminum foil. What an amus-
ing sight we must make, I thought. Though Matt was my double,
he was also my opposite. I noticed his hands, scarred and leathery
beyond his years from coyote trapping and fence building, and
contrasted them with my own, which only labored through holding
a pen or using a graphing calculator.*

While Elena became salutatorian at St. Mary's Academy, Matt
skipped much of high school to build fence. She planned on attending Brown University, while he thought of joining the marines,
as Ormand had done. Matt represented a way of life far different
from Elena's life in Portland. His was the kind of life I would have
lived, had I grown up with my father.

After that first meeting with Matt, Elena went to Monument
with me whenever we had time. On each visit, she sought him
out.

*I returned to Monument this summer to visit Matt. My grandpa
had died, leaving nothing to explain his life other than the coyote-
skinning knife my dad inherited. I've always prided myself on my
ability to understand different kinds of people, but my own grandfather remains an enigma.*

*Spending time with Matt helped me understand my grandpa's
choices. Although Matt is my exact age and bears a striking resemblance to me in both looks and personality, he couldn't live
more differently. He's continuing the tradition of our grandfather
and his father—living ruggedly, building fence. His house is a
ramshackle structure surrounded by over a dozen junker cars.
The doors are constantly unlocked so a rotating assortment of
stray dogs and the fence builders who live with him can get in and
out.*

*The transience disturbed me. I'd come to learn more about
Matt and my grandfather, but found myself trying to convince
my cousin to leave Monument. "Why don't you join the Ma-*

rines?" I asked. "Or come to Portland and enroll at the community college?"

Matt would shake his head. "Nah, I don't think so."

And I began to understand why he wouldn't be leaving Monument anytime soon. It wasn't so bad. Although the town is economically depressed, people there can live independently, free from many constraints of modern life. If Matt's too tired to build fence one day, it just doesn't happen. If he feels like taking the afternoon to go fishing with his friends, he does it.

At the same time, I knew it would be naïve to consider Monument any sort of Utopia. Like many small communities in eastern Oregon, the town is plagued by unemployment and methamphetamine use. "There's no future in Monument," I heard people repeat during my time there. But I knew they wouldn't leave. What waits for them in a city like Portland? Strangers, financial hardship and a completely foreign, fast-paced lifestyle.

As I drove home, back to the city, I couldn't stop thinking about Matt and his friends. Sometimes I imagine what our lives would be like if the random genetic lottery had cast us in opposite circumstances: Matt studying in Portland and me skinning coyotes in Monument.

Before moving ahead with his life, Matt had to clear his police record of DUIs and traffic violations. My girls had been amazed that he once consumed seventeen tallboys before being apprehended on a DUI. Neither daughter drank, unlike some of their high school classmates.

During the time Matt had been a guest of Grant County, he gained twenty pounds.

"Every morning, I got to cook for myself," he said. "All the eggs I wanted, bacon, sausage, ham on Sundays. I could really pack it away." He flexed his bicep. "Nothing to do all day but lift weights and watch TV."

Matt was a handsome boy, broad-shouldered and sandy-haired. While he and Elena had sat on the hood of Ormand's pickup, he taught her how to flip a cigarette and catch it in her mouth.

Matt lit up and exhaled. He asked Elena, "Do you know what to do when you're in the joint and somebody wants you to be his bitch?"

She didn't.

"You hit him with all you got." He tapped the ash off his cigarette. "You knock him flat and keep hitting him until the bastard doesn't try to get up again. You make him hurt so he doesn't mess with you."

Elena listened intently. I doubted she would need to use those tactics at Brown. Even so, she held her own with Matt on his terms.

"Do you know how many cars my brother stole?" she asked.

Matt shrugged.

"Seventy," she said. "And that was just in Lane County. He stole a bunch more down in Roseburg, and they still have a warrant out for his arrest in Jackson County. He's been in jail a lot longer than you."

Matt flipped his cigarette away. "Cool!"

■ ■ ■

Now, Elena and Kira were packing for the reunion. Elena appraised herself in the mirror. "I look funny in these jeans, don't I? What do you think, Kira?"

"I guess," Kira said.

"They look fine," I said, thinking she already had stacks of jeans.

I lost. The girls went to the mall with Kathy's Nordstrom card.

On the Fourth of July, we packed the car with clothes, sleeping bags, pillows, fishing gear, athletic shoes, toiletries, CDs, and a CD player, since the car had only a tape deck. I loaded the ice chest with sodas, a six-pack, apples, cheese, turkey, and half a dozen yogurts. I had trouble with the heavy food in Eastern Oregon. I wasn't used to it anymore and I couldn't eat chicken-fried steak, broasted chicken, or sixteen-ounce T-bones.

"We don't need all this food." Kira tapped the reunion announcement. It says, 'Food provided!'"

"Just in case," I said. "It's pretty remote."

"I need to buy insect repellent," Elena said. "Mosquito bites make me swell."

"You have to move those Nordstrom bags," I said. "I can't see out the back."

"Well, we're all set and ready to go," I told Kathy.

"Have a good time." She didn't look as though she would miss us much.

■ ■ ■

It took three and a half hours to reach Pendleton, counting coffee and bathroom breaks. One of the girls complained of a small bladder.

In Pendleton, I insisted on eating, but the girls protested. Eager to get to Lela's cabin, they wanted to hurry. "There'll be food at the reunion!" Kira insisted.

"I want you to eat something now."

Kira pointed at the map. "It doesn't look too far."

"We're off the freeway," I said. "We'll go through mountains, then follow a winding road along the Middle Fork of the John Day."

Against their protests, we stopped at Denny's. The food was mediocre, but I didn't want any surprises. The girls reluctantly split a bowl of soup and a small dinner salad.

After the waiter learned I was turning fifty-five the next day, he gave me the 10 percent discount. "We like to honor our seniors," he said. Thinking of myself as a senior was disheartening.

When we were on the road again, everyone's mood improved.

"Do you think we'll find any gold?" Elena asked.

"You just might," I said. "My father had a gold mine up on Big Creek, so there's got to be gold around. Big Creek is just a couple of drainages away."

"Matt will know how to pan for gold," Elena said.

After going south on highway 395 for two hours, we turned onto a rough county road that wound along the river. The country was

beautiful with ponderosas and red firs, hillsides blanketed with
tamaracks. The girls became impatient after an hour's drive with a
top speed of forty miles per hour.

We passed a few abandoned homesteads and a tumbled-down
sawmill.

"Who owns all this?" Kira asked.

"We do," I said. "It belongs to the government. Forest Service
and Bureau of Land Management. Now the tribes are buying up
land, too."

"Is there a place to change before we get there?" Elena asked.

"The same place you go to the bathroom out here. Wherever
you want."

When I estimated we were twenty minutes from the cabin, I
pulled the car onto a meadow alongside the river so the girls could
get themselves ready. The new jeans, makeup, and hair took half
an hour. I walked through a grove of ponderosas along the river,
checking possible fishing sites. A sign posted to one tree said the
river was closed to fishing in order to protect the wild-salmon run.
Well, I'd fish on the creeks.

At Granite Boulder Creek, which was more of a trickle, we
turned onto a dirt road and followed it through the woods for a
mile. Dust rose everywhere, covering the car. I saw some big tire
tracks. Winnebagos and motor homes, I figured.

"Those people look mean," Kira said. "This can't be the place."

A man and a woman sat on a tilted porch in front of a dilapi-
dated cabin. The man wore a greasy brown barn coat, and the
woman had on jeans and a sweatshirt with a cowgirl design. The
man held a barking dog that was trying to lunge at the car.

"Stay here, Bandit," he said.

I realized that Kira had never met Ormand before. Now that
she'd mentioned it, he did look mean, but he wasn't.

"That's Ormand," Elena told Kira. "But where is everybody?"

"Now that we're here, there's five," I said. "That's my aunt
Lela."

She stood, dusted off the seat of her jeans, and started limping our way. She paused to wave a welcome. Lela had been a looker in her day and still had a pleasant smile and animated features. "I'm so glad you came and brought the girls," she said as we hugged. "Don't worry about Bandit. He barks at his own feet."

I introduced Elena and Kira, who hugged Lela, too.

"Those girls are growed taller than you," Ormand said. When he smiled, the mean look disappeared. "You better stop feeding them." He lurched off the steps and we hugged each other. He smelled like whiskey.

Bandit nuzzled and licked the girls and me.

"He'll love you to death," Lela said. "He's a big baby."

"Is Matt going to be here?" Elena asked.

Ormand shook his head. "Matt's fishing in Alaska. He went up to Dutch Harbor and hired on as a deckhand."

Elena's expression sombered.

"I'm thinking about going up there myself," Ormand said. "Them outfits are always looking for a good cook."

I didn't smell any barbecue, and I was puzzled by scraps of lettuce and tomatoes lying in the dirt a few feet off the porch. Two pickups sat behind the house—Ormand's beater GMC and a shiny red Tacoma. Where were the motor homes? Where were the people?

"You girls better come inside here," Lela said. "I'll get you some chocolate cake. You like chocolate cake, don't you? And I still got some milk in the cool can." As she hobbled toward the porch, I could tell how much her knee hurt. She paused, glancing at the vegetable scraps in the dust. "I guess I shouldn't have tossed away the rest of that salad."

"Your cake is better anyway," Ormand said.

Inside, we sat on an ancient sofa with odd depressions and stick chairs with peeling varnish. Old pictures of the Pendleton Round-Up decorated the walls. While we ate cake, Lela asked the girls about their studies, activities, and boyfriends.

"When I was your age, I loved to dance. But now my knee is plumb give out. Ford, my first husband, he was a wonderful dancer." She seemed to enjoy the memory. "I wish you could meet my kids, all your cousins, but they left to watch Garrett play in a baseball tournament."

"Aunt Lela, Craig and I are going outside for a minute." Ormand signaled for me to follow.

"That cake was delicious," I said, still thinking about the missing barbecue.

On the porch, Ormand lit a cigarette and offered me one. I took it out of camaraderie. "Where is everybody?" I asked. "I saw motor home tracks coming in. Was there a fight?"

Ormand shook his head. "No fight. I guess you could say we had a little bit of a fracas last night. That's what Dad would call it . . . just a fracas. A few people got sore jaws and ribs. Nothing's broke."

"What happened?"

"Oh, there was a little disagreement about cards. Dean didn't like the way Andy was dealing, so they got to jawing at each other. Then Bob had a few words to say and I got in on it somehow. It's kind of blurry. A couple people got knocked down, but then we all made up again."

"So why did everybody go?"

"Well, a lot of people didn't come in the first place because of health reasons or other family commitments. And today, they left early, since Monument was putting on an all-class reunion. I stayed behind to help Lela pack up. I guess you and your daughters kind of missed the crowd."

I wasn't too happy that I'd driven six hours for this, but at the same time, I half-expected a Lesley reunion would go haywire. "Well, at least it's good to see you and Lela."

"That's right." Ormand flicked his cigarette so it landed by the vegetables. He headed for his pickup. "I've got something I want you to see." He reached across the driver's seat and picked up a black revolver. "Take a look at this. It was Dad's."

I recognized the pistol. I opened the cylinder to make certain it was empty. "It's a Colt Python three-fifty-seven Magnum—a classic."

Ormand smiled and nodded. "This is the standard all gun makers try to match. It's worth about seven hundred dollars."

"We sold a few when I worked in my uncle Oscar's guide service."

"It was stolen when Dad was sick, but I knew who took it, so I could get it back. One of Opal's no-good boyfriends wound up with it and I threatened him with the sheriff, so he 'found' it in exchange for a hundred bucks."

Somehow, it felt strange to be holding the same pistol my father had carried.

"Dad used to win marksmanship tournaments with this Colt at the Umatilla Army Depot. He was a crack shot." Ormand reached under the seat and brought out a half box of cartridges. "Want to give it a try?"

"All right. I'm going to tell the girls what's going on so they don't get too excited."

Everybody came out to watch. Ormand lined up four beer cans and handed me the pistol. I loaded it, apologized ahead of time for poor marksmanship, and nicked one can with the fourth shot. My ears rang from the firing.

"Dad carried this all the time when he was gold mining," Ormand said. "He had a lousy partner. A lot of shady types came to his mining cabin, and Dad always kept the pistol close by."

The girls declined Ormand's offer to let them try.

"Hey," he asked them. "If two Lesleys get divorced, are they still brother and sister?"

We all laughed at that one, even though I'd heard it before.

Ormand flipped the cylinder open to make certain it was empty, then had me double-check. He handed the pistol to Elena. "This was your grandfather's," he said. "If they'd had Olympic shooting events in his day, Dad could have won a gold medal."

Elena seemed uncomfortable and started to hand back the pistol. "It's pretty heavy."

Lela took the pistol from her, aimed at the cans, and held steady. "It's heavy for me, too. I keep a little thirty-two automatic by my bed back in John Day. It's lighter for a woman."

Kira wanted to hold the pistol. She used a two-handed grip, as Lela had done.

"Do you want to try it?" Ormand asked.

"Why not?"

He loaded it for her and she aimed at the cans. When she fired, the pistol bucked. "That really hurts my wrist," she said.

Ormand took the pistol from her. He drilled one can on the third shot, but that was all. Maybe I wasn't such a greenhorn after all.

"There's a little burr in the trigger pull," he said. "I'm going to file that down. Still, it beats shooting off firecrackers."

■ ■ ■

After Lela closed up her cabin, everyone headed for the fireworks display in Prairie City.

The girls were a little downcast. "I wanted to see Matt," Elena said.

"He can earn big money fishing in Alaska." I remembered going to Ketchikan and longshoring to earn money for graduate school. I had loved Alaska.

"The gold panning didn't happen," Elena said. "Maybe I should go fishing in Alaska."

"You'd have an adventure," I told her. "They say there's two hardy men for every woman up there."

"I'm sorry this reunion didn't work out better for you, Dad." Kira leaned over the front seat. "Maybe it wasn't such a good idea. I hope you're not too disappointed."

"I'm glad to be here with you two," I said. "And it's always good to see Lela and Ormand."

On the outskirts of town, people had set up lawn chairs on the ground or on the flatbeds of farm trucks. Teenagers flirted inside pickups parked along the fence lines. The Strawberry Mountains glowed pink and crimson as the sun went down.

Beautiful country, I thought. But hard to make a living if you don't inherit a ranch.

I took out the cool can and we picnicked, waiting in the dusk for the fireworks to begin. On the Fourth of July, I like to imagine that all the celebration is just a prelude to my birthday. Prairie City put on a humdinger of a display.

The next morning the girls snuck out of the motel room early and bought a cake decorated for the Fourth of July. They scraped off the old letters and wrote "Happy Birthday, Dad" with a brown frosting tube, the only color available in the small grocery store. Five red candles represented fifty years and five blue ones stood for a year apiece. The single white candle meant one to grow on.

As I blew out the candles, I remembered my uncle Oscar's saying: "We're a small outfit, but we're a hell of an outfit." Both girls have wonderful voices. I cried with happiness when they sang. Fifty-five, the double nickel, and even if most of the Lesleys hadn't shown, we had a celebration.